The Culturally Competent Educator

Dedication

To my third grade teacher, Mrs. Gowdy, who saw my potential in 1970 and opened doors I didn't know existed.
You personalized my learning journey, pushing boundaries and lifting limits, showing me how far I could truly soar.
Your gift of differentiated instruction, before it had a name, shaped not only my future but the educator I became.

The Culturally Competent Educator

Connecting Equitable Practices for Instruction, Assessment, and Grading

Almitra L. Berry

FOR INFORMATION:

Corwin
A SAGE Company
2455 Teller Road
Thousand Oaks, California 91320
(800) 233-9936
www.corwin.com

SAGE Publications Ltd.
1 Oliver's Yard
55 City Road
London EC1Y 1SP
United Kingdom

SAGE Publications India Pvt. Ltd.
Unit No 323-333, Third Floor, F-Block
International Trade Tower Nehru Place
New Delhi 110 019
India

SAGE Publications Asia-Pacific Pte. Ltd.
18 Cross Street #10-10/11/12
China Square Central
Singapore 048423

Vice President and Editorial Director: Monica Eckman
Senior Acquisitions Editor: Megan Bedell
Senior Content Development Editor: Mia Rodriguez
Content Development and Operations Manager: Lucas Schleicher
Senior Editorial Assistant: Natalie Delpino
Production Editor: Tori Mirsadjadi
Typesetter: C&M Digitals (P) Ltd.
Proofreader: Theresa Kay
Cover Designer: Scott Van Atta
Marketing Manager: Melissa Duclos

Printed and bound by CPI Group (UK) Ltd, Croydon, CR0 4YY

Library of Congress Cataloging-in-Publication Data

Names: Berry, Almitra L, author.

Title: The culturally competent educator : connecting equitable practices for instruction, assessment, and grading / Almitra L Berry.

Description: Thousand Oaks, California : Corwin, [2025] | Includes bibliographical references and index.

Identifiers: LCCN 2024051617 | ISBN 9781071981726 (paperback) | ISBN 9781071981733 (epub) | ISBN 9781071981740 (epub) | ISBN 9781071981757 (pdf)

Subjects: LCSH: Educational equalization. | Culturally relevant pedagogy. | Educational tests and measurements. | Effective teaching. | Grading and marking (Students)

Classification: LCC LC213 .B47 2025 | DDC 379.2/6—dc23/eng/20250208
LC record available at https://lccn.loc.gov/2024051617

This book is printed on acid-free paper.

25 26 27 28 29 10 9 8 7 6 5 4 3 2 1

CONTENTS

ABOUT THE AUTHOR

Almitra L. Berry, EdD, is the CEO, founder, and principal consultant of ALBerry Consulting, Incorporated. She is a nationally recognized speaker, author, and consultant on the topic of culturally and linguistically diverse learners in America's K–12 education system. Her research focuses on equity and academic achievement in majority-of-color, low-wealth, large, urban school districts.

Dr. Berry is author of the book *Effecting Change for Culturally and Linguistically Diverse Learners*, which addresses the educational needs for culturally and linguistically diverse learners, focusing heavily on provision gaps, equity, and addressing related challenges during the coronavirus pandemic.

She is a graduate of the University of California, Davis, holding a BA in political science/public administration. She holds an MEd in curriculum and instruction and an EdD in educational leadership with a specialization in curriculum and instruction. She has held multiple credentials, including a California reading endorsement, language development specialist (LDS), and bilingual/cross-cultural language acquisition and development (CLAD/BCLAD) for Spanish language instruction.

Dr. Berry has worked with educators, leaders, and school boards throughout the United States. She has presented at scores of state, national, and international conferences on the topics of equity, leadership, curriculum reform, and meeting the needs of historically underserved and disenfranchised learners.

Her work aims to introduce educators to a culturally relevant pragmatism that regards the culturally and linguistically diverse learner as one who brings to school a divergent order of reality. That reality influences the culture of school, the equity of policy, and the efficacy of instructional methods. She calls upon educators and educational leaders to evaluate policy, curriculum, instruction, supervision, and professional learning with a lens focused on equity.

INTRODUCTION

Over the last thirty-one years, I have had the pleasure, the honor, and the privilege to provide instruction to some of the most marginalized learners in our schools and to those who serve them. As a classroom educator, I had my 30 to 150 learners each year. As a consultant, I have served countless schools, districts, and classrooms. But no matter how many schools I work with, there always seems to be a need to keep doing the "on-the-ground" work.

There are always more instructors and administrators who need guidance in providing equitable instruction to children. This being the case, I decided it was time to once again put pen to paper (or keystrokes to screen) to reach a broader audience.

I use the word *learner* and the term *provide instruction* with specific intent. Because I am not a *teacher*, but rather an *educator.*

Let's unpack that, shall we?

In my final years as a classroom educator, I based my spelling instruction in word morphology. I knew that my sixth graders were learners of color from homes of low financial wealth, an impactful **comorbidity** resulting from a confluence of social, economic, racial, cultural, and linguistic factors. Providing instruction in word morphology gave them an opportunity to apply their knowledge of roots and affixes to more words than any other method. So, let's use that same approach here.

comorbidity—in school demographics, the presence of two unalterable demographic markers in a learner that have historically impacted academic success through no fault of the learner

The word *learner* comes from the verb *learn.* One who learns is a learner. A learner gains or acquires knowledge or skills by study, experience, or being taught. Study and experience are active, being taught is passive. I argue that people, both children and adults, who actively participate in instructional activities have higher outcomes. Learners engage in instruction, they do not simply sit and receive it or just *get taught, told, trained.*

The word *teacher* is rooted in the verb *to teach*, which means "to give instruction." The affix *–er* means "one who." *Teach* is rooted in an Old English word that means to "show, present, or point out." So, a *teacher* is *one who shows, presents*, or *points out.* Teaching, then, is unidirectional or one-sided, as if I have all the knowledge and information to impart to my learners and they have nothing to give back to me. The idea that people, both children and adults, are merely empty vessels into which we can pour information exudes elitism.

Nothing could be further from the truth.

In this resource, I primarily use the word *educator.* It comes from the Latin word *educare*, which means to "lead out." Once again, the affix *–or* means *one who.* An educator guides. They lead their learners out of one state toward another. It may be from a lack of knowledge of how to read, write, think, or calculate to a state of literacy and numeracy. It could be out of a state of not knowing history or science or a world language and into one where they can make sense of worlds past, present, and future, by integrating the knowledge gained from a study of these subjects. Where you do find the word *teacher* in this book, note the context. There is a reason for its use in those instances.

Educating is an active relationship between two parties: the educator and those the educator leads. And true educators can only lead when learners in their classrooms choose to learn, to follow. Put a pin in that, it will make complete sense in another chapter or two.

As an educator, I have much to learn from those I instruct. This is how I am able to provide the instruction learners need; not simply provide information I want to give.

I was first called an equity warrior many years ago by a superintendent who was referring to my unrelenting passion to hold those in power accountable to meeting the needs of every child. This was long before the term *equity* was popularized and became the "in" thing in education and was demonized by those who seek to oppress our marginalized culturally and linguistically diverse learners.

Over time, I've come to define and identify the characteristics of **equity warriors**, those who I greet and salute in every episode of my podcast *Educational Equity Emancipation.* Are you an equity warrior? How many of these characteristics do you possess?

- **Promoter of Fairness:** actively working to ensure that resources, opportunities, and advantages are distributed fairly among all individuals and groups in your district, school, or classroom.
- **Challenger of Bias and Discrimination:** actively working against biases, prejudices, and discrimination; advocating for those who may be disadvantaged because of their race, gender, socioeconomic status, ability, or other marginalized identity.
- **Seeker of Systemic Change:** recognizing that many inequities are rooted in systemic and structural issues, actively seeking changes in policies and systems, not just individual behaviors or attitudes.
- **Lifelong Learner:** committed to continually learning and educating yourself about issues related to equity and social justice, especially in public schools and as related to children.
- **Active Ally:** standing up for and supporting marginalized groups; working to use whatever privilege you hold to effect positive change.
- **Striver of Inclusion and Representation:** striving for diverse and inclusive representation in all areas, such as curricular materials, instructional methodologies, decision-making processes, policy development, and leadership roles.

equity warrior—one who actively advocates for equity; one who works to ensure no person, especially no child, is disadvantaged by prejudice or bias

This Book Is for You

Yes, you. I wrote this book not only for the educators, but for the teachers, in the hopes that they will become educators. I wrote it for the school and district administrators who already serve as or are considering becoming instructional leaders, not merely managers. I wrote it for those still in college who are exploring careers as educators and for those transitioning from paraprofessional roles into classroom instructor positions. And yes, for the professors and practicum supervisors who support that work. Each of you has a responsibility to provide instruction: to children in classrooms, to adults in professional learning and development, to those you lead, and to your peers in day-to-day discussions about what's happening in your classrooms.

There's another term you will read frequently in this text: *provide instruction. Provide* comes from two Latin words: *pro–* "before" and *videre* "to see." To provide is "to see before." Instruct comes from two Latin words also: *in–* "upon or towards" and *struere* "pile up." The affixes *–ion, –tion,* and *–sion* all do the same thing. They are often added to verbs and form nouns of action. Instruction is literally *piling upon.* So when we provide instruction, we take part in an act that piles upon our learners that which we know they need because we see the needs before us.

I am not a teacher. I am an educator. I see the needs of the learners in front of me. This extends beyond the academics, to an understanding of who they are as whole people. I make myself aware of their languages, their cultures, their lived experiences (including their prior experiences in our classrooms), all that they bring with them, to give them what they need in order to be successful: socially, behaviorally, and academically.

Working through this book will improve your ability to see the complex and comprehensive needs of your learners (children or adults!) and give them what they need to be successful. Through your learning, you'll not only work to build success for others, but for yourself as well. You will become a better, more skilled, and more culturally competent educator.

Why Equitable Classroom Practices?

As an educator, I have witnessed tremendous inequities over the last twenty-odd years, particularly when coaching others in providing instruction in English (and Spanish) language arts and literacy to marginalized learners. These inequities are often rooted in implicit bias, presenting themselves in subtle, and sometimes not-so-subtle, ways. They present in words spoken, gestures used, attitudes taken by *teachers* and administrators. Not educators, teachers. Not educational leaders, administrators. They present in policies and practices that uphold educational caste systems where marginalized learners are forever seen as unable to achieve. Personally flawed. Uneducable. They present when adults dismiss poor outcomes with a shrug of the shoulders and blame the victims saying, "Well, those kids . . ."

Author's Perspective: White in America

Though not a race nor an ethnicity, I use the term *White* as I use the terms *Black, Latine, Indigenous*, and *Asian American*. I reference *White European* as a culture, although there is no singular culture. Just as there is no singular Asian American culture, or one of any other broad racial or ethnic group. I make the distinction to identify a group of people in the United States whose ancestors may have immigrated to the United States from any number of European nations. Why?

Because one's typical lived experience in the United States is distinctly different based on the history of who holds social and political power in the country. Since the United States became a country, power has been held first by people of English or British ancestry, then by people who came from (or whose ancestors came from) other Western European countries whose physical characteristics allowed them to present as physically similar to those with English ancestry. Most notably, the presence of fair, or "white" skin.

Like it or not, we are each given a label of race. Isabel Wilkerson wrote, "While the requirements to qualify as white have changed over the centuries . . . what lies beneath each label is centuries of history and assigning of assumptions and values to physical features in a structure of human hierarchy" (Wilkerson, 2020, pp. 18–19).

Like it or not, admit it or not, we all see color. There is no such thing as racial colorblindness. We all see characteristics of human beings: from skin tone to hair color to height, weight, gender, etc. But in the United States, those with white skin benefit from the power that the country's history, and the history of European colonialism of Black and Brown countries, afford it.

The difference in the lived experiences of White Americans, regardless of their ancestral origins, lies in the fact that is easy for them to assimilate into the social and political power dynamic because of the country's systemic and institutional racism that assigns human value based on race.

Culture is defined as the information, norms, values, behavior, and morals of a group. Culture lies in beliefs and systems transmitted socially not genetically. The politically powerful define and promote what they deem to be positive aspects of the dominant, or White, culture. And they publicly ascribe to and promote it as the norm for the United States. The existence of that White American culture does not require all White people to consciously ascribe or contribute to it.

Just as what is perceived by the politically and socially dominant group as Black, Latine, Asian American, or Indigenous culture does not require all people of those groups to consciously ascribe to their perceived culture. White American norms and the perceived superiority that they promote have become so infused into the fabric of American society, that those who present as White benefit by association based on skin color.

Since I was a marginalized learner with multiple comorbidities, I recognize from a very personal place, as well as an academic place, the damage that inequity does. And that is just one of the many reasons why I am committed to helping others understand how *what* we teach and *how* we teach it is critical. It's critical if we desire to be educators, not teachers. It is critical if we believe that every child deserves a high-quality education that will lead to the opportunity for them to become whoever they choose to become.

Inequitable practices result in low achievement. Low achievement relegates children to lives of social and economic disadvantage. It fuels the school to prison pipeline. It results in poorer health and shorter lives.

It is my hope, that as you not only read, but learn through engaging with the content of this text, you will put into practice those things that will improve learning, instruction, grading, assessment, and the culture of your classroom for your learners. It is my hope that you will come to see your instructional content, the literature, the texts, and the tests you put in front of your learners as they do: as either connecting to their own lived experiences or building walls—marginalizing them even further. And that when the latter is the case, you eliminate that which is harmful.

It is my hope that you will see that equitable practices can literally change lives.

About This Professional Learning Book

I've written this book with learner engagement in mind. Your engagement as a learner, and the engagement of the learners you serve every day in your schools and classrooms. So, if you haven't already done so, prepare a journal for your journey through this text. The questions I ask throughout are not mere hypotheticals. Think, reflect, journal, and act on them. The text is interactive. You'll want to mark up your book, take notes, and have a place for completing the many activities you find in each chapter, because you will be prompted to research, examine, plan, and implement.

Where possible, I provide you with examples of what things should (or might) look like in the classroom, along with nonexamples—what things should never look like in the classroom. These examples and nonexamples are not all-encompassing. I cannot imagine every context of every reader of this book. What I have done is drawn upon my more than 20 years of working with schools and districts across North America, coaching in classrooms, and providing professional learning to nearly one thousand school districts. From that experience, that learning, I have a warehouse of examples. Your context may be slightly different, but hopefully, the examples will be a sufficient guide.

Chapter 1 is where we establish a simple definition of equity. It's one that's easy to memorize and apply across contexts. Here you'll also learn the four equity indicators and learn to evaluate four areas common to all schools and districts. And I'll give you exemplars: what each looks like and what each should never look like.

In **Chapter 2** we turn our focus inward to consider our individual identities and then outward to understand systemic bias and racism.

In **Chapter 3** we develop a baseline of inclusivity, identifying who our learners are and how we can begin to develop cultural competency to support them in our schools and classrooms.

In **Chapter 4** we look at the foundations of creating a culture in your classroom or school that is safe and inclusive of all learners.

In **Chapter 5** we begin evaluating instructional practices based on Equity Indicator 2: Standards. We focus on what is necessary to recognize and how to respond to the learning needs of culturally and linguistically diverse learners.

In **Chapter 6** we turn our attention to instructional content, examining the materials we use based on Equity Indicator 3: Impartiality. We look for representation and consider how bias, stereotype, and misrepresentation find their way into our content and impact our learners.

In **Chapter 7** you'll also learn how and why to develop media literacy along with strategies for supplementing and enhancing existing instructional materials to make what you have work until the next curriculum adoption.

In **Chapter 8** the foundations of equitable assessment are laid. Then, in **Chapter 9**, we explore principles and strategies for creating equitable assessments and implementing equitable assessment practices through a culturally relevant lens. Specific strategies are laid out in grade-level bands to help you implement strategies most appropriate to your assigned grade level.

Similarly, in **Chapter 10** the foundations of equitable grading are laid. **Chapter 11** provides you with grade-range specific strategies for communicating grading policies and practices with parents and caregivers, and **Chapter 12** provides you with a guide to implementing an equitable grading system in your classroom.

Chapter 13 is an opportunity to reflect on the work you've done through the course of the text. You'll use the lens of the four equity indicators as your metric and think about your journey on the Pathway to Cultural Competence.

Finally, you'll find several appendices with additional exemplars, tools, and background information to supplement your learning.

Extending Your Learning

In several chapters, you'll find a section titled *The Work of the Professional Learning Community* with specific activities that are best supported by a community of educators. If you have not already done so, now is the time to create a PLC to work through the content of this text. There will be many times you'll want someone to navigate the topics along with you. Your PLC is also always the best venue for discussing the *Reflect and Act* activities and the *Mindset Meter* self-assessments at the end of every chapter, as well as more involved activities in Chapters 12 and 13.

Your collective experiences and collective intelligence will provide a deeper understanding, and perhaps greater exposure to the inequities that may be at work in your organization.

If you are not reading this book as part of a community of educators, but rather on your own, you may want to create your own community.

Of course, I'm always curious to hear what is happening in schools and classrooms. Feel free to email info@askdrberry.com with your questions and anecdotes.

I am not a *teacher*, but rather an *educator*. I hope, as you read and work through this text, that you are both a learner and an educator, too. Enjoy!

EDUCATIONAL EQUITY IN THE K–12 CLASSROOM

CHAPTER 1

The Simple Definition of Equity

Have you ever wondered, when you sit in the quiet of your own thinking and reflecting space, "Am I really doing what is equitable? Am I providing instruction or leading or speaking with an equity mindset? Am I looking through the lens of equity? And how do I know?"

If you've ever had that thought, you're not alone! I've had it. So, what is **equity**? Many of us struggle to define it. We think we know it when we see it, but cannot explain it succinctly to those outside of our world of education. It is a term that is used daily. We say that we want equitable education, but for whom? How do we get it? What needs to change? How do we know when we've achieved it?

To truly get at equity, we must first agree that each child is an individual.

I am a Black American. My parents escaped the Jim Crow South in the 1950s, settling in California. Education was important to them, as was making sure our speech had no vestiges of Black Vernacular or a Southern accent. My English was flawless. My grammar impeccable. But I was a child steeply rooted in the culture of Black America. My father was a Black Panther and practicing Muslim. My home culture did not reflect the White European-American middle class "norm" upon which U.S. schools and curriculum were built. My parents were emigrants, yet multi-generational racialized Americans. The disconnect between my own lived experience and the instructional materials—remember

Dick and Jane?—was more a chasm than a gap. Were it not for an amazing third-grade teacher, Mrs. Gowdy, I'm not sure where I would have landed. I know I was not alone.

The diversity of lived experiences of our learners is vast. I cannot list them all, nor can we imagine that we know or understand them all. When the culture of home is distinctly different from that of school, the learner is culturally diverse—whether you can *see* their culture or not.

We have identified and unidentified exceptional learners such as hearing, visually, verbally, or physically impaired, and neurodivergent.

And we have learners who are multiply diverse. Perhaps both culturally and linguistically or linguistically and neurologically, or some other combination.

There are no cookie-cutter kids, so there can be no simple cookie-cutter solutions to equitable access. What's an educator to do?

Well, let's start with a simple definition of equity. The National Equity Project (n.d., para. 1) defines it as "each child receives what they need to develop to their full academic and social potential." I define equity simply and broadly as *without bias against or favoritism for.* When talking about our thoughts, mindsets, and actions as educators being rooted in equity, we must provide an educational experience for each child without bias against any child based on their language or culture or ability or neurodivergence . . . or gender or race.

How do you define equity? Take a minute to reflect and write your own definition in your journal.

equity—without bias against or favoritism for

The Four Equity Indicators

To grade ourselves on educating through a lens of equity, we must have a consistent form of measurement—a metric. How can we quantify, or count, or measure equity? How can we measure bias or favoritism through a scientific, **quantifiable** lens?

quantifiable—anything that can be measured or counted using numbers, e.g., Lexile levels, test scores, number of books read.

Let's look at four indicators of equity (Figure 1.1) and how we can use those to measure whether our curriculum materials, instructional practices, disciplinary actions, policies, procedures, and pretty much everything else in our educational systems are truly equitable—showing no bias against or favoritism for any learner or their lived experience.

We'll rely on these four indicators of equity:

1. Meritocracy
2. Standards
3. Impartiality
4. Asset allocation

Figure 1.1

The Four Equity Indicators

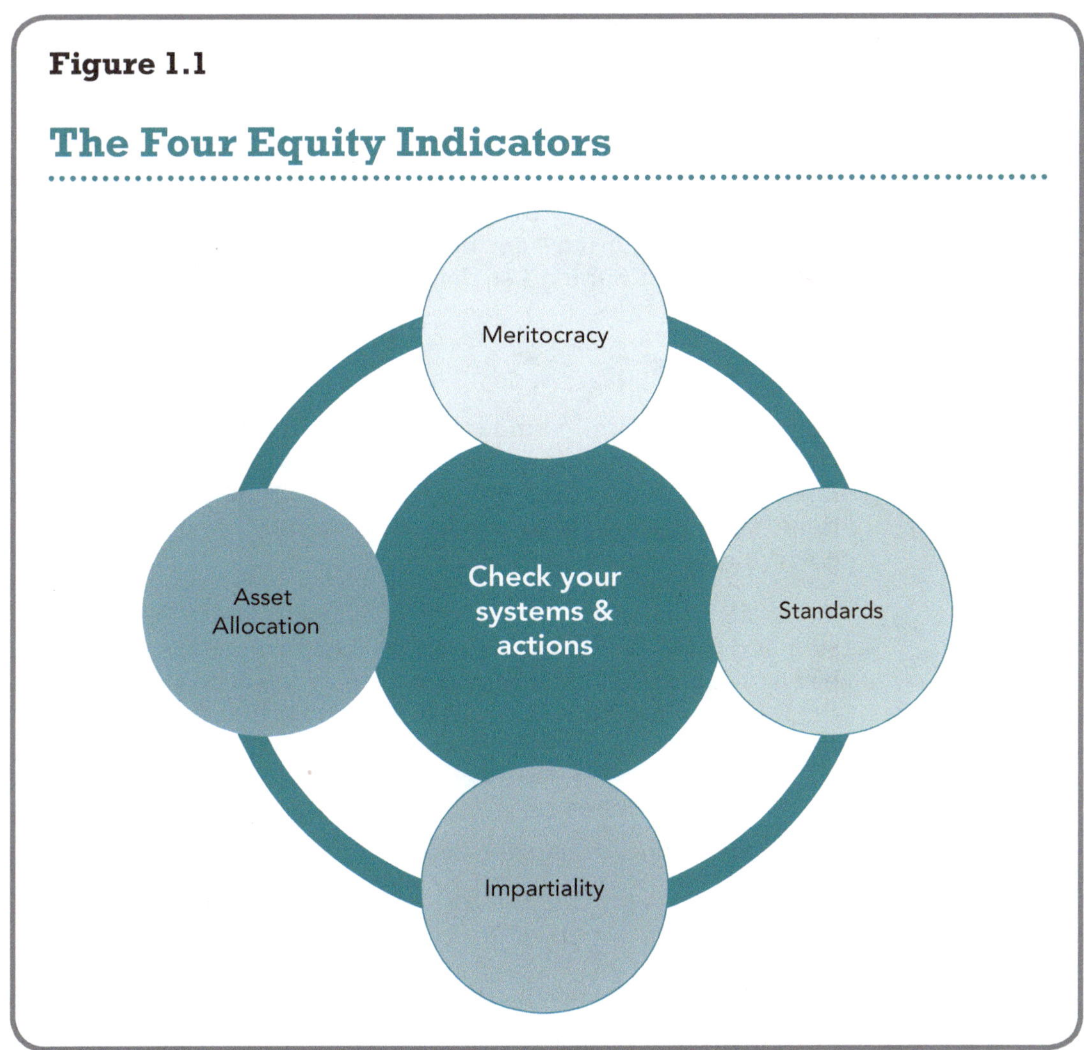

I chose these four indicators after conducting research on achievement indicators and educational equality in other developed and developing nations. UNESCO examined the condition of education through a global lens, viewing quality education as a "fundamental human right." For each of these indicators, an essential question will guide your examination as we check our classroom culture and instructional materials and practices. Each indicator is a source of data, an opportunity to check your outcomes against an ideal. The data informs us of how we are doing: we as educators and our students as learners and future global citizens.

MERITOCRACY

Meritocracy is the idea that power is held by people based on their ability. There are two essential questions to ask here:

- *Who has the power in your classroom?*
- *Are we using that power for the good of the marginalized in our school community?*

In a truly equitable system, those holding the power should be those who have the ability, the desire, and the commitment to use that power for good; for the good of the marginalized, without bias against those who may not be marginalized. We'll get more into this concept in Chapter 4 so don't worry if it feels hazy.

STANDARDS

We typically think of standards as "the knowledge or skills that every student should learn and be able to do at each grade level" (Institute for Educational Sciences, n.d., p. 1). Consider that and think more broadly: who enrolls, who attends, who achieves literacy and numeracy on time?

Think also about the standards of educators—our professional standards and the Educators' Oath in the Practitioner's Perspective box on page 13. We must consider not only the academic targets of the learners, but our adherence to standards that target our skills in crafting and delivering instruction so that every learner can demonstrate mastery. There are two essential questions to ask here:

- *Who is demonstrating mastery?*
- *Are we taking action that results in demonstrating ongoing mastery year over year?*

In a truly equitable system, the standards are not the high bar that only some (children and educators) will reach, but the minimum proficiency for each person. That means that the instruction we provide and how we provide it is determined by what is required for each child to meet that minimum level of proficiency. When we reflect upon our daily work, we ask the two questions above to shape the next day's work serving our learners.

Examine your own state's professional standards for teaching. In which standards are you demonstrating mastery? In which are you not? What actions could you take to demonstrate mastery year over year?

Practitioner's Perspective

Doctors take the Hippocratic Oath. What if educators also had to take an oath to teach? What would that oath look like? Perhaps something like this:

"I will apply pedagogic measures for the benefit of all children according to my ability and judgment; I will keep them from illiteracy and innumeracy. I will neither use an inappropriate method, nor will I make a suggestion to this effect. I will not teach to a test. I will teach for the benefit of children, remaining free of all intentional injustice, of all mischief, and in particular, of low expectations for children who come to learn" (Berry, 2023, p. 40).

IMPARTIALITY

Impartiality is another way of saying "fairness," or "without bias," but in this instance, it is more specific. The two essential questions we ask here are:

- *Who has representation?*
- *Am I accurately and appropriately considering the cultures of all those affected, or am I acting from a middle-class, White European, Western cultural bias?*

In a truly equitable classroom, every policy, practice, and curriculum instrument must be examined to ensure that you are not harming children by subliminally providing instruction that the children, their lived experiences, their races, their cultures, their people, and their languages are not the norm. For example, minor microaggressive statements such as, "Huh, that's different" in response to a learner's expressed thought or dress, or banning peer support or collaboration because it's viewed as cheating, puts the learners' cultures at odds with yours. Not recognizing all cultural holidays on the class calendar, or questioning why certain learners do not want to dress up for Halloween is partial. Oppression occurs in many forms, and omission is one of them. We often use the metaphor of "mirrors, windows, and sliding glass doors" when discussing the importance of representation and diversity in literature. We'll go deeper into that in Chapter 3.

Mirrors, Windows, and Sliding Glass Doors

Using the metaphors of *mirrors, windows,* and *sliding glass doors* to describe literature is rooted in the work of children's literature scholar Rudine Sims Bishop (2012). When examining literature for diversity of representation, it's about how learners see not only themselves, but others in books.

Mirrors are books where learners see themselves, their cultures, their languages, their lived experiences. Sometimes the characters physically look like them or members of their families. Sometimes the characters come from similar cultural or linguistic backgrounds. Or it could be that they share common lived experiences, even common traumas. The big idea is that learners see themselves reflected in the literature.

Windows are books that provide learners views into the cultures and lived experiences of people who are different from them. Windows give learners diverse perspectives. Here they learn to empathize with people who may not look like them or share common culture but may share lived experiences or thinking. The big idea here is that learners see other cultures and develop multicultural awareness.

Sliding glass doors extends the window metaphor. Learners not only "see" other cultures but are provided an opportunity to "step into" the lived experiences of diverse peoples, even if only for a moment. Learners enjoy an immersion into the lives and worlds of people and cultures they may never otherwise experience. The big idea here is that learners deeply experience other cultures, further developing empathy and multicultural awareness.

ASSET ALLOCATION

Asset allocation is about creating constructive inequality to remedy the historical oppression of marginalized learners. The essential questions here are:

- *Is there positive structural inequality?*
- *Am I choosing and allocating resources to create opportunity and excellence for all involved?*

In a truly equitable classroom, you work to remedy or eliminate gaps and disproportionality. This means that assets or resources (like time and small group instruction) are committed in a targeted way to provide what is needed for those who need more, all the while ensuring that you do no harm to any other learners. When you allocate classroom assets equitably, you do your part to eliminate disproportionalities in areas such as referrals to special education or suspensions and expulsions from your classroom.

The Four Equity Indicators at Work

To see how we can examine our schools and classrooms through the lenses of the four equity indicators, we'll use two areas common to every K–12 system: foundational skills and discipline. Why these two? Simple. Everyone involved in the day-to-day operations of school has some connection to both. You either provide or are impacted by them. And every learner encounters and is impacted by both at some point in their educational journey.

FOUNDATIONAL SKILLS

Meritocracy

I've yet to meet an educator that doesn't state they want all their learners to read, write, think, and calculate with mastery at grade level. After all, it becomes more difficult to provide content instruction to older learners who lack basic skills. They tend to have more disciplinary issues. Their futures as productive citizens are not nearly as promising as those of learners who are higher achievers.

But do we always do what is in the best interest of our learners? Are children who are racially, culturally, or linguistically diverse equally successful in foundational skills in reading and mathematics when it comes time for state testing? Are there achievement gaps fueled by a **provision gap**?

provision gap—the difference between demonstrated academic ability as measured by high-stakes assessments, often annual state testing, and the required benchmarks of a grade level; the gap that is created by the use of ineffective instructional methods and culturally inappropriate curriculum

When we look at test score data, which groups tend to have the largest gaps? These are the learners we are marginalizing when we do not use our power for good.

Standards

Mastery of foundational literacy skills means the learner can read grade level material with **automaticity**, **prosody**, and high-level comprehension without scaffolds or supports. We serve learners best when those responsible for determining the instructional methods and materials for each child, especially at kindergarten and Grade 1, ask the two essential questions over and over: *Who is demonstrating mastery? Are we taking action that results in demonstrating ongoing mastery year over year?* When we take it down to the level of *each* child, we move away from decision-making based on price or preference and toward data-based decision-making rooted in equity.

At the higher grade levels and across content areas, our learners rely on those foundational skills. And you rely on your learners having mastered those skills so that they can master the standards for your content area and grade level. As a community of educators in a system rooted in equity, we must hold one another accountable for making choices that result in equal outcomes. We must work with one another not only in our siloed departments and grade levels, but across them.

We make certain our choices, including providing professional learning for those who deliver instruction, are in the best interest of our learners. We make certain that our choices for children who are racially, culturally, or linguistically diverse result in their mastery of foundational skills. We make certain to not create achievement gaps fueled by provision gaps.

automaticity—the ability to read connected text without spending cognitive energy processing low-level details

prosody—the ability to read connected text orally with intonation and appropriate emotion in various contexts

Through the frame of standards, when we look at outcomes across the grades, we look again to see which groups tend to have not only large, but also enduring gaps. We identify the subject areas where these gaps present themselves. We analyze when these gaps appear. Which learners are we marginalizing by our inaction or refusal to respond to the needs of each child? What materials selection or methodological approaches need to be modified, strengthened, or abandoned?

Impartiality

An important indicator of impartiality is representation. You might be thinking it's easy to have representation when providing reading instruction. After all, it's all about literature, right? And you're right. Representation in literature is fairly easy, so let's focus on mathematics. What does impartiality look like when providing foundational math instruction?

Keep in mind, it's more than just who learners see, it's also about the ways we teach. How do you engage your learners? Do you use tools that will spark curiosity and engagement from learners who are historically marginalized through teaching from a White, Western perspective? Is content presented in ways that *accurately and appropriately consider the cultures of all* the learners in your classroom?

The genetic roots of many Black learners in North and South America reach back to the Yoruba people of West Africa, generally from areas that are now Nigeria, Benin, and Togo. Their traditional divination practices, the Ifá divination system, uses a binary system based on a binary principle of 0s and 1s. If this sounds familiar, it is because it is quite similar to the one found in modern computer science.

Babalawos, Ifá diviners or priests, use either an instrument known as an Opele or palm nuts thrown on a tray to create binary patterns. Each pattern corresponds to an Odu, which is a combination of specific symbols. Each of the 16 basic Odus and 240 permutations is associated with a significant body of verses full of wisdom, advice, and references to historical and mythological events.

What may interest and engage Black learners in your classroom, and others as well, is that while the modern binary system is generally attributed to seventeenth-century German mathematician Gottfried Leibenz, the Ifá system has existed since the tenth century, and possibly even earlier.

In addition, the Ifá system is still practiced today, not only in Africa, but among the Yoruba diaspora communities around the world. And that diaspora is likely represented in your school or classroom, but the learners themselves may not even know they are a part of it.

Asset Allocation

If our goal is to have all learners read, write, think, and calculate with mastery at grade level, then we must allocate the necessary resources in a manner that ensures just that. This may mean using a different, more explicit and systematic curriculum. It may mean smaller class sizes. Perhaps it means more time in instruction. And in an equitable system we may need to create this structure of "positive inequality" while maintaining or improving the achievement of learners who are already at grade level.

Foundational skills are just that: the foundation. Without equity in foundational skills, we cannot achieve equality in other areas such as advanced placement coursework.

DISCIPLINE

Meritocracy

Every classroom has issues that arise out of disciplinary challenges. Research tends to support that learners who lack academic skills typically have more disciplinary actions taken against them. Unlike foundational skills that can be remediated so learners catch up, the actions taken against learners for disciplinary infractions often have life and death consequences in the near term.

For children of color and children with special needs, particularly behavior disorders, encounters with the justice system occur far too frequently. To alleviate this, school systems are turning to alternative policies, such as eliminating the use of force by school resource officers and instituting restorative practices to replace punitive actions.

Here we must ask if children who are racially or culturally diverse are disproportionately represented in punitive disciplinary actions in our schools. When we look at suspension, expulsion, and arrest data, which groups tend to be overrepresented in comparison to their percentage of the overall population? These are your disenfranchised learners. They are likely victims of bias and it may not be the children, but the adults who require intervention. Perhaps the classroom instruction that is being provided is not meeting the needs of the learners. Perhaps as educators we lack the cultural competence to connect with racially or culturally diverse learners. Perhaps we even fear some learners because of our lack of cultural connectedness.

Standards

You might wonder what standards have to do with discipline. Recall the definition of standards: "the knowledge or skills that every student should learn and be able to do at each grade level" (Institute for Educational Sciences, n.d., p. 1). We do not have state or national standards for behavior, however we do have expectations. We expect children to *know how* to behave. Those expectations are generally prescribed by community and cultural norms. But whose culture?

And in the absence of written behavior standards and high-stakes assessment of their mastery, we don't teach behavioral norms. We tend to simply expect adherence to norms that inevitably vary from classroom to classroom, year to year.

This has lifelong academic and social implications for our learners. Consider that the United States has the world's highest rate of incarceration (Prison Policy Initiative, 2021). Though it accounts for only 4.23% of the world's population overall, 25%

of the world's prison population is in the United States (United Nations Department of Economic and Social Affairs, 2022; United States Census Bureau, 2024). Mass incarceration is not simply a symptom of our learners' behaviors after leaving school. It is a systemic issue with its roots in how we teach or fail to teach behavior and how we discipline learners while they are in our classrooms.

In an equitable system, standards of behavior are taught. You can teach standards of behavior for your classroom. If the standard isn't met, you should strive to find ways to teach them without further harming any individual.

One of my behavioral pet peeves was the language learners used to address adults. Call me "old school" or a bit of a "Southern traditionalist," but where I come from, adults are addressed as "ma'am" or "sir." In my California classrooms, I made that expectation clear. It was an expectation for not only when they were in my classroom, but at any time on campus. And while some may find that a bit unrealistic, not only did my learners adhere to it, I received accolades for their exemplary behavior outside of my classroom. Other educators appreciated the carryover effect. After a while, my learners taught their peers and siblings to address adults in the same manner. And my learners were all Title I, all learners of color, attending school in what most would describe as "the worst neighborhood in town."

Impartiality

If comprehensive data was collected about who is disciplined in your classroom, what would it show? Think about who you discipline and what you discipline them for. Who is represented? Are **culturally and linguistically diverse learners (CLDLs)** more often disciplined? Is there even greater disproportionality for those learners who are Black, Latine, or Indigenous? Do your Black and Latine learners see themselves as discipline problems? More importantly, are your classroom disciplinary practices a mirror teaching them this?

> **culturally and linguistically diverse learner (CLDL)**—learners whose home culture is not mainstream, middle class, and White and/or whose language background reflects anything other than School English

Here, we adults need the sliding glass doors. We need to walk through them to experience the lives of our learners and develop greater empathy for their lived experiences. Then, we must examine our disciplinary practices to develop an equitable system.

In an equitable system, impartiality of discipline comes from working to develop cultural competence and becoming an antiracist educator. It comes as you work to establish restorative practices and eliminate encounters with the school- or community-based justice systems. We cannot change overrepresentation unless and until we change our systems and our mindsets. That change begins in your classroom and in your mind.

Asset Allocation

Think about your classroom discipline and any disproportionality there. If our goal is to reduce overall punitive disciplinary actions while at the same time eliminating disproportionality and encounters with the juvenile justice system, then we must allocate the necessary resources in a manner that does just that. Examine your curriculum and instruction for representation. Develop cultural competence and an antiracism mindset. Create a system of restorative practices in your classroom and eliminate retributive practices. (For more information on **restorative and retributive disciplinary practices**, see Appendix A.) In an equitable classroom we do these things by allocating resources where needed while maintaining the safety and security of your entire classroom community.

restorative practice—a conflict resolution approach focusing on repairing harm and rebuilding relationships emphasizing dialogue, accountability, and understanding the impact of one's actions, fostering community and trust among participants

retributive practice—an approach to discipline centered on punishment for wrongdoers, emphasizing the infliction of penalties proportionate to the offense; prioritizes deterrence and retribution

The good news is, by doing the work in this book, by studying and engaging in thoughtful reflection at each prompt, you will be well on your way!

Creating disciplinary equity is more about our behavior and actions as adults, rather than simply those of the learners. We must shift our mindsets, our behaviors, our beliefs (see Tables 1.1–1.4). Some of that shifting comes in the form of developing cultural competency. Some comes from professional learning and growth. Some from redesigning our systems. And while you may not be able to change the system, what you model in your classroom just might be the shining exemplar that becomes a catalyst for systemic change.

Table 1.1

What Meritocracy Looks Like in Schools and Classrooms

EXEMPLARY CLASSROOMS LOOK LIKE THIS . . .	. . . NOT THIS
Foundational Skills	
At grades K–3, classroom instruction is clearly differentiated in ELA and math with learners who are below grade level receiving explicit, systematic instruction that meets their needs.	At grades K–3, classroom instruction in ELA and math is the same for all learners regardless of their current performance level.
Struggling learners receive instruction that accelerates their learning so they may close any gap within two years.	Struggling learners may not be identified, do not receive differentiated instruction, or the "differentiation" is remediation rather than acceleration. Instruction does not support closing gaps.
Achievement gaps either (a) do not exist between subgroups, or (b) are on a trajectory of closure within two years.	Achievement gaps exist between subgroups and are not on a trajectory of closure within two years.
Discipline	
Learners removed from class for behavior are not disproportionately of any one race, ethnicity, gender, or other identity group. Any behavior that receives punitive treatment is addressed equally and at all times, regardless of who commits the infraction.	Learners removed from class for behavior may disproportionately be of a particular race, ethnicity, gender, or other identity group. Behaviors that receive punitive treatment are not addressed equally. Favoritism is shown to particular racial, ethnic, gender, or other identified groups.

Table 1.2

What Standards Look Like in Schools and Classrooms

EXEMPLARY CLASSROOMS LOOK LIKE THIS . . .	. . . NOT THIS
Foundational Skills	
Elementary core curriculum is chosen based on a demonstrated scientific instructional methodology and implemented with a level of fidelity that ensures all learners demonstrate grade-level proficiency in literacy and numeracy skills at each grade level.	Core curriculum is chosen based on something other than science that backs the efficacy of the instructional methodology; and/or implementation lacks fidelity; and/or more than 5% of learners lack grade-level proficiency in literacy and numeracy skills at each grade level.
Discipline	
Standards of discipline are written.	No consistent standards exist for behavioral expectations in each grade level.
Behavioral norms are consistent from classroom to classroom and matriculate from grade to grade.	Each instructor uses their own norms and judgment to determine what is appropriate behavior.
Instruction in behavioral norms and social-emotional skills is provided as part of the regular course of instruction.	No instruction in social-emotional skills is provided.

Table 1.3

What Impartiality Looks Like in Schools and Classrooms

EXEMPLARY CLASSROOMS LOOK LIKE THIS . . .	. . . NOT THIS
Foundational Skills	
Curriculum provides mirrors, windows, and doors in both ELA and math, so that learners can connect to the content through a variety of perspectives representative of themselves and other culturally and linguistically diverse peoples.	Curriculum tends to be White Eurocentric in perspective. Little or no representation of culturally and linguistically diverse peoples, or their contributions to the content area are found.

EXEMPLARY CLASSROOMS LOOK LIKE THIS . . .	. . . NOT THIS
Discipline	
Racial, ethnic, gender, learning ability, or socioeconomic-status subgroup disproportionality does not exist in disciplinary data.	Racial, ethnic, gender, learning ability, or socioeconomic-status subgroup disproportionality exists in disciplinary data.
Classroom management supports a culture where all learners can see themselves as positive behavior models.	Poor classroom management results in a culture where CLDLs are more often seen as disciplinary problems.

Table 1.4

What Asset Allocation Looks Like in Schools and Classrooms

EXEMPLARY CLASSROOMS LOOK LIKE THIS . . .	. . . NOT THIS
Foundational Skills	
CLDLs and learners-of-promise receive explicit, systematic curriculum and targeted instruction that meets their needs, resulting in at- or above-grade level outcomes in all subjects.	Resources are not allocated in a manner that will effectively support the academic achievement of CLDLs and learners-of-promise.
Learners at- and above-grade level receive curriculum and instruction that meets their needs so that they continue acceleration at a pace commensurate with their abilities and enrichment in line with their interests.	Learners at- and above-grade level receive curriculum and instruction that results in disengagement due to slow pace or low-interest and that may result in under-performance.
Discipline	
Sincere and consistent efforts are made to intervene early using restorative practices in the classroom, particularly for learners who appear to struggle with compliance or exhibit behaviors which may be deemed disruptive or destructive.	No early intervention exists. Early warning signs are ignored or dismissed.
Teachers seek out mental health resources for all learners, particularly for learners who appear to struggle with compliance or exhibit behaviors which may be deemed disruptive or destructive.	No resources are available or sought out.

Conclusion

In this chapter, we've covered a simple definition of equity and the Four Equity Indicators of meritocracy, standards, impartiality, and asset allocation. We considered how those indicators present themselves in foundational skills and disciplinary actions. You'll revisit these indicators many times in this text. So, if it feels a bit murky still, not to worry. The content will spiral and scaffold. Spaced repetition is a proven strategy for reaching mastery.

In Chapter 2, you'll develop an understanding of implicit and explicit bias. We'll examine racism's four tiers, bias, and their roles in equitable instruction.

Reflect and Act

Reflect on any questions and notes you wrote while reading about the four equity indicators. Now examine your own classroom, school, or district—depending on the capacity in which you serve. In your journal, respond to these questions: Where do you see inequity? What do you think is the most egregious of those? Which do you think should be addressed first? Can you use the four equity indicators to begin the work? What additional learning or supports might you need?

Use the following mindset meter as a self-assessment. The mindset meter probes different levels of understanding. Use it to make connections between the chapter content and your beliefs and behaviors. Reflect. Think. Plan. Record your responses in your journal.

●●● MY MINDSET METER

Complete the mindset meter as a self-assessment of this chapter's content.

Knowledge: The purpose of equity in the classroom as I understand it from this chapter:

____

____

____

____

Comprehension: The four equity indicators as I understand them from this chapter:

____

____

____

____

Application: How I can use each of the equity indicators in my daily work:

____

____

____

____

Analysis: I can draw these conclusions about (in)equity based on what I learned in this chapter:

____

____

____

____

Synthesis: This is how I will begin or continue to work through the lens of equity:

____

____

____

____

Evaluation: I used to think . . . but now I think . . .

____

____

____

____

If you are completing this work as part of a book study or professional learning, you may find there are great variances in the way you and your peers respond. This is because your lived experiences and your cultures may be more diverse than you think.

CONSIDERING YOUR OWN IDENTITY

CHAPTER 2

Setting a Baseline

We dive deep into cultural and linguistic diversity in this book; however, with any new learning, it's good to get a baseline. Let's get yours. This is my favorite activity, and one I start any day-long or longer professional learning session with. It's not quite the same in this context, so, I've made a few alterations. It's the best we can do. Please participate. This is an essential entry in your journal.

identity—the conception, qualities, beliefs, and expressions that make a person or group distinct, encompassing aspects like culture, ethnicity, gender, and personal experiences; who or what a person is; similarity or affinity to a group

Start by identifying 7 to 10 characteristics that inform your cultural **identity**. They might be things that relate to where you are from, geographically. They could be your race, ethnicity, language, marital status, gender identity, sexual orientation, religion, worldview, artistic skills, athletic skills, special interests, political affiliation, etc. Who are you?

Now, put an asterisk next to the two characteristics that you feel most strongly inform your identity.

Thinking about just the two characteristics marked with the asterisk, with whom in your workplace do you share those? Not one or the other, but both. If you don't share both with anyone, identify who you share each one with. Is there a large number of people or a small one?

Looking at that list, does this suggest that you are an insider? That you have a place of privilege in your school organization? Or are you an outsider, marginalized, with little insight, visibility, or influence in relation to, or with regard to those who hold power?

If you identified characteristics that suggest you have insider status in your school or organization, please answer these questions:

- Identify people in your school or organization who do not share those two characteristics. What are their names?
- Be brutally honest. Can you identify or imagine ways in which their outsider status makes it harder to achieve things in your organization, or to navigate the dominant environment?

If you identified characteristics that suggest you have outsider status in your school or organization, please answer these questions:

- Identify people in your school or organization who do not share those two characteristics. What are their names?
- Be brutally honest. Can you identify or imagine ways in which their privileged status makes it easier to achieve things in your organization, or to navigate the dominant environment?

Now, think about your learners. How many of them share those two most important characteristics with you? How might their privileged or marginalized status impact their daily navigation of school?

Understanding Implicit and Explicit Bias

As educators, our understanding of implicit and explicit bias plays a critical role in the learning environment and learner outcomes. Our responsibilities as educators includes fostering an inclusive classroom and school environment, instruction, and discipline conducive to learners' personal, social, emotional, and academic growth. These goals are undermined by the existence of implicit and explicit bias in our texts, our methods, our policies, our practices, even our classroom decor. These implicit biases affect our learners' self-esteem, motivation, behaviors, academic outcomes, and their futures.

I like to use an iceberg metaphor (see Figure 2.1) to help understand bias. If we were to spot an iceberg while safely on shore or in a sturdy, seaworthy boat, we would see only what is above the water. But what do we know about an iceberg? We know that what we can see above the water is only the tip of the iceberg. Much more mass lies below the surface. And though we cannot see it, it can do a tremendous amount of damage before we even know it exists.

Figure 2.1

The Iceberg of Bias

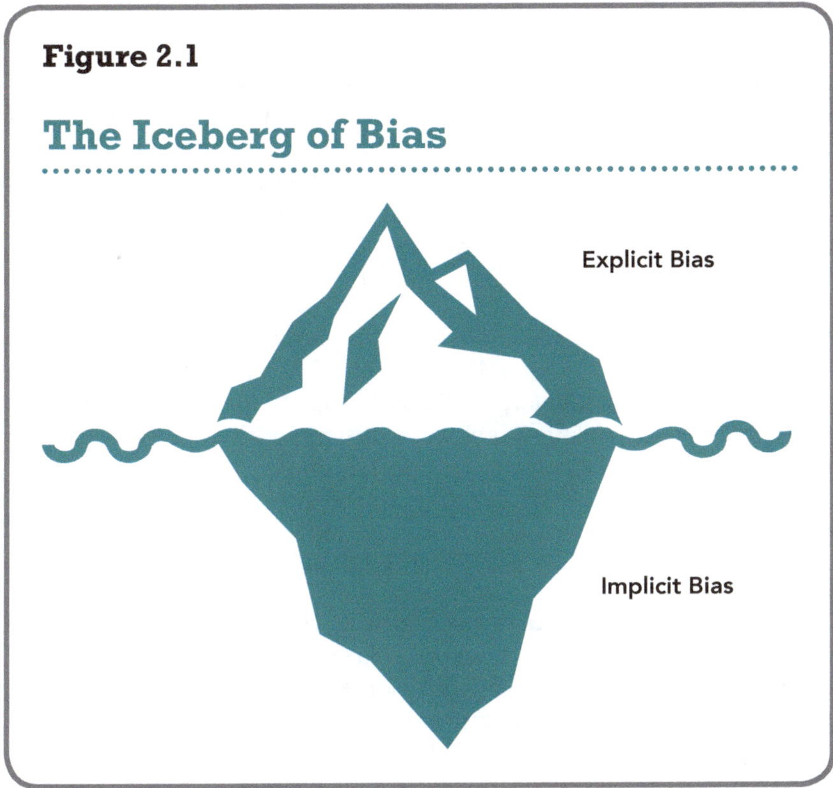

Source: iStock.com/Veronika Oliinyk

Explicit bias is the tip of the iceberg. It refers to those conscious prejudices that humans hold toward others based on race, gender, age, religion, culture, and other known or assumed social or genetic factors that we can name, see, and call out. In our schools, the existence of these biases often leads to discriminatory practices in grading, placement, assignment, and discipline. For marginalized groups who are the targets of discrimination, **explicit bias** creates an openly hostile environment. Bias shows up in teacher expectations about performance and behavior, in unfair grading practices, placement in honors and advanced coursework. It limits learners' opportunities, hindering their academic, personal, and psychological growth and development.

explicit—stated clearly and in detail, leaving no room for confusion, misinterpretation, or doubt

explicit bias—the conscious and intentional prejudices or stereotypes individuals hold toward others, based on race, gender, age, religion, culture, and other known or assumed social or genetic factors that we can name, see, and call out, usually in a way that is unfair and/or harmful

Implicit bias is the part of the iceberg that lies below the surface of the water. The part we cannot see. These are the unconscious attitudes or stereotypes that humans hold toward others based on things such as race, gender, age, religion, culture, and other known or assumed social or genetic factors.

But unlike explicit bias, implicit bias is often subtle. And in that subtlety lies a horrific insidiousness. It manifests in a variety of ways, from teacher and administrator body language to the way we ask questions of certain learners—and which questions we ask of them. It manifests in who we call on in class and when or how often we do so. It subtly favors some learners over others. In that favoritism lies inequity—a favoritism for.

Research informs us that teachers implicitly hold lower expectations for learners of color (Mizrav, 2023; TNTP, 2018), and believe that girls are less proficient in STEM subjects (Ireland et al., 2018) and that boys, especially Black boys, are more likely to be discipline problems (Butler-Barnes & Inniss-Thompson, 2020; Townsend, 2000). These implicit biases negatively affect our learners' self-perception, engagement, and both academic and disciplinary outcomes (Butler-Barnes & Inniss-Thompson, 2020).

Overcoming implicit biases, something you may not even know you hold, is difficult. I offer you a first step: recognize that you have them. It's okay. We all do! Some implicit bias is harmless preference, like loving all animals, but treating cats with more affection than dogs. However, those implicit biases that impact what instruction we provide and how we provide it, who we discipline and how we discipline—those biases have lifelong social, economic, and psychological impact.

Those biases do harm.

Engaging in professional learning, ongoing self-reflection, and anti-bias training is a next step. This work is a precursor to implementing classroom strategies, examining and changing instructional materials, instructional methodologies, policies, and practices to mitigate if not eliminate implicit bias from our schools and classrooms.

Whether implicit or explicit, bias may be personal (held by an individual) or institutional, baked into the system of K-12 or compulsory education, or your specific school or school district or system. When the bias is something that is part of the structure of an institution such as school, we refer to it as **systemic bias.**

Let's look now at how implicit and explicit bias impact providing instruction and learning.

implicit bias—a natural phenomenon that exists in all humans, based on observed, taught, and reinforced behavior and ideas that cause prejudice in favor of or against a thing, a person, a group, or a culture, usually in a way that is unfair and/or harmful

systemic bias—pervasive, ingrained prejudice within a system or institution that results in unequal treatment or outcomes for a particular group, often based on race, gender, or other characteristics.

Identifying Systemic Biases

We can never achieve equity unless we work to understand, identify, and root out the subtle practices, policies, and patterns that measurably favor some while disadvantaging and damaging others. Remember the measurements discussed previously: meritocracy, standards, impartiality, and asset allocation. The questions that you ask for each of those will help to determine whether equity or inequity exists.

Curriculum, or what instruction we provide, may reflect systemic bias with a source being the developer of the curriculum. Typically, educational publishers develop instructional materials to meet the demands of the three largest U.S. markets: California, Florida, and Texas (Bradley, 2021); their instructional standards and frameworks. This means that the materials, images, narrative and expository texts, even the version of history presented, are rooted in the perspectives of those who hold the power to determine what content will be sold or banned in those three states (Ravitch, 2003).

In some areas of the country, the perspectives and achievements of Black, Indigenous, and other People of Color (BIPOC) peoples and historically marginalized groups may be absent, misrepresented, distorted, or worse yet, explicitly banned. If history lessons highlight the accomplishments of the founders while ignoring the holocausts perpetuated on Indigenous peoples and enslaved Africans, it signifies systemic bias. If your high school's literary canon is devoted to the works of White men, while ignoring the contributions of women and authors of color, it signifies systemic bias. If the authors of your textbooks are disproportionately of one race, it signifies a culturally biased perspective and thus, systemic bias.

The Literary Canon

On winning the Nobel Prize in Literature, Toni Morrison said, "Our silence has been long and deep… In canonical literature, we have always been spoken for. Or we have been spoken to. Or we have appeared as jokes or as flat figures suggesting sensuality" (Gates & Senna, 1993).

Morrison's critique of the American canon, the body of literary works most widely recognized, studied, and taught in literature classes is supported by several studies (Applebee, 1989, 1992; Hansen, 2005; Kumar, 2022). The U.S. high school canon has essentially remained unchanged for more than 30 years. These texts are typically considered of high artistic quality, significant to American culture, and influential in shaping literary tradition. Yet, to Morrison's point, omit authentic voices of people of color.

The ten most commonly cited authors and their works are (Applebee, 1989, 1992; Barron, 2021; Cawley, 2015; Kumar, 2022):

- William Shakespeare: *Romeo and Juliet*, *Hamlet*, *Julius Caesar*, and *Macbeth*
- Mark Twain: *The Adventures of Huckleberry Finn*
- Nathaniel Hawthorne: *The Scarlet Letter*
- J.D. Salinger: *The Catcher in the Rye*
- John Knowles: *A Separate Peace*
- Tennessee Williams: *The Glass Menagerie*
- William Golding: *The Lord of the Flies*

Less often cited are the following:

- Harper Lee: *To Kill a Mockingbird*
- John Steinbeck: *Of Mice and Men* and *The Grapes of Wrath*
- George Orwell: *1984* and *Animal Farm*
- Jane Austen: *Pride and Prejudice*

Of these 11 authors and 16 titles:

- only two authors are women
- none of the authors are BIPOC
- none of the authors identified as being queer (LGBTQIA+)
- none of the protagonists are persons of color
- where people of color are portrayed, their characters are neither fully developed, nor truly humanized

The canon as indicated here is White Eurocentric and centered on cisgender men. It entirely excludes works by authors from diverse backgrounds and perspectives.

It's more difficult to identify a middle school canon, or a K–5 canon. And that's not a bad thing. It may mean that educators and commercially published ELA curricula have acted to diversify literature at the lower grades.

And recent efforts to diversify the high school literary canon to include more works by authors of color, women authors, and authors from varied socio-economic and cultural backgrounds have been met with increasing bans on titles and authors who present and represent diversity of race and identity, even the Nobel Prize winning Toni Morrison.

Instruction, or how we teach, may reflect systemic bias rooted in our own personal biases, the instruction we received from various schools of education, and professional learning. Instructional bias surfaces in methods that favor certain ways of learning, knowledge, experiences, and engagement. Many learners of color come from cultures that value collectivism and are steeped in oral traditions. Those learners engage through conversation and working with one another. In some cultures, helping others is a moral imperative; however, in our classrooms, methods may favor individualism.

We first tend to teach as we've learned. We mirror the methods that worked for us or do what our professors told us to do. Given that higher education faculty is 67% White European (National Center for Education Statistics [NCES], 2021), and that 80% of our educators are White Europeans (NCES, 2022), we can readily deduce that we've learned methods favoring a White Eurocentric ideology.

Our systems assign grades based on individual achievement. (More about grades in Chapters 8 to 12.) We create individual assignments. I've been in classrooms where students are asked to distribute points among themselves, potentially passing the propensity of bias to the learners to victimize one of their own. We call on learners as individuals. Unlike on a popular game show, they are not offered a *phone a friend* option to collaboratively think through their understanding. They are often told they are right or wrong, without nuance or consideration of cultural interpretations, especially when discussing literature. And again, literature tends to be overwhelmingly White Eurocentric and authored by cisgender men, particularly in states and districts engaging in banning books due to their diversity content.

Disciplinary practices also reveal systemic bias. Across the United States, in school systems large and small, suspensions and expulsions are disproportionately meted out to Black and Latine learners. Data published by the National Center for

Education Statistics annually report that students of color, particularly Black and Latino boys, are more likely to be suspended or expelled and more likely to have law enforcement actions taken against them compared to their White peers for the same or similar infractions (NCES, 2020). This indicates a bias in disciplinary actions.

Identifying Personal Biases

It's important for educators to not only understand what personal biases are, but also to acknowledge that they have them. This acknowledgment is a critical step for educators to ensure that they're providing equitable, inclusive, and effective learning environments for every child. Much like what happens with identifying systemic biases, we cannot as individuals truly work toward equity unless we do the work on ourselves to understand, identify, and root out our own practices, our own patterns that measurably favor some while disadvantaging and damaging others. Here again, we can use the Four Equity Indicators to measure our personal biases: meritocracy, standards, impartiality, and asset allocation. And once again, the questions that you ask for each of those will help to determine whether equity or inequity exist because of your own personal biases.

ANOTHER LOOK AT CURRICULUM, INSTRUCTION, AND DISCIPLINE

Curriculum may reflect our individual biases when the source of the curriculum development is the individual educator. In addition, our unchecked biases can affect the material that we choose to present in our classrooms, which may potentially lead to a narrow, biased curriculum. When we are aware of our biases, we can more intentionally select a broad range of resources and topics to present a more balanced and comprehensive view of the subject matter. When you leverage meritocracy, you use your power to select and implement curriculum that is unbiased. But how do you do that?

Many elementary teachers may look toward the units they have developed and the choices they make about which units are taught to whom and when. Secondary teachers in the content areas should examine their curriculum choices as well. When our personal biases mirror the systemic biases in our schools and school districts, our classroom choices may simply go to underscore and further enhance the damage that's done to our learners. A personal audit of our curriculum choices, where those choices are personal choices would serve to inform you as to whether or not your choices are disproportionately reflective of a single perspective or your own personal biases.

Instruction or how we teach is greatly subject to our own personal biases. We tend to teach in the manner in which we were taught. And if we were taught in systems of education that have continued to carry on systemic biases, we will reflect those same biases in our own methods. We also know that not every child learns the same way, and so if we fail to notice and recognize the differences in the ways that each of our children does learn, and simply teach in a manner that we desire to teach, or that we like to teach, then we are further damaging children through our own implicit biases.

Reflect on the second essential question of impartiality: *Am I accurately and appropriately considering the cultures of all those affected, or am I acting from a middle-class, White-European, Western cultural bias?*

Why are you providing instruction and using the strategies or methods you are? Is it because of the science supporting the methods? Is it because they are what you were taught in teacher's college? Is it because you enjoy the methods?

Our classroom disciplinary practices also reveal our individual implicit biases. If our classroom rules are grounded in our personal belief systems and not what is necessarily beneficial for all children, then we are exercising our personal biases. When children behave in a manner that is culturally appropriate and culturally affirming to them, but their behavior does not fit your personal cultural beliefs, you must determine if your personal biases are interfering with your ability to be culturally affirming to your learners. Consider who you allow to turn in homework late, who you send to the office for disrespect or for other behaviors that truly do not interfere with the conduct of class, particularly if you do not equally punish every child for engaging in the same behavior.

Finally, resource allocation can reflect personal biases based on the assignments that we choose and the resources that are required to complete them. If you have disparity in socioeconomic groups in your classroom, you have unequal learning environments that may disadvantage students from under-resourced homes. If you assign work that requires the use of materials or resources from outside of the classroom, your personal biases are interfering with the success of your students. As educators, we must examine what every child has in terms of resources. Even better, we should not require that children use or acquire resources outside of what is available in the classroom or at school. You should not have to use your personal funds to fill those gaps either! Look for classroom-level grants and seek donations from local philanthropical organizations and businesses that may employ learners after graduation.

Have you ever assigned a task or project you thought would be great for students only to later realize that not all students had the capacity to complete it? Most teachers have at some point. Many times this is quite innocuous and we would not have thoughts that it would be harmful to children, but here's a simple example of something that is inequitable and quite often damaging to children.

Let's say we assign children the task of completing a family history or a family tree. Without careful consideration and planning, we may overlook that some children are in foster care and some children may not have information about any ancestors beyond the parents or caregivers with whom they currently live. There may be children whose parent (or parents) are incarcerated. There are those children who have come from circumstances where they have lost contact with their parents. Some have parents who have been deported. Some children come from communities of warfare and strife.

Quite commonly, we don't consider that many of our children cannot trace ancestry back to a grandparent or beyond two, maybe three generations most.

This is an example of how children's lived experiences are different from the lived experience of the educator. What may bring us as teachers joy may bring trauma to some of the children we are educating. An alternative is to have early learners complete a community web instead. Focus them on the people who make up their community, while still teaching the concepts of relationship and interconnectedness. At the upper elementary grades, learners can extend this to an exploration of their personal identities, cultures, and social elements through project-based learning. Middle and high school learners can research and articulate how their personal histories, cultures, and the broader historical contexts (local, state, or national) have shaped their current identities and perspectives.

Racism: The Four-Tiered Model

We cannot discuss equity in any setting in any organization without first acknowledging the existence of racism and the existence of race as an element that impacts our culturally and linguistically diverse learners. Later in this chapter, I suggest several books for those who would like a more in-depth exploration. I'll endeavor here to give you enough background to make sense of the content in this book.

Racism is not as simple as we would like to believe it is. It is not simply about how some people think, believe, and behave. Racism is about power. Racism comes in many forms and is baked into our society. Many of us are familiar with either a Multi-Tiered Support Services (MTSS) or RTI (Response to Intervention) systems. Typically, those are three or four tiered systems. You may think of racism in much the same way. Figure 2.2 provides an illustration—the model of those four tiers of racism as concentric circles. I created this visual to encapsulate the work of numerous researchers, all of whom agree on the varying types of racism but label the types differently. If you have worked with other models, they should readily align to this one.

Figure 2.2

The Four-Tiered Model of Racism

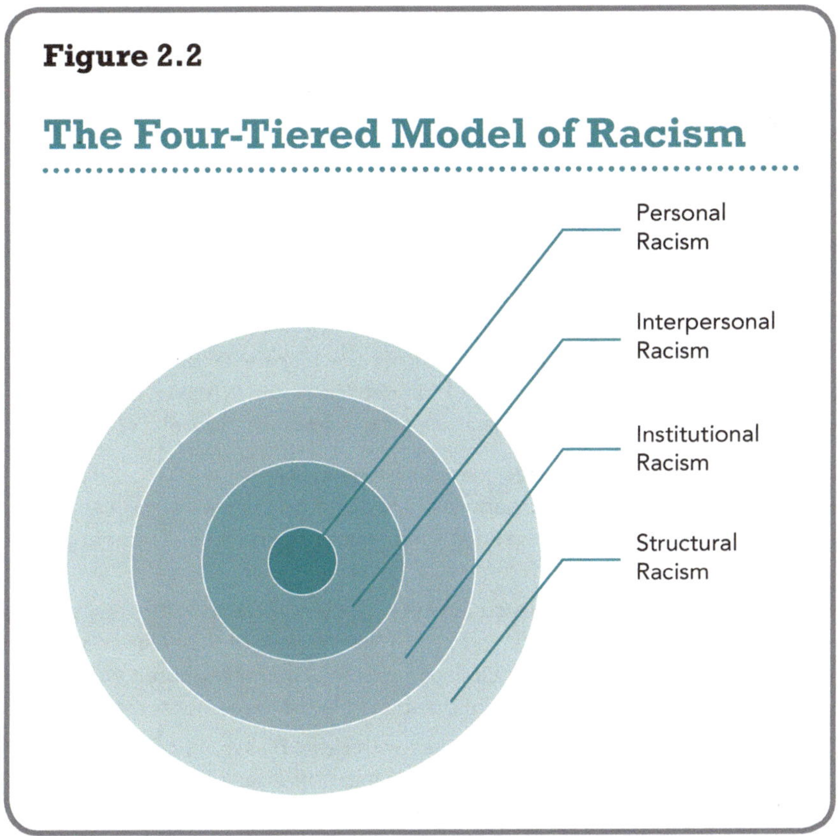

Table 2.1 provides a definition of each tier and what it looks like in the classroom. Through understanding this four-tiered model of racism we can analyze the full context of what is required to create equity in our schools and how race and racism play a role in that.

Table 2.1

The Four Tiers of Racism Explained

TIER	DEFINITION	WHAT IT LOOKS LIKE IN SCHOOLS AND CLASSROOMS
1. Structural racism	Racial bias among institutions and across society (national, state, and regional	• Laws, rules, and policies exist that provide an unfair advantage to some learners, White learners in this case; unfair or harmful treatment is meted out to learners of color because of their race.

(Continued)

(Continued)

TIER	DEFINITION	WHAT IT LOOKS LIKE IN SCHOOLS AND CLASSROOMS
	departments of education)	• Persistent and pervasive achievement gaps exist between Black and White or Brown and White learners at the state level • Funding disproportionality exists by race • School district boundaries are gerrymandered, supporting inequitable funding
2. Institutional racism	Racial bias that occurs within institutions of power (schools and districts)	• Learners of color are disproportionality suspended and expelled, even for infractions that White learners are not • Persistent and pervasive achievement gaps exist between Black and White or Brown and White learners at the school or school district level
3. Interpersonal racism	Racial bias that is personally mediated between two or more individuals	• Jokes, harassments and threats, and microaggressions occur on the part of educators directed at their learners or between learners of different racial groups • Instructors with racial bias disproportionately send Black and Latino learners out of their classroom for disciplinary concerns that are ignored when a White child engages in the same behavior • Administrators with racial bias mete out punishment for similar offenses differently for learners of color than their White counterparts • Persistent and pervasive achievement gaps exist between Black and White or Brown and White learners at the classroom level
4. Personal racism	Individuals hold racism in their heart and act on that behavior. Private beliefs and biases about race and racism are influenced by their culture.	• The sorting process is influenced by race • Instructors may ask students of color to Anglicize their names to make them easier to pronounce • Instructors may adjust their courses to omit content that incorporates events, topics, or literature of people of color • Expectations of success are lower for learners of color than for White learners • Language used to praise or correct learners of color is different from that used to praise or correct White learners

Recommended Readings on Racism

In this list, I am including books I have read that I believe can impact and inform you as an educator, and that have a connection to, or bearing on, the people in K–12 schools. Some may not seem closely connected to the business of school, however I lean heavily on them when working with educators on the issues of race and racism in school. Some of these are referenced in this book.

- *A Different Mirror: A History of Multicultural America* by Ronald Takaki. 2008. Back Bay Books
- *Caste: The Origins of Our Discontent* by Isabel Wilkerson. 2020. Random House.
- *Courageous Conversations About Race, Third Edition* by Glenn E. Singleton. 2021. Corwin
- *Dispatches From the Race War* by Tim Wise. 2020. City Lights Books
- *Everyday Antiracism: Getting Real About Race in School* edited by Mika Pollock. 2008. New York Press
- *How the Word Is Passed: A Reckoning With the History of Slavery Across America* by Clint S. Smith. 2021. Little, Brown and Company
- *Let's Talk About Race* by Nancy A. Dome. 2022. Lioncrest
- *Minor Feelings: An Asian American Reckoning* by Cathy Park Hong. 2020. Random House
- *Nice Racism: How Progressive White People Perpetuate Racial Harm* by Robin DiAngelo. 2021. Beacon Press
- *Punished for Dreaming: How School Reform Harms Black Children and How We Heal* by Bettina L. Love. 2023. St. Martin's Press
- *Racing to Justice* by John A. Powell. 2012. Indiana University Press
- *Stamped From the Beginning* by Ibram X. Kendi. 2016. Hachette Books
- *Street Data: A Next-Generation Model for Equity, Pedagogy, and School Transformation* by Shane Safir and Jamila Dugan. 2021. Corwin
- *The Making of Asian America* by Erika Lee. 2016. Simon and Schuster
- *What Truth Sounds Like* by Michael Eric Dyson. 2018. St. Martin's Press

Conclusion

In this chapter, we've developed an understanding of implicit and explicit bias. You've considered your own identity and analyzed racism's four tiers, and their roles in equitable instruction.

In Chapter 3, I introduce my Culturally Appropriate Response to Instruction (CARTI) Framework. We'll focus on step 1 of the framework, cultural awareness, and its relationship to the first equity indicator: meritocracy. You'll get explicit guidance on working to develop or improve your level of cultural awareness in preparation for the first day of school.

As you engage in the reflect and act exercises below, take your time. Focus on your instructional setting, daily work, and lived work experience in your setting. Keep in mind you'll find differences between your and your peers' responses. Be mindful. Seek to speak your truth and have tolerance for theirs.

Reflect and Act

Reflect on the identity exercise you completed in the Introduction. Consider the content of this chapter. How does your new understanding influence your responses? Has anything changed? How so?

Reflect on the questions and notes you wrote while reading this chapter. Now examine your own classroom, school, or district. Where do you see inequity, systemic bias, racism? What do you think is the most egregious of those? Which do you think should be addressed first? Can you use the metrics of the four equity indicators to begin the work? What additional learning or supports might you need?

●●● MY MINDSET METER

Complete the mindset meter as a self-assessment. Make connections between the content of this chapter, Chapter 1, and your lived experience.

Knowledge: I can define and cite examples of the four tiers of racism in my own words:

____

____

____

____

Comprehension: I can explain the difference between implicit and explicit bias as I understand it from this chapter:

____

____

____

____

Application: I can make use of my learning from this chapter to:

____

____

____

____

Analysis: I think my own implicit bias shows in this way:

____

____

____

____

Synthesis: This is what I can change to solve the impact of systemic bias in my school/district:

____

____

____

____

Evaluation: I used to think ______ but now I think ______.

____

____

____

____

CHAPTER 3

INCLUSIVITY

DEVELOPING YOUR OWN CULTURAL COMPETENCE

The Framework for a Culturally Appropriate Response to Instruction (CARTI)

The CARTI Framework (Figure 3.1) is a practical, socio-culturally relevant approach to teaching culturally and linguistically diverse learners. This five-step framework has a single, central focus: academic achievement. At each step of the framework, we are reminded that every curricular and instructional decision is based on improving life outcomes for the learners in your classroom, your school, and your district.

When I first developed the framework, I focused on English language arts and reading. My work since then has been impacted by the growing need to address equity not only in the academic domains, but in the behavioral domains as well. Our learners cannot thrive academically if disciplinary equity is not present as well.

Over the next several chapters, we will work through the CARTI Framework, one step at a time. Each step can be synthesized with and evaluated by the four equity indicators you learned about in Chapter 1.

Figure 3.1

The CARTI Framework

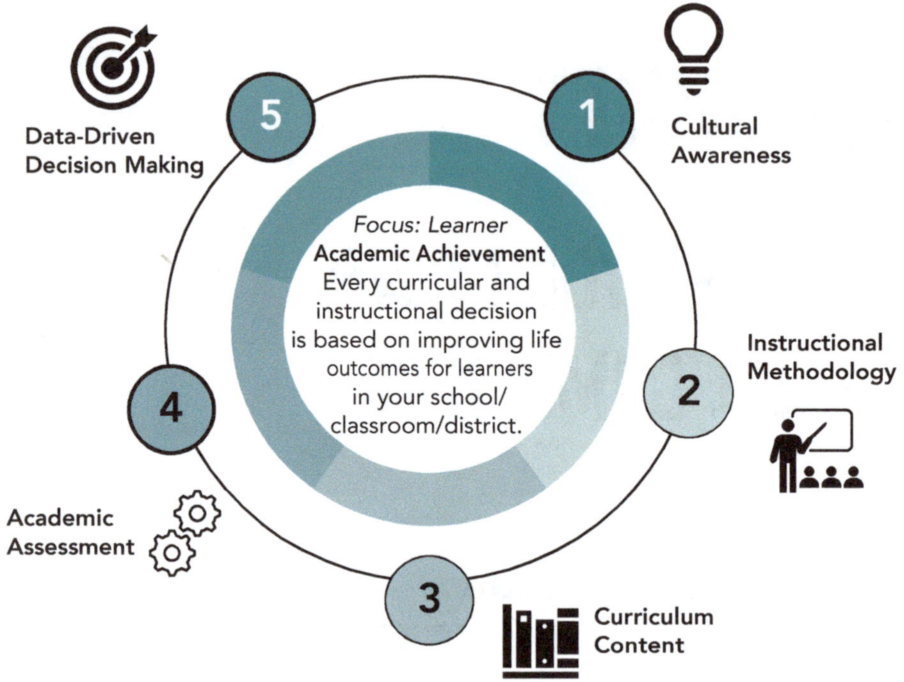

1. **Cultural Awareness**

   Educators constantly work on improving their levels of awareness and connectedness to the full range of cultures of the learners.

2. **Instructional Methodology**

   Educators use scientifically proven methods for delivering content. Methods are validated with learners who look like educators' own learners.

3. **Curriculum Content**

   Educators choose and use content that is not only rigorous but also culturally appropriate to support learner engagement.

4. **Academic Assessment**

   Standard-protocol-based learner assessment provides data that can be used to drive decision making. Assessments are validated in demographics like those of educators' own learners.

5. **Data-Driven Decision Making**

   Decisions about instructional placement, pace, grouping, and content are based on the data from quantitative and qualitative assessment.

Step 1: Cultural Awareness

Before we begin to explore the concept of inclusivity and how we build and maintain a culturally connected classroom, let's consider the work of step 1 of the framework (see Figure 3.2) and how it connects to equity.

Figure 3.2

The CARTI Framework: Step 1

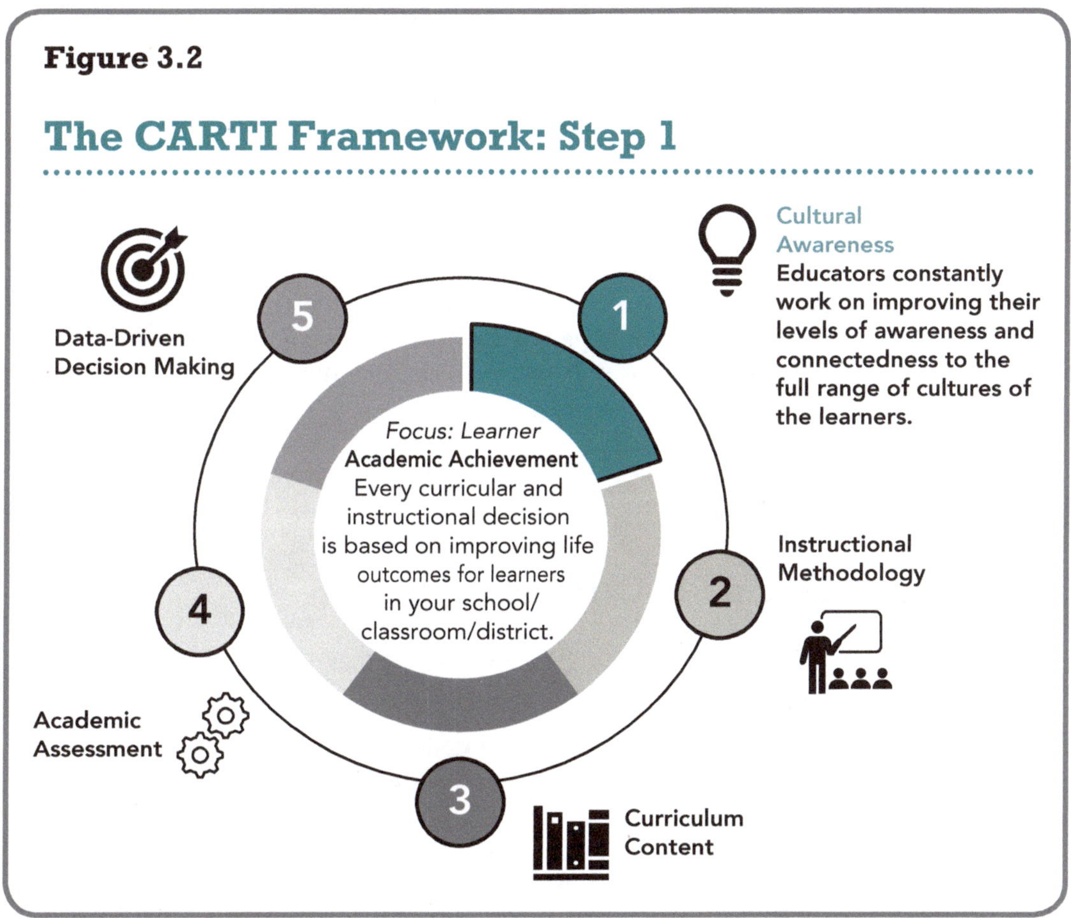

Equity requires understanding. It requires us to affirm, validate, and respect every child who walks into our schools. This is facilitated through our development of cultural awareness. We must commit to constantly improving our levels of awareness and connectedness to the full range of cultures of our learners.

cultural awareness—awareness of the information, norms, values, behaviors, and morals of groups of people who share an identity; awareness of the socially transmitted norms, values, behaviors, and morals of a group of people

Becoming culturally aware is a first step toward developing cultural competence or cultural proficiency (these two terms are often used interchangeably). This skill development is a process that makes explicit the values and practices that enable individuals (educators and learners) and organizations (schools and districts) to interact effectively across the various cultures they are comprised of.

When I work with educators, I describe it as a pathway from unconscious incompetence to unconscious competence based on the conscious competence learning model (Jones et al., 2006; Poore, 2014). An action-oriented journey that can be embarked upon as a matter of personal choice, or as a goal for school improvement. The pathway consists of three zones across four stages (see Table 3.1).

Table 3.1

Pathway to Cultural Competence

THE FEAR ZONE		THE LEARNING ZONE	THE GROWTH ZONE
Unconsciously Incompetent	**Consciously Incompetent**	**Consciously Competent**	**Unconsciously Competent**
Ignorant of the value of cultural diversity, enjoying of privilege, engaging in destructive behaviors (demonization, oppression)	Aware of your cultural ignorance and incompetence, but may be open to professional learning and personal development	Aware of cultural differences and learning to respectfully navigate multiple diverse cultural settings; recognize what you don't know	Respect, value, and affirm cultural differences; welcomed in culturally diverse spaces; can communicate your knowledge and instruct others
Doing harm, allowing harm, and denying resources	May be ignoring or doing harm, allowing harm, and denying resources	Calling out those who do harm, allow harm, or deny resources	Actively working to systemically eliminate doing harm, allowing harm, or denying resources
Destructive Behaviors	Passive Behaviors	Proactive Behaviors	Transformative Behaviors

The first stage in the first zone, the fear zone, is unconscious incompetence. Educators in this stage are ignorant of the value of cultural diversity. They likely enjoy racial or economic privilege which benefits them while harming others. To maintain that privilege, they engage in destructive behaviors such as demonization of other cultures and identities and oppression of others who are culturally diverse. They may use their power to do harm, allow harm, or deny resources to learners through their instructional practices or classroom management and disciplinary actions.

The second stage in the fear zone is conscious incompetence. Educators who are consciously incompetent are cognizant of diversity. They are aware of their ignorance of its value and their lack of understanding of how to use culturally responsive practices and relate to culturally and linguistically diverse learners. Because of this, they tend to engage in passive behaviors often tolerating destructive behaviors of other educators. They may forfeit their power. And in so doing, they ignore or allow harm perpetrated by themselves or others.

They inflict this harm through toxic instructional practices as well as damaging classroom management and disciplinary actions. They may ignore that learners who are culturally and linguistically diverse are denied resources to support their academic success, and they may deny those resources themselves.

Those in the fear zone may only participate in professional learning for cultural awareness when it is mandated. They may not be engaged during that learning. They may not implement what is taught. However, engagement and implementation are required to move from one stage to the next.

When an educator shifts to conscious competency, they move into the learning zone. Educators who are consciously competent are aware of cultural diversity. They have learned to navigate multiple diverse cultural settings and contexts. They have metacognitive knowledge, but do not yet have metacognitive regulation. They know what they don't know, but they cannot instruct others on how to do what they do.

Educators who are consciously competent engage in proactive behaviors. They call out their peers, certainly their subordinates, and perhaps even their leaders, who do harm, allow harm, or deny resources to learners. Unafraid, they voluntarily engage in professional and personal learning for growth and development.

The final zone is the growth zone and means that someone has become unconsciously competent. These educators intrinsically and openly respect, value, and affirm cultural differences—and do so without having to consciously consider their words or actions. These educators are welcomed in culturally diverse spaces. They are comfortable in those spaces while not offending those who occupy them. They have both metacognitive knowledge and metacognitive regulation. They can communicate their knowledge and instruct and lead others still in the fear and learning zone. Their behaviors are transformative. These *equity warriors*, like those I described in the Introduction, actively work to systemically eliminate practices and policies that do harm, allow harm, or deny resources to learners.

If you'd like to take your own formative assessment, you may use the Educators' Cultural Awareness, Knowledge and Skills Survey (ECAKSS), available at www.surveymonkey.com/r/ECAKKS. As you continue with your work, you may wish to return to the survey annually to assess your growth.

Cultural awareness not only recognizes, but also embraces, values, and respects the differences and similarities within and between groups of people from different cultural backgrounds.

Cultural awareness involves:

- **Self-awareness:** Understanding one's own culture, including biases and assumptions about other people or cultures.
- **Understanding and respect:** Learning about other cultures, traditions, beliefs, and ways of life. This often includes understanding and respecting cultural nuances, rituals, symbols, and social norms.
- **Empathy and open-mindedness:** Being open to experiencing and learning from cultures that are different from one's own, and empathizing with the experiences of people from those cultures.
- **Adaptability:** The ability to communicate and interact effectively with people from different cultural backgrounds, which may involve adapting one's behavior to respect other cultures.

Cultural awareness is an important skill for educators to master. It helps foster effective communication, reduces conflicts, and promotes inclusiveness and mutual respect in our schools and classrooms. Increasing cultural awareness can help educators, schools, and districts understand and respect differences, which can lead to more effective and equitable academic and disciplinary interactions and outcomes.

In Chapter 2, you reflected on your identity. Here, let's continue to explore the broad scope of identity. Then we can move on to examine the question, "Who are our learners?"

Look again at your responses to the identity exercise in Chapter 2. Identity is not only about who we are from a physiological or biological perspective, but also about who we are from a social, cultural, and psychological perspective. How did you identify physiologically? Biologically? Socially? Culturally? Psychologically? What other aspects of identity inform who you are? Have they always been there or has your identity changed or evolved over the years?

Just like you, as our learners grow from preschool through high school, various aspects of who they are and how they identify will change. Some of the greatest changes and challenges to identity come during adolescence due to their heightened desire to fit in with their peers. The inputs to their identity (Figure 3.3) and the influences of family, peer groups, socialization, politics, and their lived experiences all come into play.

Figure 3.3

Identity Inputs

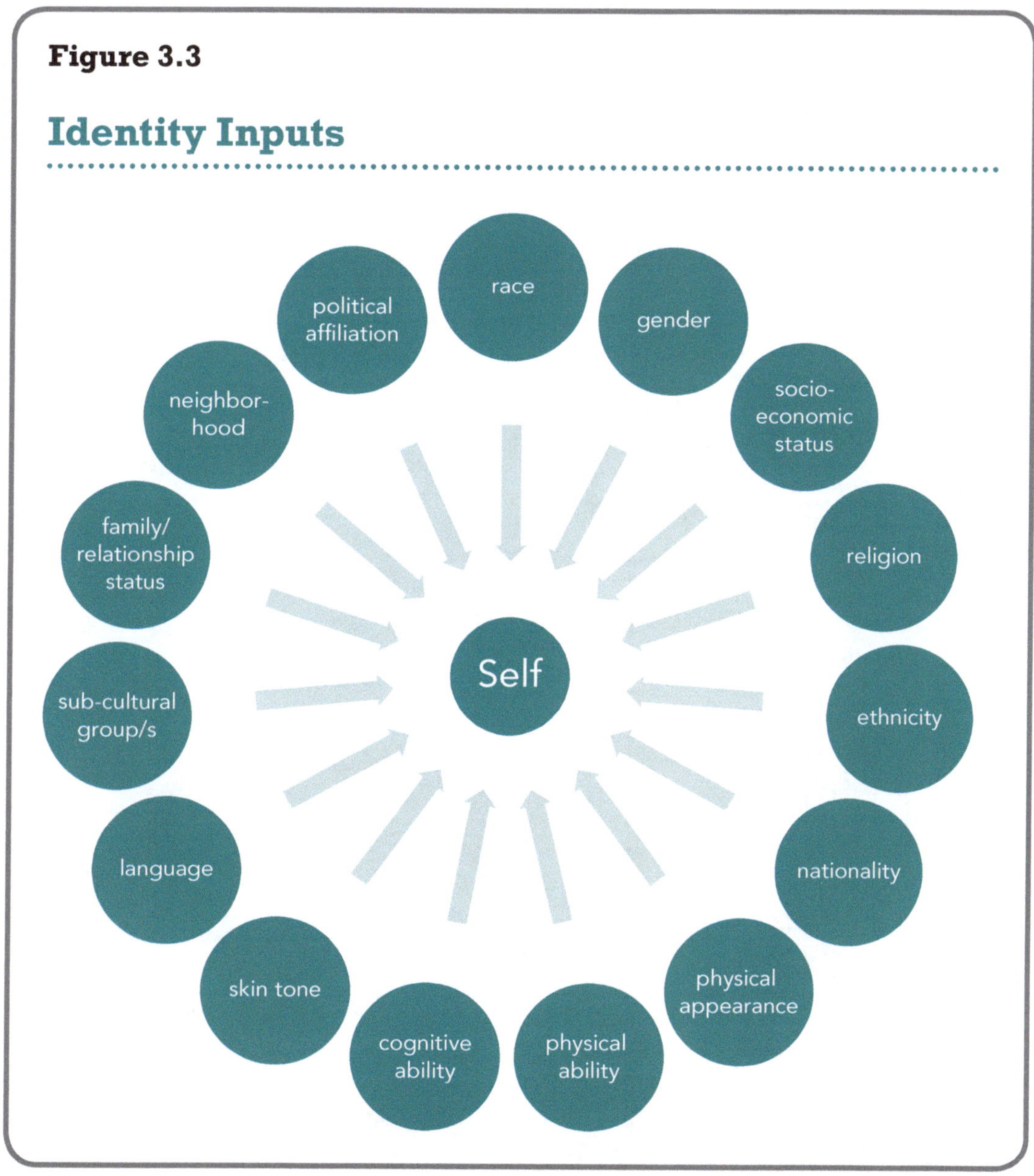

Before moving on, take a few moments to reflect on who your learners are. Use Table 3.2 as a model for your work. I've started a few columns for you. Add more columns to address the identities

Table 3.2

Identifying My Learners

RACE	GENDER/ IDENTITY	AGE OR AGE GROUP	RELIGION	LANGUAGE	ETHNICITY	NATIONALITY	SOCIAL CLASS	PEER GROUP	ABILITY
White Black/ African American Latine/ Hispanic Chinese Filipino					American South American Central American European				Gifted 504 IEP

of your learners. Consider the various aspects of identity and list all the descriptors you can think of for each of those aspects. For example, for languages, what are the languages (world and sociocultural) that your learners speak? (Refer to Appendix B for a short list of sociocultural languages common to the United States.)

Where do you need to become more aware and connected to the full range of cultures of your learners? How can you use community resources to do so? If school has not started, do the best you can based on what you know. When the instructional year begins, open this activity up to your learners. Ask them who they are. Ask them how they identify. They may have characteristics that neither I nor you thought of! Ask how you might get to know them, their cultures, their communities better. Then do so.

Equity Indicator 1: Meritocracy

Remember that meritocracy is the idea that power is held by people based on their ability. Let's reconsider our two essential questions in the context of the inclusive, culturally connected classroom.

- *Who has the power in your classroom?*
- *Are we using that power for the good of the marginalized in our school community?*

When you answered this question in Chapter 2, did you respond that you held the power? Do you believe you do? And if so, do you hold it exclusively? And in the previous reflections, did you contemplate how you now go about using that tremendous power for the good of your marginalized learners? If not, take a minute to do so now. And when you're ready, let's dig in!

We want to begin making sure that all our learners have a place, a learning environment that is equitable, not simply accessible. You must create a culture in your classroom that validates, affirms, and respects each child and what they bring to the classroom. This is how you begin to leverage your power for good. It is not enough that each learner can walk into the classroom and receive the same books as everyone else. It is not enough that they all have the same desks, and access to the same technology. It is not enough that they all have a qualified educator leading their classes and a counselor who knows their names and understands their goals and challenges. Those items reflect equality. Equity is different.

Now I imagine there is someone reading this with a case of *what-about-ism.* What about the learners who identify as behavior problems, delinquents, violators of the law and personal safety? What about the ones who disrupt the learning environment? What about the . . .? You get the idea.

What about them?

This can be addressed by you best as you get to know your learners. Who they are. No, the school community is not solely responsible for every aspect of a child's growth and development, and certainly not the challenges they may face based on their current socioeconomic status. However, educators in schools serving marginalized learners have a tremendous opportunity—perhaps a moral imperative—to create schools that empower each child with the academic and social-emotional skills to make informed choices and take actions to improve their life outcomes.

The essential questions of meritocracy guide us in considering where, if at all, we as educators fail our children. Is it at the very beginning? Are they victims of a sorting process in kindergarten where we determine, because of an aspect of their identity, that they do not warrant valuing, affirming, and respecting them, their culture, their background? Did we fail to use our power to create a safe classroom environment? Did we fail to use our power to provide instruction that met their needs? Did they, perhaps, after a year or two of not having their instructional needs met, decide to check out or wreak havoc? When we monitor our behavior based on the criterion of meritocracy, these are they questions we must ask about how we are using our power.

Now, let's get to learning and changing. Let's begin to develop your culturally connected, inclusive school or classroom.

Before the Year Begins: Developing Your Own Cultural Competence

If you've ever taught kindergarten, parented, or just hung around a 4- or 5-year-old, you know they are fond of asking the simplest of questions: "Why?" And they'll ask it repeatedly until they get an answer they are satisfied with. We should be more like kindergartners when it comes to developing our own cultural competence.

The Five Whys is a framework for root cause analysis—a method of problem solving. And the problem for you to solve here is personal. It's about getting to an outcome of personal cultural competence. We'll look more closely at root cause analysis after we develop an outcome statement, a goal.

Setting goals is vital for a purposeful and fulfilling career in education. Goals provide direction in our work life and give us a benchmark for determining whether we're actually succeeding or not. A goal is a desired outcome, a vision that you plan and commit to achieve. A goal serves as a roadmap toward a specific destination. It should fuel your ambition, enhance your focus, and motivate you to overcome challenges. Your goal should facilitate the process of decision-making as the school year progresses and help manage your progress by providing measurable benchmarks. Ultimately, it should lead to personal (perhaps organizational) growth, improvement, and a sense of accomplishment.

Let's start by jotting in your journal three to five high-level, perhaps *pie-in-the-sky* goals about cultural awareness for you in your role. Think of these as big buckets, not the grain that goes in them.

Not all goals are created equal. In doing equity work, always write SMART goals. A SMART goal is a well-structured objective that integrates five key characteristics: Specific, Measurable, Achievable, Relevant as well as Realistic, and Timely or Time-bound. It's specific, offering a clear definition of what is to be achieved. It's measurable, providing a means to track progress. It's achievable, yet challenging enough to inspire action, to require work. It's relevant, aligning with broader objectives and realistic—no pie in the sky. Lastly, it's timely and time-bound, having a clear deadline to foster urgency and focus. SMART goals streamline efforts, making goal achievement inspirational, manageable, and rewarding.

Create a SMART goal you can reference for the work in this text. Perhaps you've worked on SMART goals in the past and this is a familiar exercise. If not, Appendix C takes you step-by-step through SMART goal setting. Write your SMART goal in your journal.

The inclusive, culturally connected classroom is about fully embracing racial, socioeconomic, gender, and other diversities; creating agency, ensuring everyone's voices are heard and valued; and creating a welcoming school environment for all. Inclusion promotes a sense of belonging and value for everyone irrespective of their backgrounds, identities, or circumstances.

Review the work you did identifying your learners (Table 3.2). When you developed your goal, did you incorporate one or more elements of identity diversity? Did you consider race, language, or gender identity? Depending on the named groups that make up your learner demographic, there may be diversity of language or religion. We cannot ask learners or faculty about many elements of diversity, like sexual orientation, religion, political perspectives, etc.; however, we may know about them. Learners themselves may have shared. Or parents and caregivers may have provided the information to better help you understand their child and meet their academic and social needs.

Looking at your goal, are you confident that you are creating inclusivity for marginalized learners in your context? Perhaps you're a school or district leader and your goal is focused on the diversity of your staff. Or a curriculum leader focused on finding representation for marginalized learners. The same considerations classroom instructors should give hold true for adults that you supervise as a leader.

As you work on your goals, you might create a separate goal to give the identity groups agency, and to effectively support new and diverse new members as they come into your system. Some goals may require a cultural shift and professional learning, creating psychological safety to make all that happen.

Let's take a last look. Does your goal include one or more elements of inclusion? Does it work to fully embrace racial, socioeconomic, gender, or other diversities? Are you creating agency? Are you ensuring everyone's voices are heard and valued? Does it work toward creating a welcoming school environment for all? You need to answer *yes* to at least one of those questions. And the more the better.

Now back to that young child's question. Why? Why do you need to achieve the goal you set? Why do you need to do the work? Table 3.3 has a graphic organizer we'll use to work through this.

Table 3.3

Five Whys Organizer for SMART Goal Analysis

	PROBLEM	WHY?	WHY?	WHY?	WHY?	WHY?
	SMART Goal	What We See on the Surface	Sub-causes	Hard-Core Truth	Status Quo	Root Cause
Your statement or question						
Your responses						

This work is referred to as root cause analysis. It's a method of problem solving that's designed to pinpoint the exact, or root, cause of a specific outcome or outcomes. In our case the reason why you find that your work on cultural connectedness must be done. Once the root cause is determined, we can reset for a solution from a more informed perspective.

Sometimes the root can be completely removed. In becoming culturally competent, it is our task to dig up the root and bring it to light. It must be named and dealt with openly to eliminate its impact on the outcomes you seek to change. The only way to truly effect systemic change is to get at it from the root. This is a critical task for school leaders and equity warriors.

Start by writing your SMART goal (or an abbreviated version) in the first row of the **problem** column of Table 3.3. I refer to it as a problem because you've identified it as an issue of cultural awareness that needs to be addressed to create an inclusive classroom or school. Here's an example of a goal:

> *I want to culturally connect with 85% of the 32% of my learners who are Southeast Asian who don't have faculty representation a population of learners with whom I failed to connect last year, as measured by learner self-reporting on my end-of-year learner evaluations, growing to 98% by June 2030, at a rate of 20% growth to goal each year.*

And here's an abbreviated version:

> *Culturally connect with my Southeast Asian learners.*

Next, we reframe that problem as a question.

> *Why is it that I don't culturally connect with my Southeast Asian learners and why haven't I previously recognized it as problematic?*

This is an example of the first why. It is what we see on the surface. It's shallow. It may not have been visible if we are in the fear zone of the pathway. Write your first question in the **What We See on the Surface** column.

Write a quick and simple response to the question in the row below it. This will frame your next why question. Look at your response and be critical. Is this a result of destructive or passive behaviors stemming from cultural incompetence identified in Table 3.1? Is it something that your school or district has allowed to become part of the culture of the organization? Has it been tolerated because it maintains the status quo for those who hold power and do not use it for the good of those most marginalized?

Now ask why again. This is a sub-cause, or second why. It digs into the rationale for allowing the behaviors, policies, or practices to exist. In my experience, when educators examine their rapid responses to that question, they find that behaviors, policies, and practices exist because they are not easy to remove or revise, pointing to the intermediate causes of the problem.

All the responses to this point are aboveground issues and outcomes. They are things that you can easily see. To get at the root, you must continue the exercise by asking three more whys, each of which digs deeper. You'll uncover some hard-core truths, then the hidden objectives of the status quo, and ultimately the root cause. Unless and until you address the root cause, you cannot truly understand the importance, the urgency, of accomplishing your goal.

I can give you broad-brush academic whys. Moving into the growth zone, developing transformative behaviors, and becoming unconsciously competent requires that you dig. You must find your whys. You'll also find your passion for building and maintaining an inclusive, culturally connected classroom.

Expand Your Cultural Knowledge

When I began my role as a national consultant for an educational publisher, the company president gave me a bit of sage advice. He said that when I was about to begin working in a state or community that was new to me, to "always fly in day or two ahead. Read the local newspapers. Eat in local restaurants. Drive around. Get to know the community."

Those words stuck with me. And I did as was suggested. It made a tremendous difference in my ability to connect with the educators I worked with, and with the learners in their classrooms. It made a tremendous difference in my ability to feel at ease in their communities and avoid offending community members. And after these twenty-odd years of working with schools in 45 states, I can recall something fairly unique about the culture of each of those communities.

Now, I'm not suggesting you need to travel the world. That would be absurd. Especially on an instructor's salary. However, here are five free to almost-free ways that you can learn about the various cultures in your community.

CULTURAL FESTIVALS AND EVENTS

Various ethnic communities host cultural festivals, parades, and events to celebrate their traditions and customs. You may find food festivals, dance and music performances, or art exhibitions.

If you work at a high school, there may be learner clubs or affinity groups that represent the cultures and are willing to provide information about their community events. These events are often free or low cost and offer a hands-on experience.

LIBRARIES

Your school or local library is likely to have books, films, and music from various cultures. Public libraries often host talks, presentations, book clubs, or reading groups focused on different cultural topics. Some libraries have language clubs or conversation groups where you can practice a new language and learn about the culture at the same time.

COMMUNITY CENTERS, CULTURAL CENTERS AND MUSEUMS, AND RELIGIOUS INSTITUTIONS

I often tell participants in my workshops, "If you want to understand a group's culture, go to church." You don't have to convert, just attend, and observe. Community and cultural centers, cultural museums, and religious institutions often host cultural events and activities. They may also offer free or inexpensive culture-specific classes on cooking, language, dance, art, and so on. Take a class! It's a great way to learn and participate in cultural traditions.

HIGH SCHOOL, COLLEGE, AND UNIVERSITY EVENTS

Educational institutions often have clubs and organizations dedicated to celebrating and educating others about different cultures. Look for events or lectures that are open to the public. If you don't work at the high school level, but there are high school cultural clubs, talk to the school's administrators about attending. College and university event calendars can be found online.

VOLUNTEERING

Volunteering with organizations that work with diverse groups is a great way to immerse yourself *in* the community while giving *to* the community. You could help at a local international festival. You can tutor multilingual adult learners. Perhaps you're moved to assist a resettlement organization working with immigrants and refugees. Through these activities, you will have opportunities to interact directly with people from different cultures and learn from their experiences.

Those are my top five. Each of these experiences is an opportunity to learn about your learners from outside of the classroom. It's about acting as ethnographers, gathering stories about those in your classrooms from the margins of their own communities. In short, it is data gathering from the streets of your learners' communities. Of course, you may have learners whose cultures are not well represented in the community. Talk to them if they are in middle or high school. Talk to their parents and caregivers if they are younger. Ask what you can do to better understand their culture to support the learning of their child.

You can always pick up a book and read, take an ethnic studies course, or watch a documentary. Those are great starting points. But immersion into a culture is a completely different experience that will truly broaden your horizons and develop your cultural empathy in ways that a book or documentary or course cannot.

Being immersed in a culture, getting to know the people, increases empathy. Through firsthand experiences you learn about their lived experiences, challenges, and perspectives. You encounter different philosophies and have opportunities to engage on a personal level, exposed to nuances that you'll never get from a book or documentary. You learn to communicate in a whole new way—not from a socially dominant perspective—but rather adapting so that you interact effectively. Give it a try!

During my second year, I taught U.S. History at a comprehensive high school. One day, I was approached by a group of Vietnamese learners. I wasn't sure why this handful of learners—not all of whom were mine—came into my classroom, and I was a bit taken aback.

One learner, whom I'd had the prior year, explained that they wanted to start a Vietnamese Club, to have a place where they could connect and share their culture. After all, there was an African American learner union. The Mexican American and Chicano learners had MEChA (Movimiento Estudiantil Chicano de Aztlán). The Filipino learners had the Fil-Am club.

The Vietnamese learners explained that when they approached the administration, they were told they couldn't have a club without a faculty sponsor. I think this was the first time I really thought about the importance of representation for ethnic minority learners. Though our city had a sizeable Vietnamese population, I hadn't realized until that moment that there were no Vietnamese faculty on staff at this high school serving nearly 3,000 learners.

Of course, I accepted!

I learned a tremendous amount about Vietnamese culture and traditions in carrying out my (very minimal) duties. For a big event, I even wore an *ao dai*, the national traditional dress for women. And I'll admit, they had a hard time finding one to fit me! But they were tenacious.

In preparation for the school carnival, 30 or so showed up at my house, with a few grandmothers in tow, to wrap spring rolls. I will never forget the pile of shoes at the front door, the energy, the love, the desire to help me learn a few phrases in their language, the camaraderie and connections this group of teens brought to my home, and into my life.

Conclusion

In this chapter, I introduced you to the CARTI Framework. We focused on step 1 of the framework, cultural awareness, and its relationship to the first equity indicator: meritocracy. You considered where you are on the Pathway to Cultural Competence and perhaps even took the Educators' Cultural Awareness, Knowledge and Skills Survey (ECAKSS) as a formative self-assessment. You've identified who your learners are and made a plan to develop or improve your level of cultural awareness in preparation for the first day of school.

In Chapter 4, you'll develop a plan to create a safe and inclusive classroom culture. You'll focus on creating a space that is psychologically safe, where your learners can engage in instruction, express their ideas, and challenge other's ideas safely and respectfully. We'll examine the danger of microaggressions, their potential to destroy a safe and inclusive culture, and how they must be interrupted.

As you engage in this chapter's Reflect and Act exercises, have fun! Don't be discouraged if you run into challenges. They may simply serve as a baseline and opportunity for more reflection and growth. If you are part of a book study or PLC, you may wish to make the scavenger hunt either competitive or cooperative.

Reflect and Act

Conduct a scavenger hunt. This is a fun way, especially if working with a PLC, to find resources to support your immersion into the various cultures of your community. Here are some items to get you started:

- Find a book of poetry published in the last five years by a person of an identified racialized/ethnic community representative of your learners.
- Find a podcast hosted by a person of one of your identified racialized/ethnic communities. Bonus points if the podcast has something to do with education!
- Find three films featuring Black leads that aren't about trauma, slavery, or the civil rights movement. (The movie *The Help* doesn't count.)

- Find a local radio station or radio show featuring music from one of your learners' identified racialized/ethnic communities other than Black/African American.
- Find a memoir by a woman who identifies with one of your learners' identified racialized/ethnic communities with a very different life experience from your own.
- Find three books appropriate for your grade level that feature protagonists from three of your identified learners' racialized/ethnic communities (for example, Salvadoran, Korean, and Ukrainian).
- Find a local news outlet, online or print, focused on one of your identified learners' racialized/ethnic communities.
- Find a TV show that centers on each of the following in a lead role:
  - An Asian/Pacific American (APA) or Asian/Pacific Islander (API) woman
  - An Indigenous person
  - Someone from the LGBTQIA+ community
  - A Middle Eastern/North African (MENA) person not portrayed as a terrorist
  - A Latine person not portrayed as a criminal, or domestic or agricultural worker
  - A trans person played by a trans actor
- Find a movie that passes the DuVernay Test (named for director Ava DuVernay), a film or show in which ethnic/racialized people have fully realized lives rather than serve as scenery in White stories.
- Find a film made in the country of, and about one of, your identified learners' racialized/ethnic communities.

Reflect on how the scavenger hunt experience has enhanced your understanding and empathy. Now examine your own classroom, school, or district—depending on the capacity in which you serve. Where do you see inequity?

●●● MY MINDSET METER

Complete the mindset meter as a self-assessment. Make connections between the content in this chapter, previous chapters, and your lived experience.

Knowledge: The meaning of inclusivity in the classroom as I understand it from this chapter:

____

____

____

____

Comprehension: Here's what I can say about where I am on the Pathway to Cultural Competence:

____

____

____

____

Application: This is how I can develop my knowledge about the cultures of my learners:

____

____

____

____

Analysis: I can draw these conclusions about inclusivity in my school or district based on what I learned in this chapter:

____

____

____

____

Synthesis: This is how I will begin to create an inclusive classroom culture:

____

____

____

____

Evaluation: I used to think ______ but now I think ______.

____

____

____

____

CREATING A CULTURE OF EQUITY FROM THE FIRST DAY OF SCHOOL FORWARD

CHAPTER 4

Establishing a Safe and Inclusive Classroom Culture for Every Learner

Establishing a safe and inclusive classroom culture is not a solo venture. Yes, you set the tone. You lead. You create the atmosphere. But if you can't get your learners to participate, you won't have a culture, just an authoritarian state. Of course, if you're reading this book, it may be a benevolent authoritarian state, but even that fails the indicator of meritocracy if you aim to support equity.

Often when we talk about a *safe* classroom, we think of physical safety. There are systems, policies, and procedures in place for that. I want us to focus on a part not often addressed when we focus on instructional practices as merely actions and methods used to deliver content. Let's focus on a part of instructional engagement essential for learning: **psychological safety**. Psychological safety refers to our need to feel safe to engage in a cognitive sense. Safe to be open to learning. Safe to engage. Safe to speak up and contribute to the conversation. Safe to think outside the box and express thoughts without fear of ridicule, embarrassment, or punishment by one's peers, instructors, or leaders.

Think about it. What if you were dropped into a completely foreign environment? A place where you knew no one, or perhaps knew nothing about the place, its leaders, and its government. Imagine that. What fears might you have? Would you be suspicious of anyone or anything? Of course, you would! Isn't that the same as the first day of school for many learners? Isn't that the new instructor experience?

There are four stages of psychological safety that we should attend to in creating and maintaining a safe and inclusive classroom culture: inclusion, learning, contributing, and challenging (Clark, 2020). Let's look at each in turn. For each, you will create a norm to help establish safety in your classroom. Keep in mind, your classroom should be grounded in equity, so this psychologically safe space should also be an equitable one. Go back to your definition of equity and the Mindset Meter in Chapter 1. And remain rooted in the difference between equity and equality.

psychological safety—the need for people in a group (classroom, school, organization) to feel safe to participate, to learn, to speak up without fear of punishment, ridicule, or embarrassment.

Creating an Environment of Inclusion

The first step to psychological safety is creating an environment of inclusion. A place where every learner feels welcomed, valued, and affirmed. And this must be a genuine state. We have a basic human need to feel included. Until that need is met, we cannot begin to learn. We do this by working to create a classroom or school that welcomes every child without prejudgment. We create environments where every learner has worth, valued for simply being human.

To create such an environment, we must first overcome our own implicit and explicit biases, our "passion for superiority." How? How do we overcome what John Adams (1777) wrote was the "one Principle, which predominates in human Nature so much in every stage of Life, from the Cradle to the Grave, in Males and females, old and young, black and white, rich and poor, high and low"? The passion, drive, quest for being the most knowledgeable or most powerful person in the room must be suppressed to create a classroom that is inclusive of every child.

You must first start by loving yourself. It's hard to be inclusive if you have low self-esteem (Bleckmann et al., 2023), since self-esteem functions as an index to your own inclusion experience with others. Low self-esteem is connected to exclusion. Stay with me. Think about where you are on the pathway to cultural competence. How can you manifest energy or desire to include others if you're in the fear zone, still grappling with recognizing your own implicit and explicit bias that sees others as less than? You're still reading this, so you are progressing! Continue to work on your cultural awareness and sensitivity, and lean into a bit of colloquial wisdom: fake it 'til you make it. Practice until you come to a point where authentic conviction takes hold.

The first step is to create a basic statement of the inclusion norm. Something akin to, *Everyone in this classroom has a place here. In this space, we respect and value everyone, simply because they are human.*

That's the norm I use when conducting professional learning workshops. What is or will be your norm for an inclusive environment? Take a moment to think and jot one down in your journal. You can always revise it later.

Now that you have named your norm, claim it. Put it on a poster. Display it prominently in your classroom. Put it in your syllabus. Make it a part of the first days of school routine by stating it and having your learners recite it.

Think back to the discussion of standards and discipline in Chapter 1. Your inclusion norm is a standard. It is knowledge and a soft skill that every learner should comprehend at a high level and be able to practice in your school or classroom. More than simply an expectation, you will need to provide instruction on it. It must become part of your culture.

Here are five strategies you can use to support inclusion safety in your school or classroom:

1. Ensure your environment reflects a wide range of cultures, languages, and perspectives. Think about equity indicator 3—impartiality. *Who has representation? Are there mirrors, windows, and sliding glass doors not only in your curriculum, but in what adorns your walls?*

2. Develop and implement equitable classroom practices. Good news here! This book provides plenty of those in the chapters on instructional practices. Keep reading.

3. Establish, articulate, and support anti-bias and anti-discrimination policies and practices. Develop and implement lessons that instruct on the value of diversity, and support understanding of the policies. You may choose to create a

classroom or school charter that outlines expected behaviors. Completing this as an activity with learners supports a collective commitment to an inclusive environment. Sharing this with parents and caregivers, asking for their commitment, supports an even broader understanding and collective commitment.

4. Use language that is inclusive and nondiscriminatory and hold your learners to the same standard. Be sensitive. Respect learners' identities and preferred pronouns. Encourage your learners to do the same. In some states, legislation prohibits the recognition or use of any pronoun outside the one assigned at birth. If that is the case in your state, consider having a private conversation with the learner or their caregivers to express your empathy and help them understand your legal dilemma.
5. Engage learners in activities that build community through collaboration. Community building activities can serve to create empathy, awareness, and understanding. They can break down stereotypes and create a common culture among your learners of diverse backgrounds. There's more on those activities in the chapters on methods and assessment.

Creating an Environment Where Everyone Learns

When everyone feels included, everyone can learn. This is the second stage toward a psychologically safe environment. We have a basic human need to learn, to understand, to satisfy our natural curiosity. In the classroom, we sometimes must spark that curiosity. After all, not every child wants to learn every subject. Math was never my jam. Ever! I did it because I had to in order to achieve my other goals. But not all our learners are intrinsically motivated.

And even in an inclusive environment, there may still be fear of failure. The children who sit in your classrooms are not blank slates. They bring into the classroom their lived experiences from other classrooms. If the learner's previous experiences have included being in classrooms where the teacher showed no concern or empathy, they will not feel safe until they know that your classroom is different.

I've come to own the philosophy that our children don't fail our classes. We fail to instruct our children. Some of that failure comes from unsafe spaces where we cultivate a culture of callousness. Here again, when developing learning safety in your classroom, you'll need a basic statement of the norm. You want to grant permission for every individual to engage in all aspects of the learning process. My norm is this: "This classroom is a place of respect for learning and growing. We respect and value everyone's contributions, questions, and engagement." And by everyone, that includes you, too. Safe for you to learn from them. Now, what's your norm for the learning environment? Take a moment to think and jot one down in your journal. You can always revise it later.

Here are five strategies for creating learning safety in your classroom. These strategies rely heavily on an instructional paradigm that makes the strategies part of every lesson.

1. Implement culturally responsive instructional methods like those in the methods chapters in this book. Select and implement culturally responsive curricula. You'll find guidelines for evaluating and selecting culturally responsive curricula in Chapters 5 and 6.

2. Affirm not only who each learner is, but their abilities and efforts. Do so routinely. Use the *3 Glows and a Grow* process (see page 68). Positive reinforcement builds confidence. And when you acknowledge each learners' efforts and celebrate their achievements, you remove the fear of risk taking, creating an environment where they will stretch and take chances without fear of embarrassment or reprisal.

3. Establish clear expectations and consistent routines. This creates a stable and predictable learning environment. When learners know what to expect from you and your instruction, it may reduce anxiety (provided the expectation is positive). Lower the affective filter—the psychological barrier that can affect learning—to support learners engaging more fully in the instruction.

4. Practice and provide instruction in soft skills and emotional intelligence. Unfortunately, as I write this, there is pending or passed legislation in several states that bans or limits instruction in social-emotional learning (Abrams, 2023). Please be aware of what is and is not allowed in your district and implement accordingly. Self-awareness, empathy, clear communication, adaptability, teamwork, and collaboration—to name a few—are soft skills critical to success not only in the classroom, but also in life and most careers.

5. Give learners voice, agency. Involve them in decision-making processes about classroom norms and activities. Empowering learners in making decisions gives them a sense of ownership over their environment. For those historically marginalized, it helps create a feeling of more than safety, it creates mutual respect.

Affirming Learners With Three Glows and a Grow

Three glows and a grow. It's a simple formula that helps keep learners engaged, excited, and continuing to develop, even as you sometimes relay heavy constructive guidance. The idea is that for every area of weakness that you need to share with the learner, their caregiver, or another instructor, you also note three areas of strength.

Let's say you have a multilingual learner who struggles with English syntax in their written work. In their primary language the adjective comes after the noun, not before it as in English. But before you mark up their errors, stop. Take a breath. And find three things the learner did well. Find the good.

Perhaps they captured the essence of the assignment quite nicely. If it's science, their response is technically correct. Maybe it's history, and their facts are in order. Or it's literary interpretation and their response clearly indicates a deep level of understanding of the theme of the work. Well, there's one glow right there. Name it.

- Absolutely correct! Mixing silver nitrate and ethanol can result in a serious fire!
- Excellent articulation of the challenges and successes of the Second Continental Congress!
- Wonderful interpretation of the unconscious evaluation of each of the character's own existence against an almost invisible controlling narrative!

Perhaps the assignment is neatly presented. Let's say it's biology, and their illustration of an cell is superb. Or it's geography, and their hand drawn map is precise, reflective of a clear understanding of mapmaking. Or it's a text-to-text connection and text they chose shows insight. Well, there's a second glow! Name it.

- Meticulous detail in your illustration of the cell!
- What a precise map! I can see you captured all the elements necessary for navigating the terrain!
- Your text-to-text connection shows tremendous insight! Bravo!

Or maybe it's something as simple as getting a proper heading on the paper, with their name, class period, date, and assignment written legibly and in the correct order! Name it. *Yes!! You nailed the heading!!!*

And then, name the one most important element of growth that is needed for that learner to master so that they can continue to improve. If syntax hinders their ability to communicate, to understand, or to demonstrate their knowledge, name it. But don't just mark it up and leave it there. Give feedback as guidance on how to do better. *In English, the adjective comes before the noun. You'd write "an orange dog" instead of "a dog orange." Let's have you rework the underlined areas using English syntax. If it helps, you can write them first in Spanish, then in English to help make the connection.*

Now you may have noticed the generous use of exclamation points in the glows. That is intentional. It lets the learner know that you are excited by what they are doing right. And they should be excited too! Avoid the use of exclamation points in the grow statements—whether spoken or in print.

My book *Effecting Change for Culturally and Linguistically Diverse Learners* (Second Edition published by Shell in 2022) extensively covers feedback delivered at the point of instruction. I'll point you to Chapter 8 in that text for a thorough discussion of feedback.

Creating an Environment Where Everyone Can Contribute

Human beings have a deep and unrelenting desire to participate. It's no fun riding the bench. When learners feel safe to contribute their thoughts, ideas, and opinions, they are that much more likely to engage. This is the third stage of psychological safety. Think about those times when you felt safe to speak up and contribute ideas. How did it feel when even the silliest (in retrospect) ideas were accepted without judgment? Now think of a time when your contributions were diminished or ridiculed. Which is the environment you want in your classroom?

Contributing is more than learning. When there is true safety to contribute, mistakes are viewed as opportunities for learning rather than reasons for failure. Work to create a supportive and nurturing environment where continuous learning and improvement is valued. (More about this in Chapter 4 on grading schemes.) Teach your learners the value of collective intelligence and the benefit of diversity of thought. This fuels ingenuity and creativity, problem-solving, and effective decision-making. Your learners need to feel safe taking risks.

Ask yourself this question:

> *Do you respect and value only those learners who are diligent and high achieving, or do you acknowledge that wisdom and solutions can come from the most unexpected contributors with origins in lived experiences divergent from yours?*

Use your answer to that question to create your contributor norm. Take a moment to think and jot one down in your journal.

Here are five strategies for creating contributor safety in your classroom/s. These strategies, too, rely heavily on an instructional paradigm that makes the strategies part of every lesson. But by applying these strategies diligently, you'll create a classroom that is the ideal environment for intellectual growth and participation.

1. Encourage risk-taking. View mistakes as a natural part of the learning process. It helps if you can call out and laugh at your own mistakes. Even when learners don't provide a "correct" response, celebrate their attempts and willingness to contribute. Use the *Glows* format. Find and use examples of pop culture icons who learn from errors. Even Steph Curry (my favorite basketball player) only hits 94% of his 3-pointers and he is the NBA's all-time leader in 3-point shots. What examples will resonate with your learners?

2. Vary opportunities for learners to contribute. Not everyone is comfortable expressing themselves in the same way. Provide various modes of participation, giving equal weight to each. (See Chapters 10 and 11 on grading for more about this.) Whether it's group discussion, journaling, written essays, or creative projects using multimedia, provide avenues for all learners to contribute in a manner that suits them.

3. Establish ground rules for interaction. Emphasize respect, active listening, and equitable sharing of the floor. While learners may be involved in establishing the rules, you must ensure that they are consistently and equally applied. Your learners can be tasked with that as well, holding one another accountable to the guidelines.

4. Use structured dialogue techniques to guide discussion. For example, "think-pair-share" or "turn-and-talk" or even a "grand conversation" or "Socratic seminar." Not only do these techniques support learners in knowing what to expect, they allow learners to prepare their thoughts and contribute in a managed and respectful setting.

5. Acknowledge and value all contributions. This is another layer of affirming the learner. Your own active listening and thoughtful responses to each and every contribution is a public acknowledgment that every learner is valued, respected, and safe. This encourages further participation.

When I taught struggling sixth graders, reading aloud was challenging. Many of my learners started the year four or five years below grade level. But read aloud they did. On a voluntary basis. During reading instruction, they learned strategies for word attack. They knew how to use morphographic clues, context clues, and apposition to make sense of unknown words. And they learned, because of the culture established, to respect the person reading—no matter the challenges or lack of fluency they exhibited.

There was never an eye roll or giggle or sigh when someone was disfluent. Our culture, established beginning day one and reinforced through the strategies described here, set the tone. They encouraged one another. They were quiet, respectful, and patient when a peer worked to sound out a word, check with me that they had pronounced it correctly, and then reread the entire sentence so that they could read the word in context and derive meaning from the passage.

It was a beautiful thing. The concept of psychological safety was not something I was taught in teacher's college. It would be years before I knew what it was. But even then, I knew there was something special about the culture of my classroom. These decades later, as I occasionally hear from former learners, they affirm my suspicions.

Creating a Safe-to-Challenge Environment

The fourth stage of psychological safety is the safety to challenge the status quo. Challenging the status quo can be a daunting task, especially when we are placing that task in the hands of developing young minds in an environment where they have little or no power.

Asking our learners to question accepted norms, methods, or ideas can result in a tremendous amount of learning and problem solving in a safe classroom. However, it can also trigger resistance or backlash in classrooms that are less evolved. Getting to this level of safety is not easy. Learners may fear that challenging the status quo will result in criticism, judgment, or even punishment. They might worry about being perceived as disrespectful, negative, or troublemakers, and these fears can silence valuable perspectives and ideas.

Work to make your classroom a space where learners receive encouragement to question and challenge the established way of doing things. Welcome their proposed new ideas, suggested changes, and expressed dissenting opinions. Make sure they know there's no reason to fear retaliation such as a low grade or office referral. This freedom will foster creativity, innovation, and a desire to learn and grow.

Creating this environment requires you to listen, show empathy, value diverse opinions, and respond constructively to criticism levied by your learners. Modeling these behaviors sets a tone for your classroom. You demonstrate that it's not just safe but beneficial to question, innovate, and occasionally disrupt the status quo. True learning takes place when gnarly problems meet creative chaos with only a slight possibility that they will end up where your lesson planned for them to go.

Ask yourself these questions:

- *How will you give every learner in your classroom the responsibility to disagree? And how will you remain open and silent as you receive their ideas?*

Use your answers to create your challenger safety norm. Take a moment to jot it down in your journal.

Here are five strategies for creating challenger safety in your classroom. These require tremendous self-discipline, particularly if you are still struggling with overcoming bias. Integrating these strategies into your instructional practice will create a space where everyone has agency. And that, dear educators, is an amazing space!

1. Value dissent and provide instruction on how to do so. When learners understand that dissenting opinions have value and contribute to a deeper understanding of the content under study, not only do you cultivate safety, you support cognitive humility—an openness to the idea that there is more than one way of thinking, and that our way may not be the best way for all. Emphasize that respectful disagreement can be the best form of brainstorming and lead to innovation and growth.
2. Establish protocols for respectful disagreement. You might provide sentence stems such as "I see it differently because . . ." or "I respectfully challenge the idea that . . ." Ensure that learners disagree with ideas, not people, and word the stems accordingly. This will help your learners express disagreement in a respectful and constructive way.

3. Incorporate silent reflection—for yourself as well as the entire class. Before anyone responds, a pause of 20–30 seconds for reflection supports full consideration of the ideas presented. It is time for you and everyone in the room to consider the idea. It encourages thoughtful responses rather that immediate, perhaps off-the-cuff or insensitive, emotional reactions. During this time learners may journal, doodle, or simply sit and think. You may be familiar with the concept of "wait time" and probably already wait three to five seconds. There's other research—and my own experience—that establishes longer times in certain settings or when differentiating for some learners. I once required a three-minute wait time after some silliness in responses. It was amazing what those students came up with when forced to take time to really think. The same thing happens in the workshops I do with teachers. The silence is uncomfortable, but the outcomes are worth it.
4. Utilize think-pair-share or another strategy. Provide learners time to gather their thoughts and formulate their responses. Think-pair-share gives learners a chance to talk through their responses with one classmate before speaking to the entire group. It also may develop an ally, someone who is more confident sharing in a whole group to speak for a learner who is less comfortable.
5. Use Socratic questioning. This method provides opportunities to explore underlying assumptions, evidence, and implications of ideas being studied. It requires instruction and modeling initially but can be handed over to learners after practice.

Think about the elements that must be established to create a culture of psychological safety in your classroom. Lean heavily into the third equity indicator of impartiality. Who has representation? Then review the four norms you developed to prepare, revise, and evaluate your classroom culture plan.

Reflective Dialogue Circles

Socratic seminars and grand conversations encourage learners to engage in critical thinking (Berger & Wild, 2017). In both, the goal is to foster analytical thought and illuminate ideas. Grand conversations (Peterson & Eeds, 2007) are less formal than Socratic seminars. For the safe and inclusive classroom, and for those of you who have not used or are not wedded to either method, I suggest using reflective dialogue circles. Reflective dialogue circles are a hybrid format with several components (see Table 4.1).

Table 4.1

Reflective Dialogue Circles

INSTRUCTIONAL COMPONENT	ACTION
Shared text	Center the discussion on content that all learners have had an opportunity to share. This may be a piece of literature engaged in through independent or shared reading, historical document, current event, visual or performance art, or other content that has significant and discussable ideas or interpretations.
Learner-centered	You serve as facilitator, but the discussion is primarily learner-centered. Begin with open-ended questions related to the content. Questions should be thought-provoking and elicit complex thinking and discussion. Encourage learners to express their interpretations. There are no right or wrong answers, the focus is on sharing.
Open dialogue	Learners do not debate, but rather explore different perspectives and build on one another's ideas to develop deeper understanding of the material. There are no predetermined conclusions.
Deep, holistic, critical thinking	Encourage learners to think critically and to articulate their reasoning or evidence. Challenge learners to substantiate their statements with specific references to the text, content, or to prior knowledge. Learners should make connections to themes and ideas related to their own lived experiences, societal issues, and cross-curricular content or knowledge.
Active listening and respectful exchange	All participants, including you, listen to others so that they may respond thoughtfully. The conversation is grounded in mutual respect, with a flow that builds on the contributions of other participants, rather than jumping from one topic or thought to another.
Equitable participation	All participants contribute to the discussion. You may need to intervene, but that intervention should be minimal once the conversation is underway. The goal is for the learners to drive the conversation.
Reflection and insight	End with a period of reflection where learners can articulate what they learned, insights they gained, questions they still have, and how their thinking has changed. This is similar to the Mindset Meters at the end of the chapters of this book.

Socratic seminars, grand conversations, and reflective dialogue circles are powerful tools for deepening learning and cultivating skills in a safe and inclusive classroom. Whichever you use will promote respect for diverse ideas, and learners will learn from one another in a community of respectful inquiry.

Microaggressions at School

As you work to build a safe and inclusive classroom, there will be numerous opportunities for **microaggressions** to occur. They may be your own, or they may come from learners.

Remember the iceberg metaphor for biases? Microaggressions stem from our biases, coming up from the bottom of our icebergs. They creep into the content we teach through stereotypical narratives. They seep out of our thoughts through words, phrases, and terms that are outdated or offensive. They surface in the assumptions we make about learners' abilities, interests, or backgrounds based on aspects of their identities. They are reflected in instructional methods that are culturally unresponsive and in disciplinary actions that disproportionately impact marginalized learners.

Microaggressions are subtle, everyday behavioral, verbal, or environmental put-downs that are directed toward members of marginalized groups (Sue et al., 2008). Whether verbal or nonverbal, microaggressions are typically automatic responses on the part of the aggressor. Whether conscious and intentional or unconscious and perhaps rooted in ignorance, they have a cumulative negative effect on individuals who identify with marginalized groups: our culturally and linguistically diverse learners.

The statements made or acts committed may demean a person's race, gender, sexual orientation, heritage, age, or health status, for example, simply because they belong—or are perceived to belong—to a specific identity group. There are three types of microaggression—microassault, microinsult, and microinvalidation. Each is found too often in our instructional content and our instructional practices.

MICROASSAULT

Microassaults occur when a person intentionally behaves in a discriminatory way toward a marginalized group (Sue et al., 2008). Let's look at three examples of microassaults that could occur in a teaching context. We would hope that microassaults never happen in schools, but unfortunately, we know they do. We may have experienced them as learners ourselves or heard of them from other adults in our school environment, or seen them on social media.

The first example is a racial or ethnic slur. This occurs when a teacher or administrator uses racial or ethnic slurs when addressing or referring to a specific racial or ethnic group. This is a blatant form of racism that demeans and belittles the targeted group.

A second example is exclusion based on language or accent. This occurs when a teacher routinely ignores or dismisses contributions from multilingual learners who have strong accents, implying that their thoughts or perspectives are less valuable or irrelevant. This form of microassault makes learners feel excluded or undervalued because of their language proficiency or accent.

The third example is gender stereotyping. This occurs when a teacher consistently references outdated gender stereotypes, such as suggesting that males are better at math and science while females are more suited to arts and humanities. And what of the learner who does not identify as male or female? These behaviors can create a classroom environment where learners feel constrained by stereotypical gender norms and feel less valued if they do not conform to these stereotypes.

MICROINSULT

The second type of microaggression is the **microinsult**, a subtle, often unintentional, behavior or comment that conveys rudeness or insensitivity, or demeans a person's racial or ethnic heritage, gender, sexual orientation, or other aspect of identity. Unlike microassaults, microinsults are often unconscious and come from a place of implicit bias.

Let's look at three examples that could occur in a school or classroom setting:

> The first example is intellectual stereotyping. This occurs when, for example, a teacher, counselor, or administrator is surprised that a learner from a historically marginalized group is doing well academically and comments, "You're really smart for someone of your background!" Although intended as a compliment, this type of comment perpetuates harmful stereotypes and implies that people from certain backgrounds are not expected to be intelligent or academically successful. I can't tell you how many times I've experienced this specific microinsult myself. Countless times I've been told I was "very articulate." It was even written in my cumulative folder by my second-grade teacher. Her words, "very articulate negro."
>
> The second example is ignoring contributions. During class discussions, a teacher might consistently overlook or downplay the input from learners belonging to certain culturally or linguistically diverse, or gender groups. Even when unintentional, this behavior screams the message to learners that their perspectives are of less value or importance.

The third example is assumptions of foreignness. This transpires when school officials ask a learner of color where they're "really" from or compliment them on their good English. Not every culturally diverse learner is a foreigner. More often than not, the learners peppered by this question were born and raised in the United States. They may not even be multilingual learners! This statement implies a perpetual foreigner stereotype, suggesting that people of color, or those from diverse ethnic backgrounds, are forever foreigners—even in their own country.

MICROINVALIDATION

The final type of microaggression is the **microinvalidation**. These subtle comments or behaviors exclude, negate, or dismiss the perceptions, feelings, or experiential reality of culturally and linguistically diverse learners (Sue et al., 2008). Microinvalidations may come from a place of unconscious or implicit bias; however, they have a profound impact on the individuals on the receiving end. They inflict real damage as they invalidate individuals' experiences and identities.

Let's look at three examples that could potentially occur in a school or classroom setting:

Our first example is colorblindness. A school official (teacher, counselor, administrator, office worker) might say something like, "I don't see color, I treat all learners the same." While the intention might be to express fairness, it negates learners' racial or ethnic experiences and identities. It ignores the reality of racial or ethnic identities and in so doing, dismisses the unique experiences and challenges that learners of color face.

A second example is denial of individual experiences of racism, sexism, or homophobia. When a learner opens up about an instance where they felt they were the target of bias or discrimination, and their teacher or peers dismiss their experience, saying something like, "You're overreacting," or "I'm sure they didn't mean it like that," the learner's experience and feelings are invalidated. The learner feels unheard and unsupported.

Finally, we have the myth of meritocracy. This is related to our first equity indicator. Meritocracy is the idea that power is held by people based on their ability. However, we know this to be untrue, which is why we ask the essential questions we do. So, when educators make statements like, "Anyone can succeed in this society if they work hard enough," they discount the impact of systemic issues like racism, sexism, or classism on learners' opportunities and experiences. They fail to acknowledge that structural inequalities exist and create barriers to success for culturally and linguistically diverse learners.

microaggression—a subtle, often unintentional, form of prejudice expressed through brief verbal, behavioral, or environmental slights; remarks or actions that convey negative stereotypes or insensitivity, often directed at marginalized groups, reflecting underlying biases or misunderstandings.

microassault—explicit, intentional actions or slurs, often racially driven, meant to hurt the intended victim; usually conscious and deliberate actions or words displaying overt bigotry or bias toward a marginalized group, generally unambiguous in their discriminatory intent.

microinsult—subtle, often unintentional, verbal or behavioral communications that convey rudeness, insensitivity, or demean a person's racial heritage or identity; remarks or actions perpetuating negative stereotypes and reflecting underlying biases; subtle belittlements of a targeted individual or group.

microinvalidation—comments or actions that negate, dismiss, or nullify the feelings, experiences, or identities of individuals from marginalized groups; suggestions that a person's experiences aren't genuine, relevant, or based on real societal issues, undermining their reality or feelings.

Conclusion

In this chapter, you developed a plan to create a safe and inclusive classroom culture. You now understand how to create a space that is psychologically safe, where your learners can engage in instruction, express their ideas, and challenge one another's ideas safely and respectfully. Understanding the danger of microaggressions and their potential to destroy the safe and inclusive culture you'll work to build, you've got a basis for interrupting them—in yourself and others.

In Chapter 5, we'll shift our focus to instructional methodology. You'll examine your classroom practices with a focus on standards and a deep dive into mastery learning. The chapter will provide you with strategies to recognize and respond to the learning needs of your culturally and linguistically diverse learners.

As you engage in this chapter's reflect and act exercise, deeply scrutinize your understanding and lived experience surrounding microaggressions. You may find yourself observing the words and actions of others through a different lens now that your awareness has been raised. Own that. Think about where you placed yourself on the Pathway to Cultural Competence and what this new learning does to push or pull you in one direction or another. If you are completing this work as part of a book study or professional learning, make sure that elements of psychological safety are present in that setting. This prompt will be challenging to discuss if people do not feel that safety.

Reflect and Act

Reflect on the three types of microaggressions and the examples provided. Where have you seen these in your own context? If you have committed one, how do you feel about it now that you know of its impact? What work will you do to prevent that from happening again? What will you do when you see another educator microaggressing against a learner or other adult in your context?

●●● MY MINDSET METER

Complete the mindset meter as a self-assessment. Make connections building on what you've learned and your lived experience. Focus. Reflect. Analyze. Strategize.

Knowledge: The meaning of "the inclusive classroom" as I understand it from this chapter:

____

____

____

____

Comprehension: The purpose of creating psychological safety in the classroom as I understand it from today's work:

____

____

____

____

Application: This is how I will use discussion sessions to deepen learning and cultivate soft skills in my classroom:

____

____

____

____

Analysis: I have seen these microaggressions in schools and classrooms and can interrupt them:

____

____

____

____

Synthesis: This is how I will create a safe and inclusive classroom culture:

____

____

____

____

Evaluation: I used to think ______ but now I think ______.

____

____

____

____

INSTRUCTIONAL METHODOLOGY

CHAPTER 5

The CARTI Framework, Step 2: Instructional Methodology

As we continue to explore the concept of inclusivity and how we build and maintain a culturally connected classroom, let's check the work of step 2 of the CARTI Framework, instructional methodology (see Figure 5.1). Equity has, at its core, equality of outcomes. This means that the methods we use should be effective enough that every learner ends the year at- or above-grade level. This is facilitated through our use of instructional methods that have been scientifically proven to work with the learners that we serve. Our developing cultural awareness helps us focus on and analyze the true efficacy of the methods we employ. In developing a culturally connected, inclusive classroom, we must commit to using only those methods proven effective for our learners.

Methods are the *how* of teaching. How will you teach the material? How will you deliver instruction?

As a reminder, the second indicator of equity is Standards. As an equity indicator, standards are metrics that we use to craft and deliver instruction and to measure academic performance. Learners demonstrate their mastery of standards. There are two essential questions to ask here:

- *Who is demonstrating mastery?*
- *Are we taking action to result in learners demonstrating ongoing mastery year over year?*

Figure 5.1

The CARTI Framework

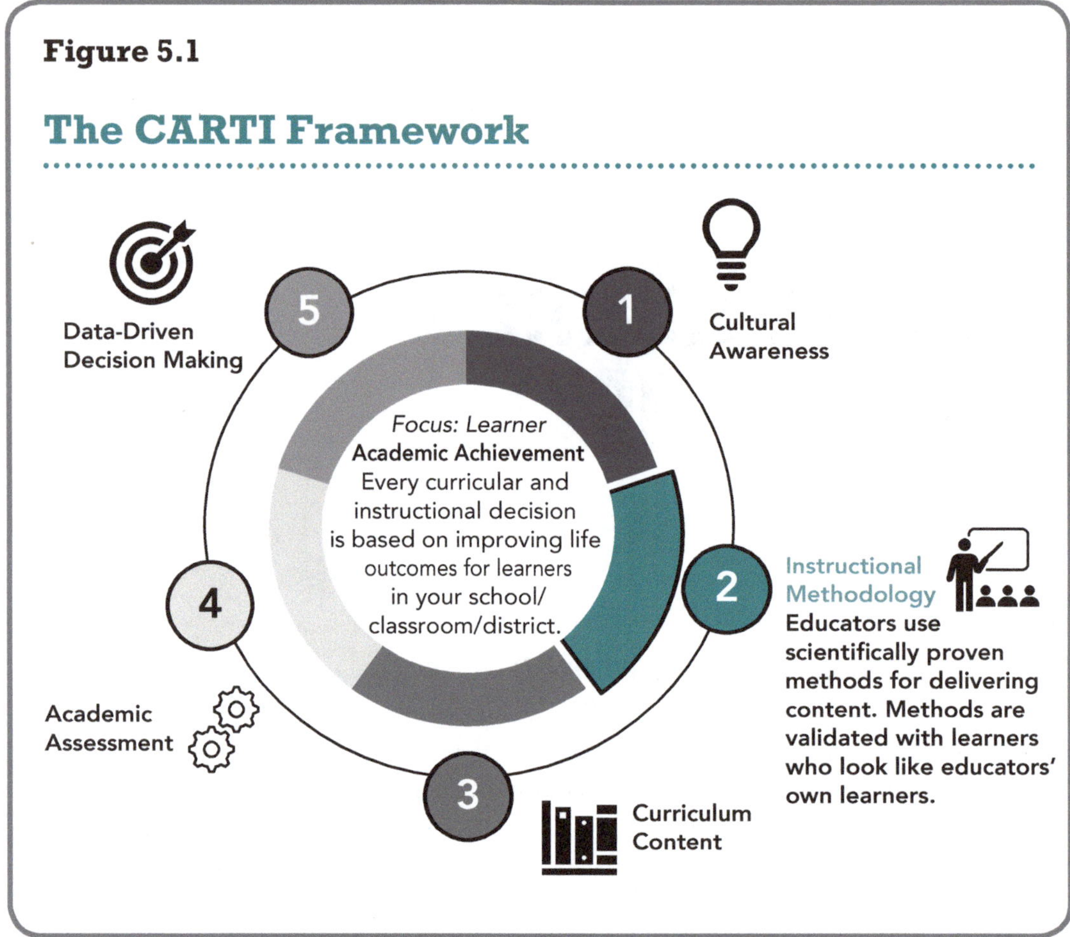

Diversity Tally Scorecard

As you move from theory to practice, you'll be examining your methods. For that, you'll need a tool—a way to keep score as you reflect on your methods and work toward improvements that will result in equitable instruction to get equal outcomes. So, let's look at the diversity tally scorecard (Table 5.1).

I've created the scorecard with headings for the most common groups of marginalized learners. Higher achieving learners are included as a reminder that when examining our methods, we don't want to neglect our higher achieving learners while we work to meet the needs of all others. Learners may fall into multiple categories. When you create your own scorecard, you'll change

Table 5.1

Diversity Tally Scorecard for Instructional Delivery

	Black Learners	Latin -A/-O/-E Learners	Other Racial Minority Learners	Title I Learners	Multilingual Learners	Lower Achieving Learners	Higher Achieving Learners
Instruction provides for differentiated instruction for these learners.							
Instruction provides engagement and motivation for these learners.							
Instruction supports critical thinking skills in these learners.							
Instruction supports the development and use of soft skills for these learners.							
Instruction supports opportunities to demonstrate comprehensive synthesis by these learners.							

the groups to reflect the learners you identified as marginalized in Table 3.2. In the first column are seven criteria for evaluating *how* you deliver instruction.

For each of the criteria (and any sub-criteria you add), you'll scrutinize its use and efficacy for learners who identify with the groups you've listed. You could write a simple "yes" or "no" in each box, or provide more detailed information to assist you in improving your practice.

Keep reading as we review the criteria. Then it will be your turn to create your own diversity tally scorecard.

DIFFERENTIATING INSTRUCTION

Are we are differentiating both content and methods, catering to the unique needs of individual learners? This is more common in the early elementary grades. It may be a necessary and overlooked element with upper elementary and adolescent learners. The content, the process, or product may need to be varied based on your learners' levels of readiness or interests.

Do a quick assessment of your delivery methods. Do you lecture, read aloud, read along? Do you show videos or play audio recordings? Do your learners read silently or listen to audiocasts of their books? Is content delivered using technology? From what different types of sources and media do learners get information? When you create your own diversity tally scorecard, list those various sources under differentiated instruction and evaluate each one separately. Take a minute to jot down those sources in your journal.

Do a quick assessment of your product requests. What do your learners turn in to demonstrate their level of mastery of the content? How much variety is there? Do you offer methods for those who are more artistic to demonstrate their learning? What about the multilingual who can write an essay in their primary language, but is struggling to demonstrate written proficiency in English? When you create your own diversity tally scorecard, list the types of products under differentiated instruction and evaluate each of them separately. Take a minute to jot down those products in your journal.

For a quick, global assessment in the row for this item, ask the question,

- *Am I differentiating instruction, using content, methods, and strategies, that addresses the needs of my _______ learners?*

ENGAGING AND MOTIVATING LEARNERS

Engagement drives participation. Participation drives achievement (Nkrumah, 2023). The methods we choose should motivate and engage all our learners. Each learner. Every learner. We must avoid stereotyping. Yes, be mindful of who each learner is, but mindful that not every learner is like every other learner that they share a category or identity with.

Rarely will we teach a subject in K–12 that every child just loves to learn. Think of your own experiences studying a subject that simply bored you. Or perhaps a subject was taught in a way that made your eyes roll back in your head. Let's avoid that! Are the methods you are using creating and promoting engagement from all your learners? Who disengages? Who are you motivating and who are you not?

As you consider this criteria on the scorecard, ask,

- *Am I providing instruction that engages and motivates my ______ learners?*

SUPPORTING CRITICAL THINKING

A variety of methods such as problem-based learning, inquiry-based learning, and project-based learning help develop critical thinking and real-world transferrable skills (Hendratmoko et al., 2023; Ssemugenyi, 2023). How are you teaching critical or higher-order thinking skills? We can't simply expect learners to use inference, evaluation, persuasion, or justification. We must provide information students can use to practice those skills—content. We must create and deliver lessons that teach learners how to use those skills—process. And we must create opportunities for them to demonstrate their ability to use the skills—product.

As above, do a quick assessment of your instructional content and processes, and the products you request from your learners. Take a minute to jot them down in your journal.

When you create your own diversity scorecard, list the content, processes, and products below critical thinking and evaluate each one. For a quick, global assessment for this item, ask the question,

- *Am I relying on content, processes, and products that support critical thinking in my ______ learners?*

DEVELOPING AND SUPPORTING SOFT SKILLS

Soft skills are those interpersonal skills that help us to relate and work with others (Cegolon, 2023). Sometimes called *people skills*, development of these non-technical social skills was severely delayed for many learners during the COVID-19 pandemic (Phogat et al., 2023; Ye et al., 2023). We must use instructional methods that incorporate opportunities for learners to develop these softs skills. This supports cultural understanding and facilitates the exchange of diverse ideas and perspectives.

Think about the grade level (or levels) you work with. What are the soft skills that you expect learners in that grade to have? Take a minute to jot them down in your journal.

When you create your own diversity tally scorecard, list the methods you use below soft skills and evaluate each of them separately. For a quick, general assessment for this item, ask the question,

- *Am I providing instruction and practice opportunities in my classroom for my______ learners to develop and use soft skills?*

COMPREHENSIVE SYNTHESIS

Finally, we will consider how our methods facilitate a comprehensive understanding of, not only our own subject matter, but knowledge and information across subjects. Our methods should enable learners to make connections from text to text, text to self, and text to world, synthesizing and evaluating the knowledge learned in one subject to synthesize and evaluate in another.

How we teach should foster learners' ability to approach a topic from multiple perspectives. Is this happening in your classroom?

For this last criteria, ask the question,

- *Does my instruction support opportunities for my ______ learners to demonstrate comprehensive synthesis?*

Alright! Your turn! Record a series of lessons over the course of a week. You can complete this diversity tally scorecard on your own or work with a peer. If you choose to work with others, keep in mind that having someone else evaluate your teaching can strain a relationship. So, take your ego out of it. This is about doing the right thing, doing enough of the right thing, and doing the right thing well. And when you find those right things, note who it works for and use them more often.

Who Has Mastery?

In an inclusive, culturally connected classroom or school, the educators and school leaders hold the power. And they hold it exclusively. That said, how do you go about using that tremendous power for the good of marginalized learners? Let's dig in!

We begin by making sure that all our learners have a place, a learning environment that is equitable, not simply accessible. It is not enough that each learner can walk into the classroom and receive the same books as everyone else. It is not enough that they all have the same desks, and access to the same technology. It is not enough that they all have a qualified educator leading their classes and a counselor who knows their names and understands their goals and challenges.

That's simply access. We want to develop and nurture mastery.

MASTERY VERSUS ACCESS

Both **mastery** and **access** are crucial aspects of every learner's educational journey; however, they refer to different components of the learning process.

Access concerns the availability and opportunity to receive an education. Access is the foundational level. With access, we ensure that every learner—no matter their socio-economic status, race, gender, disability, or other marginalized identity—has the right to attend school, to receive educational resources, and to participate in the learning process.

Access implies that no barriers are in place that would impede learning. Such barriers might be academic, social, cultural, physical, environmental, linguistic, or social. As an academic example, both the linguistically diverse learner and the learner with a cognitive impairment should each have access to differentiated instruction to meet their unique academic needs. The linguistically diverse learner should receive differentiated instruction to support developing School English. The learner with a cognitive impairment should have an IEP or 504 plan that defines their differentiated supports and services and should be provided the instruction and accommodations described in that plan.

As a socio-cultural-environmental example, both the learner at a historically underperforming school and the learner at a historically high-achieving school should each have access to instruction that will result in their ability to graduate college- and career-ready. They should each receive access to high quality curriculum and instruction that will allow them, should they desire, to be successful in Advanced Placement (AP) coursework.

Access is prerequisite to mastery. Access ensures everyone gets a seat in the classroom, while mastery ensures they fully grasp and develop grade-level or above proficiency in every subject. The challenge to developing and nurturing mastery is twofold. First, there is in the quality of curriculum and instruction. How well we teach what we teach. Then there is the depth of learning. How well learners learn what is taught. Both are essential: without access, mastery is moot; without mastery, access doesn't fulfill its potential. They're intertwined in the broader goal of an equitable education for every child.

Mastery doesn't happen overnight. It may not happen in a year. But it must be developed as quickly as possible for marginalized learners, especially struggling learners, and those with identities that have historically underperformed in your school or district. Once developed, it must continue to be achieved every year.

access—the opportunity for all learners to participate in and benefit from educational services, regardless of their socio-economic status, race, gender, disability, or other factors. It suggests equal opportunities and a lack of barriers in learning environments.

mastery—a deep and comprehensive understanding of a subject or skill, allowing an individual to apply, teach, or adapt the knowledge effectively in various contexts.

Teaching for Year-Over-Year Mastery

Mastery of learning requires mastery of instruction. We must remain mindful of *what* we teach as well as *how* we teach it.

Increasing mastery year-over-year requires choosing instructional materials that meet learners' needs where they are on the first day of school and using instructional methods that take them to where they need to be at the end of the school year.

To develop mastery, we must dive deeply into both content and skills. We must continually gauge how well each learner not only comprehends, but can apply what they've learned, working at the highest levels of Bloom's taxonomy.

Our learners demonstrate mastery not by passing a chapter quiz, unit test, or high-stakes exam, but by developing the ability to analyze, synthesize, and evaluate information in a comprehensive and meaningful way. If learners are taught to mastery, the tests take care of themselves. There is no need to prep for them. Just teach. Instruct. To mastery. Every lesson, every subject, every day.

Mastery indicates not just rote memorization but the ability to think critically, analyze, and adapt knowledge in real-world scenarios. It's about depth, competency, and the capacity to use knowledge and skills effectively in various contexts. Yes, rote memorization has its place. Math facts are math facts. Letter sounds are letter sounds. Knowing them frees up cognitive energy so that we can use them effortlessly to process larger chunks of information.

The Role of Rote

In teachers' college, I learned some routines that we now know are not in the best interest of mastery learning. Most memorable are the spelling and vocabulary routines. Maybe you can relate to lesson plans that looked like this:

- **Monday:** Introduce 20 vocabulary words in class. Homework: Write each word 3 times in alphabetical order.
- **Tuesday:** Include 10 of the vocabulary words in a class writing assignment. Choose the most difficult word as an exit ticket before recess. Homework: Write the definition for each word using a dictionary.
- **Wednesday:** Exchange and correct the homework. Include the other 10 vocabulary words in a class writing assignment.

Choose a difficult word as an exit ticket before recess. Homework: Write each word in a sentence of 5 words or more.

- **Thursday:** Vocabulary puzzle/word search/cloze as finish work during class. Homework: Study for tomorrow's vocabulary test.
- **Friday:** Vocabulary test. Exchange and correct. Finish work: Write any misspelled words 5 times. Write any missed definition.

I now know better. In fact, I learned better in my second or third year of teaching. My sincerest apologies to my learners from those first few years. One, I know it takes the average learner 30 meaningful engagements with a word before it becomes part of their lexicon. The key word in that sentence: *meaningful.*

Two, much of the work assigned was the worst kind of rote work. I was expecting my learners to memorize words and their definitions without any higher-order thinking involved. Sure, they applied their learning by using the words in sentences but it was still low-level thinking.

Does rote have a role? Absolutely! That's how I learned my math facts: addition, subtraction, multiplication, and division. It's how we develop reading fluency. You don't need to think about the various rules governing spelling and pronunciation to read the words you're reading right now. You're not consciously processing the apostrophe in the word *you're* or thinking about why it has a different meaning from the word *your*. And you're certainly not consciously processing or analyzing the punctuation.

Rote memorization has six key roles and it's important that we recognize and respect them:

1. It builds the foundation of many basic skills and knowledge, like math facts or the alphabetic principle (Ehri, 1998). Mastery of these foundations is essential in early learning for developing mastery in higher grades and across subjects.
2. It helps to strengthen neural pathways. The act of memorizing can enhance synaptic strength and create neural connections, benefiting memory development (Shaywitz & Shaywitz, 2020).
3. It teaches discipline and the habit of persistence. Learners will rely on these soft skills throughout their lives.
4. It provides immediate recall of facts or skills without deep thought. This is advantageous for subjects such as mental math, grammar, word knowledge, music, geography, and anatomy.

5. It supports the transmission of culture through songs, stories, and traditions that are passed from generation to generation, preserving cultural knowledge.

6. It boosts learner confidence—the child who has key knowledge readily available is more confident in their ability to learn additional information. This supports engagement in the classroom instruction when new material is introduced.

Yes, rote memorization is valuable. Yes, it has its drawbacks. It is a valuable tool when used judiciously and in combination with other learning strategies, such as the memory-enhancing strategies you'll find in Appendix D. Balance rote memorization with methods that support deeper understanding, critical thinking, and problem-solving skills.

rote—the technique of learning information through repetition without necessarily understanding its deeper meaning, emphasizes recall over comprehension, often leading to the ability to recite details without grasping their contextual significance.

Recognizing and Responding to the Learning Needs of Culturally and Linguistically Diverse Learners

Access is not mastery. While we may provide access, we must ensure that we provide instruction in a bias-free manner. We must show no bias against any of the identities of our learners nor show favoritism for any of the identities of our learners. Return to the identification activity you completed (Table 3.2). Review the groups in each of the columns through the lens of instructional methodology. Look through the lens of mastery versus access. Which identity groups routinely or historically lack mastery? Pay special attention to those with whom you and perhaps other educators in your setting, cannot or do not culturally connect or relate. Which identity groups are harmed by the instructional methods used in your classroom or promoted in your setting? Circle those identity groups. Be honest. No one can see this but you.

Using methods that recognize and respond to the needs of CLDLs is crucial for creating a culturally connected classroom. Some of the methods may challenge you as they may run counter to your typical routines or your philosophical beliefs about providing instruction.

That's okay. You may be uncomfortable for a while. That's how we grow. If your goal is a culturally connected, inclusive classroom, then establishing learner, contributor, and challenger safety hinges on your ability to embrace discomfort for the benefit of the learners.

Here are ten culturally relevant teaching strategies to support your diverse learners.

1. AFFIRMATION, VALIDATION, AND RESPECT

Have you ever had a learner whose name you found difficult to pronounce at first? I grew up with one of those names. One not familiar to any of my overwhelmingly White teachers. Although it is phonetically regular, I was called all sorts of things. I was also often asked, "What do they call you?" I never, ever, altered or shortened my name. I never Anglicized it. My parents had instilled in me the importance of my name to who I was and their beliefs, hopes, and plans about and for me.

You affirm, validate, and respect your learners beginning with knowing their names. Familiarize yourself with their backgrounds, languages, and cultures. These days tools on the Internet offer pronunciation guides for names from various cultures and ethnicities. When you find such a resource, share it with your colleagues.

And it is critical that you not only *know* learners' names, but that you call them by their names. Pronounce them properly. Ask learners to help you if the pronunciation does not readily roll off your tongue. You may even wish to record it so you can practice later. When we ask our culturally diverse learners to give us names that are easier to pronounce, we diminish who they are and devalue their culture. We want to affirm their cultural identities. And the simple act of working to say their names as they were given goes a long way in saying to a learner, "I see you for who you are."

Validate your learners' lived experiences and perspectives in classroom discussions, activities, and assignments. This is critical when discussing literary texts. The lenses through which your learners view a text may not align with your perspective or the guidance in the teacher's edition. That does not make it incorrect, just different. Learners' perspectives lend another set of metaphorical mirrors, windows, and sliding glass doors for both you and their peers.

2. SCAFFOLDED INSTRUCTION

The big idea in scaffolding instruction is to break tasks into manageable chunks.

With younger learners, struggling learners, and early language learners—monolingual or multilingual—you'll want to provide support structures, such as sentence starters or guided notes. Provide instruction on these structures as tools, then gradually remove the scaffolds as learners become more proficient and independent.

At higher grade levels, where longer term projects and assignments are typical, you'll want to break those big assignments down into manageable components. Let's take a 1,000-word essay as an example. Some learners may only need a prompt and they are good to go. Other learners, perhaps those more marginalized, may require additional supports and scaffolds. Perhaps they've never written anything longer than 300 words. Perhaps the prompt does not connect to their lived experiences.

Try this process. First, discuss the prompt. If there is a cultural disconnect, can you revise the prompt to remedy that disconnect and still achieve the goal of the lesson? Next, break down the essay into the various components. Provide explicit instruction on each portion, then have learners complete that portion. In this manner, you offer step-by-step instruction while building on learners' existing knowledge and skills. In time, the chunks can become larger and larger as you remove each scaffold.

Practitioner's Perspective

Once upon a time, I looked around my classroom and realized that there was no way my learners could demonstrate their learning through writing. My learners spoke English or Hmong or Tagalog or Spanish or African American English. None of them, or very few of them, actually spoke School English. This was a sixth-grade multiple subjects classroom. The social studies framework was focused on ancient civilizations. Given the diversity of languages and cultures in my classroom, and the concepts and terms students were learning about ancient civilizations, it became obvious that I needed to find a way for my learners to show they understood the content, not necessarily whether or not they could tell me about it in School English.

My learners were great collaborators. They worked extraordinarily well in small groups. Perhaps this is because a majority of them came from cultures that were collectivist, that emphasized and respected the value of community and of helping their neighbors and one another. I fostered this culture in my classroom.

Think for a moment about how you would get learners to explain the significance of the "silk roads" in the period of the Han Dynasty and Roman Empire and their locations. Or to explain the

(Continued)

(Continued)

major beliefs and practices of Brahmanism in India and how they evolved into early Hinduism. The traditional approach would be to ask students to write an essay of say, 500 words.

I might not have been able to express this at the time, but I knew two things were true: One, to take the traditional approach of expecting the children to express their thoughts and understandings in writing would have been culturally biased. It would have been slanted toward a White western, middle-class culture. Two, I knew that in the process of reading and grading those papers, I would not get a sense of what my learners actually understood. Three, I knew that a great number of my learners would fail. None of this was acceptable.

I also knew that the vast majority of my learners were not going to go to college. But their ability to think and reason was critical to developing the skills and tools they would need to enter the world of work. So after careful deliberation, I decided to let my learners work collectively and express their understanding through graphic art. Instead of asking for a 500-word essay on the significance and locations of the trans-Eurasian silk roads, I asked them to show this information using a map and 12 pictures. I gave them the option to work alone or in groups of two to four. I let them choose their own groups. Because I had fostered a culture of community and inclusion in my classroom, no child was left without a group.

What I got in terms of detail blew my mind, and this became the first of many assignments that would utilize this format. The images were clear and detailed. My learners' words may have been limited but they were well chosen. The final projects included timelines, road signs, thought bubbles and speech bubbles. And everyone contributed. These were not groups where one or two people did all the work. The culture of the classroom and the nature of the assignment allowed students to incorporate their home cultures into their work. Some learners were brilliant artists, and did the drawing. Other groups did not have an artist, so they used stick figures, but the image sequencing and the wording used was significant enough to show what they knew.

I also use something that we may tend to steer away from, and that is the oral argument. I asked my learners about their projects, and they gave me information that conveyed they had mastered the content.

I used this format often over the years to allow learners to express their understanding through graphic art. In social studies, I asked learners to give me a timeline. In ELA, I used it to check for comprehension of literature (while continuing to instruct on the skills of grammar, usage, mechanics, and writing). We got really good at "hot dog, hamburger, hamburger" folding to create eight-pane pages. My learners used the panes to provide four examples of comparing and four examples of contrasting concepts, ideas, or characters.

Unless a standard stated that a learner needed to demonstrate mastery through written form, I took the liberty of allowing them to use other methods to demonstrate their understanding, methods that allowed them to be successful.

3. CODE-SWITCHING AND TRANSLANGUAGING

The culturally connected classroom supports that entire linguistic repertoire of learners. In your classroom, you'll want to encourage your multilingual learners to use their primary or sociocultural languages to bridge languages needed to convey ideas. This may happen through code-switching or translanguaging.

In code-switching, a learner may alternate between two or more languages, including sociocultural languages, at the conversation, sentence, or utterance level. Here's an example of code-switching in a middle grades English Language Arts class discussing a novel. The learner speaks School English (SE) and African American English (AAE):

Educator: "Today we're exploring the main character's motivations. Why do you think she made the choices she did?"

Learner: "I think she was just tryin' to do right by her family, you know? She ain't wanna let nobody down."

Educator: "That's an insightful point. She was indeed trying to meet her family's expectations. What are some other factors affecting her decisions?"

Learner: "Peer pressure, yo. Folks at school be trippin' sometimes, so she mighta felt like 'go along get along.'"

Educator: "Peer pressure is an excellent point. Social environment often impacts decision-making. Thank you for adding that perspective."

In translanguaging, learners and educators also make use of multiple languages in a seamless and wholistic manner. Slightly different from code-switching, translanguaging is essential for a learner who does not know the English word for a concept they understand. Where in code-switching, the switch may be more social—a matter of fluency, comfort, or ease—learners and educators who translanguage tend to use the primary language as a necessary resource to comprehension or completing a task.

Here's an example of translanguaging in a seventh-grade science class focused on the water cycle. In this instance, the instructor also speaks Spanish, although translanguaging can occur only on the part of the learner:

Educator: "Today, we're going to learn about the water cycle, or 'el ciclo del agua.' Can anyone tell me the first stage of the water cycle?"

Learner: "Is it evaporation, maestra?"

Educator: "Correcto, evaporation or 'evaporación' is the first stage. ¿Qué sucede durante la evaporación?"

Learner: "El agua se convierte en vapor y sube al cielo."

Educator: "Exactly, the water turns into vapor and rises into the sky. Now, let's discuss condensation, or 'condensación.'"

Supporting the use of multiple languages in the classroom, whether translanguaging or code-switching, recognizes the value of multilingualism and shows respect for learners' home environments, languages, and cultures.

Encourage learners to use their entire linguistic repertoire, mixing languages to make meaning, understand content, and express themselves. At times, concepts expressed in a single word in one language and culture require explanations in English. Supporting translanguaging and code-switching not only validates their linguistic backgrounds but also leverages their multilingual skills for learning.

4. COLLABORATIVE LEARNING—WITH A TWIST

Cooperative groups are often formed heterogeneously, combining learners of varying levels of academic or linguistic proficiency with the idea being that the more proficient aid the less proficient. And that's okay.

But try grouping learners homogeneously at times, by identity groups. This practice supports culturally responsive teaching and provides numerous benefits to many marginalized learners. For example, when multilinguals who share a sociocultural or primary language have an opportunity to work together, they bring their shared language and culture into their classroom assignments. They connect with their peers in a different and meaningful way. Learners who are still developing School English are not burdened by the intimation that they need the support of monolingual English speakers to be successful.

Multimodal Learning

Text interaction plays a large role in learners' K–12 journeys. Consider using interactive read-alouds, guided oral reading, choral reading, and shared reading to provide variety in textual interaction. Each of these lends itself to a range of scenarios, from teaching comprehension skills to supporting less confident or struggling readers in developing fluency, to providing oral models for multilinguals.

You know the adage: *A picture is worth a thousand words.* Diagrams, charts, graphic organizers, and pictures are useful tools to support and reinforce verbal instructions. They provide critical context in conveying complex ideas and concepts that may be foreign to your learners. Visuals transcend language barriers and support teaching School English at the same time.

In addition to text, incorporate multimedia resources like audio or video recordings, music, software, podcasts, and interactive software. Different modalities support students' abilities and preferences as well as language proficiencies.

5. TOTAL PHYSICAL RESPONSE (TPR)

Why teach sitting down? TPR involves you using your body to teach, and learners using their bodies to demonstrate learning. TPR is a great tool for teaching action verbs, nouns, directions, prepositions, and other concepts that can be acted out. Appendix E has exemplars of what TPR can look like in the classroom.

6. CULTURAL JOURNALING THROUGH INTERACTIVE NOTEBOOKS

Have learners keep paper or digital notebooks where they can interact with new concepts. They can document their text-to-text, text-to-self, and text-to-world connections, helping to bridge cultural gaps. Encourage learners to use whatever tools and media they like in their notebooks. Allow drawings and choice of language (primary or sociocultural language, translanguaging, text language). As an added layer, establish a way for learners to share their journals with or request feedback from either you or their peers. Appendix F has sample print interactive notebooks for various grade levels that you can use in your classroom.

7. CULTURAL NORMS IN CLASSROOM MANAGEMENT

We don't generally consider classroom management in conversations around methods; however, understanding your learners' cultural norms is important in understanding their methods of engaging in instruction. Think back to the norms you wrote in Chapter 4. How many of those had a connection to behavior? Whose behavior? According to whose culture? Cultural norms may influence behaviors, behaviors that you may deem inappropriate if you are teaching through a White Eurocentric lens. While establishing behavioral norms is work done in step 1, it helps to remain mindful of this as you implement culturally responsive teaching strategies.

8. SHELTERED INSTRUCTION OBSERVATION PROTOCOL (SIOP)

While it may have fallen out of favor in some areas, the SIOP model is a research-validated approach to supporting multilingual learners. The model integrates School English and content instruction. A SIOP-based lesson includes both content and language objectives and frequent opportunities for learners-to-instructor and learner-to-learner interaction. Jana Echevvaria developed the SIOP model along with Deborah Short and MaryEllen Vogt. For resources and information about the model, visit www.janaechevarria.com.

9. FRONTLOADING

Pre-teaching, or frontloading key vocabulary and concepts, supports higher levels of mastery with less distraction or disengagement during content instruction. To support rapid acquisition and comprehension of key concepts and vocabulary, try using visuals, **realia**, and TPR. Realia in particular provide concrete experiences that support comprehension of abstract concepts, particularly for culturally and linguistically diverse learners.

realia—objects and material from everyday life that may be used as a visual aid; realistic toys that are exemplars of real objects, such as dinosaurs, cars, trucks, and tools

10. BUILDING AND ASSESSING SCHEMA

I've often said, "You can't activate schema a learner doesn't have." Before diving into new content, we should ascertain whether our learners have the requisite background knowledge to connect the new information to. Much like frontloading, building schema prior to introducing new concepts ensures that all learners, irrespective of their lived and educational experiences, have a foundation from which to learn.

You'll want to determine a baseline of knowledge and comprehension prior to teaching a lesson—even before building the schema you believe is necessary. Give a brief assessment before a lesson to find out what background knowledge learners have and what is missing. During the lesson, briefly assessing will help to gauge learners' comprehension. This knowledge will allow you to adjust instruction, or provide additional background accordingly.

schema—cognitive frameworks or concepts that help learners organize and interpret information; mental maps or structures used to organize knowledge, beliefs, and understandings; a requisite to incorporating new information into existing knowledge to support ease of comprehension

The Power of a Picture

I was in Detroit observing a first-grade class in a majority-of-color school that had a significant percentage of multilingual learners whose first language was Arabic. The teacher was a monolingual English speaker. The children sat crisscross applesauce on the carpet, hands in their laps, attending to every word as the teacher read aloud. The teacher came to a vocabulary word embedded in the story. I believe the word was *vehicles*. I watched as the teacher labored to convey the concept without simply giving the children examples. After an excruciating minute or more, a little girl ever-so-politely said, "Why don't you just show us a picture?"

Conclusion

In this chapter, we considered step 2 of the CARTI Framework: instructional methodology. You examined your classroom practices with a focus on Equity Indicator 2: standards and explored how to work toward mastery learning for all learners. And you examined ten culturally relevant teaching strategies to broaden your repertoire of instructional methods and support diverse learners.

In Chapter 6, we shift from instructional methodology to curriculum content. And we move from a focus on Equity Indicator 2 to Indicator 3: representation. You'll use another diversity tally scorecard to examine your instructional materials through this indicator. We'll break down how bias, stereotype, and misrepresentation present themselves in instructional material and the harm they cause to marginalized learners.

In the reflect and act exercises below, you'll see more planning elements. Take your time considering the prompts and recording your responses in your journal.

Reflect and Act

How do you ensure that learners feel valued and respected based on the way you teach?

Complete the diversity tally scorecard based on three to five lessons. How do you feel about your outcomes? What would you like to improve upon?

Which of the ten culturally relevant strategies have you, or will you, implement? How will you implement them? Why did you choose the ones you did?

●●● MY MINDSET METER

Complete the mindset meter as a self-assessment. Make connections building on what you've learned and your lived experience. Focus. Reflect. Analyze. Strategize.

Knowledge: I can describe what mastery in learning versus access to content looks like:

____

____

____

____

Comprehension: I can explain code-switching and translanguaging and its value in instruction:

____

____

____

____

Application: This is how I can use the instructional strategies I learned in this chapter:

____

____

____

____

Analysis: These are the practices I must sharpen to support all my learners reaching mastery year-over-year:

____

____

____

____

Synthesis: This is how I will recognize, value, and affirm each of my learners:

____

____

____

____

Evaluation: I used to think ______ but now I think ______.

____

____

____

____

CURRICULUM CONTENT

CHAPTER 6

The CARTI Framework, Step 3: Curriculum Content

As we continue to explore inclusivity and how we build and maintain a culturally connected classroom, we consider step 3 of the CARTI Framework (see Figure 6.1). Equality of academic achievement outcomes lies at the core of equity and the CARTI framework. The curriculum content and instructional material we use should be culturally appropriate, so that all learners can see themselves in it. It should foster engagement that sparks a desire to learn. And it should be rigorous to support the core focus of academic achievement.

We use tools to critique the instructional materials currently in use as well as those we are considering for adoption. These same tools may be used to question why some materials are denied acceptance even though they do pass the test of equity. Our developing cultural awareness guides us in analyzing the true impartiality of the materials we choose to use. In developing a culturally connected, inclusive classroom, we must commit to using only those materials that pass the muster of impartiality.

Our curriculum content is the "what" of teaching. *What* content will you cover for the subjects you teach? *What* materials will your learners engage with?

I realize that we do not all have true "academic freedom." If you do have complete control over the materials you choose to use, you can skip the rest of this paragraph. If you have some control, I'll provide you with strategies for modifying and supplementing the

Figure 6.1

The CARTI Framework

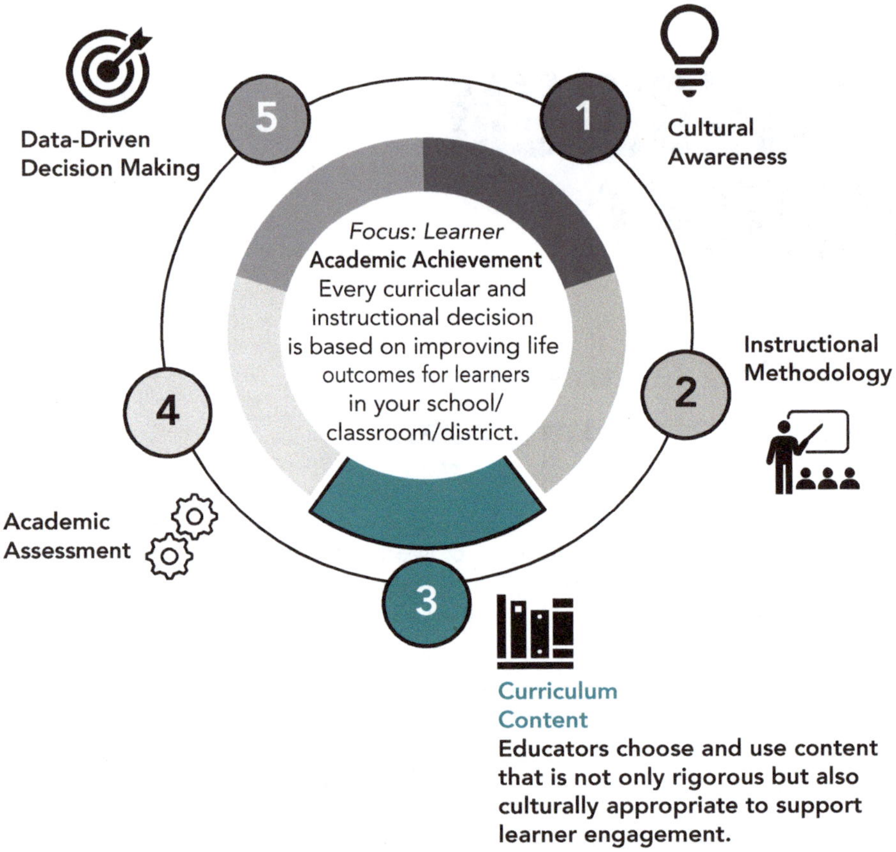

Focus: *Learner*
Academic Achievement
Every curricular and instructional decision is based on improving life outcomes for learners in your school/classroom/district.

1 Cultural Awareness

2 Instructional Methodology

3 Curriculum Content

Educators choose and use content that is not only rigorous but also culturally appropriate to support learner engagement.

4 Academic Assessment

5 Data-Driven Decision Making

materials to meet the broader goal of equity. And for those of you who have no control, who are handed curriculum, a pacing guide, and perhaps even a mandate to report your daily activities or lesson progress to a coach or administrator, I recommend reflecting on these questions in your journal:

- Why was the curriculum chosen?
- Is it working for your learners? If not, why not?
- If it is working to meet the needs of your most marginalized learners, do you have any concerns about the lack of choice?

With those reflections in mind, let's move on to impartiality.

Equity Indicator 3: Impartiality

Impartiality, as an equity indicator, is about fairness, a lack of bias. And in the context of step 3 of the CARTI framework, it's about educators choosing and using content, curriculum, and instructional materials that are not only rigorous, but culturally appropriate, to support learner engagement and success. The two essential questions we ask here are:

- *Who has representation?*
- *Are we accurately and appropriately considering the cultures of all those affected, or are we acting from a middle-class, White-European, Western cultural bias?*

In this section, we'll work on examining instructional materials to ensure that no harm comes to children by subliminally teaching that they, their lived experience, any aspect of their identities is not the norm. We'll dig deeper into the metaphorical "mirrors, windows, and sliding glass doors" when discussing the importance of representation and diversity in instructional materials. We'll get a better sense of the many forms of oppression that make their way into the materials with which our learners must engage.

DIVERSITY TALLY SCORECARD

To examine your materials, you need tools. The first and simplest tool is a way to quickly score your materials. For this, we can again use the diversity tally scorecard.

I've created the scorecard in Figure 6.2 with columns for the most common genders represented in instructional materials. There is room to add others to meet your specific context and evolving social awareness of gender diversity.

In the first column are the most common racial, ethnic, and image categories found in instructional materials. You may wish to add additional categories to match the identities of the learners you identified as marginalized in Table 3.2. These are the categories you will use to evaluate the images found in your instructional materials.

This scorecard supports a simple flip test. Start with one of the textbooks or other text materials such as literature selections used during the year. Tally each image or reference to a person in the

Figure 6.2

Diversity Tally Scorecard for Curriculum Content

	Female, Girl, or Woman	Male, Boy, or Man	Non Binary	Gender-Neutral	TOTAL	PERCENTAGE
Animals						
Asian American						
Black/African American						
Indigenous						
Latine						
Middle Eastern/ North African						
Multiracial						
Pacific Islander						
Racially Ambiguous						
People with Disabilities						
White						
TOTAL						
PERCENTAGE						

text by its gender identity and racial, ethnic, or image category. You may need to do a little bit of research to do this. For example, if you read my bio, you'll see I use the pronouns she and her. Earlier in the book, I wrote about being Black. So, in the row for "Black/African American" you will mark a tally under the "woman" column.

This task may create some challenges, particularly for White people who've ascribed to an "I don't see color" escapism. And many people who lack cultural connectedness to a variety of diverse peoples may not be able to recognize the differences in individual appearance that indicate racial and ethnic identity. I strongly suggest completing this activity as part of a PLC, and preferably, one that is racially diverse. People of color recognize the physical characteristics of their own race, a phenomena known as the "cross-race effect" or "same race bias" (Meissner & Brigham, 2001).

With children's literature, as well as images in science, and social science text, animals are typically shown without any indication of gender. You can infer, though, that a lion with a full mane is male. However, if there is no indication in the text, choose the gender-neutral column for that animal. For high school math and engineering texts, and others that lack illustrations, look at the word problems and other exemplars that are used.

Your totals for each column mean little without context. Percentages hold greater value in looking for the equal representation of people in your text. So, calculate percentages as well. With those values, you can begin to see just who has representation as well as who does not. But it goes deeper than a simple presence. As you are introduced to the additional tools in this section, you'll develop a greater understanding of the nuances of representation and the subliminal oppression that presents itself through images and text.

WHO HAS REPRESENTATION?

You could give an initial answer to our essential question, "Who has representation?" by completing the diversity tally above. The representations you tallied are the metaphorical mirrors for your learners. Think about the experience of your learners who have few or no mirrors in the texts you examined. How might they feel when asked to engage with content that either does not reflect who they are or visibly negates, omits, their existence?

Now, think about the experience of your learners with many mirrors in the texts you examined. How might they feel as their identities, perhaps their social dominance, is affirmed in the instructional material you use? What does this affirmation do to support their engagement?

Our second essential question, "Are we accurately and appropriately considering the cultures of all those affected, or are we acting from a middle-class, White-European, Western cultural bias?" requires a deeper dive, and greater context. So, let's examine the concept of White ethnocentrism first, then look to cultural and linguistic sensitivity to build the background needed to analyze instructional materials and accurately answer that question.

White Ethnocentrism

White ethnocentrism refers to the belief or assumption that the White Western European cultural norms, values, and perspectives are superior or central to others (Raden, 2003; Wilkerson, 2020). These norms, values, and perspectives are popularly attributed to the founders of the United States and are entrenched in American society throughout their evolution, maintained by social and political dominant groups (Snelgrove, 2020; Wilkerson, 2020)—the ingroup or insiders—who, regardless of their ancestry, present as White in America. It privileges "White culture" and experiences over those of non-White communities (Ryan et al., 2007). It's a significant problem in an educational setting for a number of reasons (Snelgrove, 2020).

When curriculum content is White-centric, learners are not exposed to the richness and depth of global cultures and perspectives. Not only does this deny CLDLs of those metaphorical mirrors, but it deprives all learners of a broad and deep understanding of the very diverse world in which they live and must, eventually, work. All learners need to understand and appreciate diverse cultures and perspectives to effectively navigate the global environment.

When we expose our learners to primarily White perspectives, we potentially develop, or reinforce, harmful stereotypes about non-white cultures (Greenberg & Rosenfield, 1979), leading to misconceptions and biases. We also hinder learners' critical thinking skills, because exposed to a single dominant perspective, they may not develop the skills of inference or analysis necessary to critically evaluate different viewpoints or challenge established narratives. These skills are essential to developing the culturally connected classroom where contributor and challenger safety are key components to learning.

In our classrooms, our CLDLs may feel excluded, undervalued, or oppressed when the histories, contributions, and perspectives taught do not represent their people. Our CLDLs' self-worth may be diminished, and they may disengage from the learning process. Structural racism is perpetuated by curriculum that continuously centers White experiences (Watson, 2023). Those experiences and values indirectly teach all learners that White culture is the normal culture, and theirs, by default, is *ab*normal. White ethnocentric curriculum reinforces societal structures that privilege White individuals.

Finally, as discussed previously, exposure to diverse stories, histories, and experiences helps our learners develop empathy. A White-centric curriculum deprives all learners of the chance to understand and empathize with the experiences of people from different backgrounds. While CLDLs lack mirrors, White learners lack windows and sliding glass doors. Keep in mind, though, that communities are entitled to metaphorical "curtains" and not every aspect of every learner's culture can or should be revealed to outsiders.

CULTURAL AND LINGUISTIC SENSITIVITY

We discussed cultural awareness as a key to equity indicator 1—meritocracy. In Chapters 2 and 3, we discussed sociocultural language. In the culturally connected classroom, sensitivity to diverse cultures and languages, whether world languages or sociocultural languages, is essential. That same sensitivity must extend to instructional materials.

Cultural and linguistic sensitivity ensures that content is inclusive, representative, and non-biased. Materials not only recognize the diverse backgrounds and languages of learners, but value and affirm them. When you choose and use materials with cultural and linguistic sensitivity, you enhance learner engagement. Children, just like adults, engage more when they see their cultures and languages represented. Those mirrors foster a sense of belonging and validation.

Remember the element of psychological safety? One way to promote inclusivity is by ensuring that all learners, regardless of their backgrounds, feel seen and valued, reducing feelings of marginalization. You can work to eliminate stereotypes though the selection of culturally and linguistically sensitive materials that present diverse groups accurately, dispelling myths and stereotypes.

When instructional materials validate learners lived experiences, they can relate. When we choose and use instructional materials either in learners' primary languages or with scaffolds to support their multilingualism through the use of primary language exemplars and text insets, comprehension and retention improve. Prioritizing cultural and linguistic sensitivity in teaching materials doesn't just create a more equitable classroom, it enriches the learning experience for all learners by providing mirrors, windows, and doors!

White ethnocentrism—the belief in the inherent superiority of White culture and norms, those perpetuated in American society by the social and political dominant group, leading to the evaluation of other cultures from a White-America-centric perspective.

Bias, Stereotype, and Misrepresentation

Bias, **stereotyping**, and misrepresentation are three of the most insidious and harmful practices that find their way into instructional materials. Whether occurring through ignorance or intent, the impact is the same: they do harm, allow harm, and deny resources. Remember, we also find these destructive and passive behaviors in unconsciously and consciously incompetent educators (refer to Table 3.1). Unconsciously and consciously competent educators engage in proactive and transformative behaviors, calling these instances out and working to eliminate them.

Now, let's look at ways in which bias, stereotyping, and misrepresentation not only affect learners' academic comprehension, but also their social and emotional development. How these things do harm, allow harm, and deny resources.

As learners encounter content, whether text, images, or other source materials, they simultaneously forge their sense of self and create an understanding of their place in the world. Whether mirrors, windows, or doors, materials that repeatedly portray people of certain identities as negative, stereotyped, or absent goodness and light do and allow harm (Greenberg & Rosenfield, 1979; Watson, 2023). Learners who identify with those groups potentially internalize the flawed perspectives presented, leading to decreased self-esteem and a distorted sense of identity. Learners who do not identify as such and lack cultural connectedness with those groups outside of the classroom develop negative stereotypes about those identities (Raden, 2003).

Bias and misrepresentation in our instructional materials do harm and deny resources through mirrors, windows, and sliding glass doors that provide inaccurate and skewed portrayals of history, culture, and society. Learners not exposed to the accurate, rich, and varied tapestry of humankind and world civilizations over time, receive narrow and erroneous versions of literature and history. Ignorance is fostered through denying comprehensive and accurate resources. Learners develop a lack of appreciation for the diversity of humankind and the contributions and lived experiences of the diversity of people—their peers and educators—with whom they interact daily or will come to interact as they become citizens in the global workforce.

Bias, stereotyping, and misrepresentation in instructional materials do harm by perpetuating prejudice. Instructional materials continuously expose learners to viewpoints. When those viewpoints are biased or contain stereotypes, learners may begin to see them as truths. After all, "It's in the book." Whether a mirror, window, or sliding glass door, this form of subliminal indoctrination may result in learners, all learners, carrying these biases into adulthood and perpetuating cycles of discrimination and prejudice.

Bias, stereotyping, and misrepresentation in instructional materials do harm through limiting opportunities for learners to develop empathy and tolerance. Instructional materials should broaden horizons, not constrict them. Stereotyping and bias work against this when presenting caricatured versions of culturally diverse peoples. As windows and sliding glass doors, they make it difficult for White-European learners to genuinely relate to or understand diverse peoples.

Bias in instructional materials stifles the development of critical thinking skills. No educator ever said they want their learners to operate solely at the lowest levels of Bloom's taxonomy. Yet, biased content, by its very nature, discourages questioning and promotes the acceptance of presented "facts." Biased content creates a psychologically unsafe classroom: unsafe for inclusion, unsafe to learn, unsafe to contribute, unsafe to question or challenge the materials presented.

Everywhere and every time we, as educators, fail to remove biased, stereotyping, and misrepresentational content from our classrooms, we allow harm. Tragic economic and social implications await if we as educators continue to allow instructional materials riddled with bias, stereotype, and misrepresentation in our schools. We will continue to produce citizens ill-equipped to function in a diverse global economy. In our increasingly interconnected world, recognizing, valuing, and affirming diversity are crucial for social harmony and economic collaboration.

Bias, stereotyping, and misrepresentation in instructional materials do more than just provide inaccurate information. They do harm through shaping the way children perceive themselves and others, potentially leading to lasting personal and societal ramifications. If we believe in providing world-class educations for our learners, if we believe in academic excellence, and desire classrooms that champion equity, equality, inclusivity, and critical thought, it is imperative to critically examine our instructional materials and eliminate those that fail the test of cultural congruency.

Now, let's look at the criteria you can use, the tools, to examine your own instructional materials. And remember, strategies are coming. Keep reading!

bias—a predisposition or prejudice in favor of or against something, often based on personal beliefs, experiences, or stereotypes, influencing objective judgment.

stereotyping—the act of ascribing or assigning generalized traits or behaviors to an entire group, often based on oversimplified perceptions or preconceived notions frequently rooted in cultural, racial, or gender biases

Evaluating Curriculum Content for Equity

In my work as an instructional materials reviewer, I needed a tool to use to evaluate content through a lens of equity. Through research, application, practice, and revision, I developed *The Equity Checklist for Curriculum Content*. Appendix G includes a version of this checklist. It has 65 questions to help schools and districts conduct a thorough evaluation of instructional materials. If you are part of an adoption committee, I highly recommend you recruit a group of colleagues to shoulder the load of conducting a full review using the checklist. Do not take on that task as a solo endeavor!

Here, I provide broad general categories for checking instructional materials on your own.

First, look for instructional materials that help your learners understand how knowledge is built. Look for content that creates knowledge and shapes learners' understanding of how society sees itself.

Think about how the instructional materials represent diversity. Be certain the imagery is free from bias. Think about our simple definition of equity—*without bias against or favoritism for*. Instructional material should not overlook any group—partially or completely. Of course, if you are reviewing materials to supplement gaps in core materials, you can skip this criterion.

Instructors' materials such as teachers' guides and ancillary resources should provide guidance that does not endorse generic or reductionist views about specific groups. These resources should support you with language and guidance that appreciates individual uniqueness.

Ensure that instructional materials do not provide a skewed look at influence, privilege, or representation. Materials should provide diverse interpretations of topics, situations, or communities, steering clear of simplifying or skewing intricate matters by excluding varying viewpoints.

While not always comfortable to address in instruction, your teaching material should not gloss over or sidestep uncomfortable historical truths, such as prejudice, racial bias, discrimination, exploitation, oppression, gender bias, and conflicts between groups. Dealing with this content becomes less anguishing as you continue your journey toward cultural competence.

Many educational content providers make concerted efforts to develop materials free from biased language or depictions of people. However, these things may seep into the content. Be aware and always keep an eye out. Of course, instructional material should avoid language and terms that reinforce stereotypes, biases, or sideline specific groups through linguistic signals. Unfortunately, discovering those items prior to an in-depth examination is not easy.

Sometimes, in the course of selecting materials people may rely on the aesthetic, what materials look like, through a superficial flip test. Don't succumb to simply glancing through a book without a deeper content evaluation. Be a smart and informed consumer! Dig deep!

Lastly, look for instructional materials that demonstrate a commitment to equitable instruction. Look at the teacher resource guides, the front matter in your teacher's editions, indexes, teaching notes in the margins, and ancillary resources. And if you happen to find my photo in the front matter, you'll know I've done the heavier lifting for you!

Every Content Area Has Its Biases

No content area is exempt from the possibility of bias in the instructional material. Table 6.1 provides examples of how the bias presents in curriculum and may go unnoticed. These biases may stem from systemic inequalities, unconscious prejudices, and overt discrimination.

Table 6.1

What Un/Biased Content May Look Like Across the Subject Areas

SUBJECT AREA	BIASED CONTENT LOOKS LIKE	WHAT IT LOOKS LIKE WHEN WE LIMIT BIAS
Developmental Reading Skills	Stories primarily feature characters and families who are racially ambiguous, from Eurocentric backgrounds, or animals, ignoring the diverse racial and cultural identities of learners. Text is dominated by idioms, slang, or references specific to a predominantly White, middle-class culture.	Stories feature diverse characters and families from a variety of cultural settings and compositions. Idioms, slang, or references are culturally diverse. Direct instruction and context provides understanding of connections for all learners to enhance comprehension.

(Continued)

(Continued)

SUBJECT AREA	BIASED CONTENT LOOKS LIKE	WHAT IT LOOKS LIKE WHEN WE LIMIT BIAS
Literature	American literature written primarily by White male authors dominates the canon. Stereotypes frame Indigenous and Black stories in a historical context that emphasizes subjugation and marginalization without acknowledging contemporary voices and perspectives.	World literature written by diverse authors; women, BIPOC, and LGBTQIA+ authors exist equally within the canon. Indigenous and Black stories are framed through their own voices and experiences, incorporating and acknowledging contemporary voices, without subjugation and marginalization.
Math	Word problems consistently feature stereotypical gender roles (e.g., women as homemakers, men as engineers), and reinforce societal stereotypes. Western mathematical thinkers and concepts dominate.	Word problems are void of stereotypical gender roles. Women may be portrayed as engineers and other professionals, men may be homemakers. The African and Arabic origins of mathematics and mathematical thinking lay the foundation. Content accurately frames the significant contributions from all non-Western cultures, particularly African, Arabic, and Chinese mathematicians.
Social Science	North American history focuses on European settlers and glosses over the experience and contributions of Indigenous peoples, African and Black Americans, and other marginalized minority groups. Socioeconomic issues are presented without acknowldgment of systemic inequalities and the historical context that disproportionately affects marginalized communities.	North American history focuses on all Americans, beginning with Indigenous societies who existed on the continent prior to European settlement. History provides an honest and full portrayal of the experiences and contributions of Indigenous peoples, and African and Black Americans at the hands of White Europeans. The historical contexts that created and maintain systemic inequalities serve as a frame for the socioeconomic issues that disproportionately affect BIPOC peoples.

SUBJECT AREA	BIASED CONTENT LOOKS LIKE	WHAT IT LOOKS LIKE WHEN WE LIMIT BIAS
Science	Content emphasizes the contributions of scientists who are men. Evolutionary theory may be presented as fact.	Content equitably highlights women, non-binary, and BIPOC scientists' contributions and achievements. Religious and cultural sensitivities are considered in the teaching of evolutionary thinking to support culturally diverse populations.
Music	Selections focus predominantly on Western classical and contemporary music. Music textbooks and ancillaries lack gender and cultural diversity in composers and musicians.	Selections equally focus on musical traditions from around the world and across time. Musical elements, rhythmic structures, polyrhythms, and improvisational techniques influenced by non-Western cultures are addressed. Music textbooks contain diverse composers and musicians, leading to a complete view of musical history and innovation.
Fine Arts	Western art forms and artists are emphasized without integrating art from various cultures such as African, Indigenous, or Asian art. A European perspective is used to interpret art and symbols.	Art forms from various world cultures, including African, Indigenous, and Asian, are equally integrated with Western forms. Different cultural interpretations, including learners lived experiences, are used to interpret art and symbols.
Languages other than English	European languages (e.g., French, Spanish, German) are offered disproportionately to other globally significant languages (e.g., Arabic, Chinese), reflecting a Western bias. Language is taught in isolation, with a focus on mere linguistic mechanics and possibly reinforces stereotypes.	Language offerings reflect the value of, and demand for, bilingualism in the global economy to prepare learners for careers (e.g., Mandarin Chinese, Spanish, Arabic, German, Japanese, Hindi, Russian, and Korean). Language is taught in proper cultural context.

The examples given in Table 6.1 reflect how bias can subtly or overtly infiltrate various subject areas. One often overlooked area of bias that spans content areas is a lack of diverse authors and reviewers. The content's development process is a taproot of content inequity.

Each of these biases may reinforce societal stereotypes or neglect diverse perspectives. To become un/consciously competent requires we continuously examine and revise curricula to ensure an absolutely inclusive and representative learning experience.

Selecting Diverse and Inclusive Instructional Materials

Selecting instructional materials presents a unique and complex challenge. You may be on the forefront of implementing equitable practices in your community, or even your state. You may be on a state adoption committee in a state where adoptions last for up to ten years and cannot be changed mid-cycle. Budgets tend to be a concern, no matter the adoption cycle or selection process. And, of course, not all educational publishers produce materials that meet the criteria.

So, what's an equity warrior like you to do?

If you can't change the adopted curriculum, address equity concerns through supplementation and professional learning. In Chapter 7, we'll turn to addressing bias you find in instructional materials.

Conclusion

In this chapter, we shifted our focus to curriculum content, looking at it through Equity Indicator 3: representation. You used a diversity tally scorecard to examine instructional materials and get quantifiable data—a numeric value—of how well your marginalized learners are represented in the instructional materials placed in front of them every day. We took a close look at how bias, stereotype, and misrepresentation are present in instructional materials and the harm they do to marginalized learners.

In Chapter 7, we move from evaluation to solutions, addressing and offsetting the bias in curriculum materials. I'll provide strategies for immediate implementation as well as ways to supplement and enhance the materials you currently have.

Below are two reflect and act exercises based on the activities in the chapter. (If you didn't complete the activities, do them now.) If you are part of a book study or professional learning community, these are excellent group exercises. Discuss what you found with others who teach the same content and grades as you, as well as with those who teach different content and grades.

Reflect and Act

In completing the diversity tally for instructional materials (Table 6.1), what did you notice? Which group or groups were most frequently represented? Were any groups completely omitted? What difficulties did you encounter? What thoughts do you have about the presence of metaphorical mirrors for your CLDL?

Did you check your instructional materials using the categories described on pages 273–280? What did you find? What will you do with that knowledge and information?

●●● MY MINDSET METER

Complete the mindset meter as a self-assessment. Make connections building on what you've learned and your lived experience. Focus. Reflect. Analyze. Strategize.

Knowledge: The meaning of representation in curriculum as I understand it from this chapter:

____

____

____

____

Comprehension: This is why we must analyze instructional materials for impartiality:

____

____

____

____

Application: This is how I can support my culturally connected, inclusive classroom based on what I learned in this chapter:

____

____

____

____

Analysis: I will examine my instructional materials and state content standards through this lens:

____

____

____

____

Synthesis: This is how I will address bias in my instructional materials:

____

____

____

____

Evaluation: I used to think ______ but now I think ______.

____

____

____

____

CHAPTER 7

ADDRESSING AND OFFSETTING BIAS IN CURRICULUM MATERIALS

In Chapter 6, we examined Equity Indicator 3, impartiality, and looked at the importance of representation in instructional materials. We established the "why" of representation. You now have the tools and guidance to examine your curriculum content and, for those of you with the power, to review curricula you may consider purchasing.

In this chapter, I provide additional support for those of you who may not have purchasing power. I'll give you three strategies that you can immediately implement to help develop your learners' media literacy—valuable whether you have power to select curriculum or not. Then, we consider how to supplement existing curricula by using primary sources and contemporary social commentary to fill gaps and provide a balanced or counter narrative to the bias that you or your learners find in instructional materials.

Recognizing that bias exists is one thing. Addressing it appropriately requires a concerted effort to seek out resources that meet state standards, are developmentally appropriate, and are academically accessible for learners.

Let's look first at three strategies for supplementing and enhancing existing instructional materials, and then at the work that can be done with and through your professional learning community to support meeting Equity Indicator 3, impartiality.

Developing Media Literacy

So that they accurately access, analyze, and evaluate primary and secondary source content such as the materials you may choose to supplement and enhance your existing instructional materials, your learners must develop **media literacy**. Media literacy helps individuals make informed decisions related to content consumption. If your learners lack media literacy, you need to explicitly teach it. Media literacy equips learners with the critical thinking skills necessary to navigate a complex digital landscape—to discern between credible information and misinformation. This discernment is crucial in an age where fake news and manipulated content can spread swiftly.

media literacy—the ability to access, analyze, evaluate, and create media (especially digital); an understanding of how media messages shape our culture and society; the ability to make informed decisions related to media consumption.

Media literacy is crucial, for our learners and ourselves. It is even more important as we work to understand and learn from diverse perspectives. Media literacy promotes ethical engagement with digital platforms. It helps learners understand the implications of their online actions and encourages responsible digital citizenship. Learners become not just passive consumers but active participants, who can critically create and share content. Cultivate media literacy in your learners to support learning from diverse viewpoints.

For ourselves and our learners, media literacy goes beyond comprehending content; it includes developing fluency that leads to automaticity in analyzing the motives, biases, and methods of content production and distribution.

For those of you who may feel you lack technological savvy as compared to your learners, your own media literacy is not only crucial, but a moral imperative. The *right* thing is both *scientifically* right and *ethically* right for *your* learners! That overlap, between scientifically right and ethically right is where CARTI—the Culturally Appropriate Response to Instruction—lives. Failing to teach media literacy to learners due to our own discomfort with or low level of digital literacy is not ethically right. It both does harm and denies resources to learners.

Project Look Sharp and the National Association for Media Literacy Education (NAMLE) both provide tools, activities, and assessments for each grade span. The NAMLE Resource Library is free and available at medialiteracynow.org/resource-library. Lessons and resources available from NAMLE are research-based and recommended by many state's departments of education. While these lessons have not been subject to intense scientific validation, NAMLE is focused on research, unlike other widely available media literacy lessons.

Appendix H contains lessons and activities you can use in your classroom to help develop media literacy. For day-to-day instruction, here are three easy-to-incorporate strategies to support developing media literacy.

1. Critical Questioning
2. Experiential Media Creation
3. Media Diversity Journals

Follow the five-step process for each strategy shown in Table 7.1. Establish routines for these strategies so that learners take ownership, so they can revisit and revise their work based on feedback from you and their peers as well as their personal reflection. Though implementation looks different at each grade level, the steps are appropriate for all grade levels. Younger learners will require more supports and scaffolding, while more advanced learners may readily connect, integrate, demonstrate, and reflect with minimal prompting. Having these strategies as an iterative process helps learners see the importance of continuous learning and improving their skills.

Table 7.1

Five-Step Process for Strategy Implementation

CONNECT	INSTRUCT	INTEGRATE	DEMONSTRATE	REFLECT
Connect the strategy to your content standards or objectives.	Use explicit instruction and a gradual release method to provide learners with the knowledge and skills they need to use the strategy on their own.	Integrate the strategy into lessons, journaling, group activities, and homework.	Provide opportunities for learners to demonstrate their knowledge based on using the strategy.	Have learners reflect on their learning and outputs.

STRATEGY 1: CRITICAL QUESTIONING

Connect

Start by embedding media literacy objectives within your frameworks if they do not exist. The idea is for the development of critical media literacy skills to be an integral part of learners' instructional experience.

Instruct

Provide explicit instruction, guided practice and application, and then release scaffolds as you see learners have mastered critical questioning. Provide reference guides and posters with questions your learners can use to evaluate messages. Adjust these five exemplars to serve your learners and the content:

1. What's the main message?
2. Who benefits from this message?
3. What voices are not being heard?
4. Why was this made?
5. Who is the target audience?

Integrate

Explicitly incorporate critical questioning as a tool learners must use both in and out of class. Include activities that require learners to deconstruct messages and meanings in textbooks and primary source media used in the classroom.

Demonstrate

Provide opportunities for learners to demonstrate their use of critical questioning. Opportunities include writing in reflective journals, grand conversations, and collaborative activities.

Reflect

Provide opportunities for peer- and instructor-feedback and self-reflection. Learners can use the questions developed from the exemplars above or you might choose different ones. Self-reflection that follows feedback should incorporate what was learned from the feedback.

STRATEGY 2: EXPERIENTIAL MEDIA CREATION

Connect

Look at your curriculum and the learning objectives. Identify where you can embed media creation projects that align with some of those learning objectives. Consider how creating a media project will facilitate learners' critical thinking and reflective evaluation skills.

Instruct

Develop a process that can be integrated into your content, making connections between critical thinking and reflection, the content under study, and the process of creation. This is similar to teaching the writing process in a content area, however instead of writing you're teaching media creation. You may already be doing this!

Have your learners created a play or newspaper or slide presentation? That's media creation. Simply expand the outputs to include other types of media such as short form videos (TikTok or YouTube), blogs, or video news reports, for example.

Integrate

Provide opportunities for learners to create projects in multiple formats so that they have the opportunity to think about how best to demonstrate their learning to "show what they know." You might integrate critical questioning as part of the process, having learners use the five critical questions they are already working with. This gives learners insight into decision-making processes, biases, and challenges.

Demonstrate

Include in-class time for learners to showcase their creations.

Reflect

Include a prompt that supports learners reflecting on societal impact. What are the social implications of what they've produced? What is their responsibility to their audience and society related to how they tell their story? How does their product influence public opinion and behavior?

STRATEGY 3: MEDIA DIVERSITY JOURNALS

Connect

Look for media content from national and international sources, independent outlets, and different mediums to get a more comprehensive view of issues related to the content you teach. This may be easier for ELA, science, social studies, and the arts than for, say, math. Math educators may need to use social media platforms and other contemporary sources.

Instruct

Introduce the concept of media diversity journals to learners. If they are already journaling, incorporate *media diversity* as a format for entries into their existing journals. Emphasize how journaling will help them track the diversity of peoples and opinions for topics studied in class. Build on the *critical questioning* skills from above.

Integrate

Integrate journaling by connecting it to content areas that make sense. In a literature class, learners can examine the background of the author and make connections to character diversity. In social studies, they can analyze the messages about a single event from diverse figures. For example, Frederick Douglass's take on emancipation as compared to Jefferson Davis's. In science, learners can analyze messages about climate change from geophysicists and climate change deniers.

Demonstrate

Design assignments such as presentations, essays, research papers, and discussions or grand conversations, that require learners to draw on their journals for evidence and insights.

Reflect

Provide time for learners to update their journals and reflect on their observations. This could be part of a weekly routine (e.g., on Fridays), or you could tie it to end of unit or end of theme wrap-ups. From time-to-time, prompt learners to reflect on how maintaining their journal has influenced how they consume media outside of your class and their understanding of media bias.

By nurturing media literacy, you're not just teaching learners to be critical consumers of media; you're equipping them with lifelong skills to navigate a complex information landscape, discern truth from falsehood, and appreciate the diverse perspectives that enrich our global discourse.

Digital Media Popular With Generations Z and Alpha

Media literacy goes beyond recognizing the ten forms of digital media listed below. Social media, video streaming, online gaming, and other digital platforms are omnipresent. Today's learners, members of Generation Z (or Zoomers) and Generation Alpha (or screenagers), are continuously exposed to an ever-expanding virtual world (Drugaş, 2022). These platforms shape not only how learners consume information but also influence the formation of their beliefs, attitudes, and cultural norms.

In teaching media literacy, remain cognizant of the continuously changing digital media landscape. Of course, any of these ten forms may be displaced in the future.

- Social media platforms (e.g., Instagram, X)
- Video streaming services (e.g., YouTube, Netflix)
- Online multiplayer games
- Podcasts
- E-books and digital magazines
- Music streaming services (e.g., Spotify, Apple Music)
- Virtual reality (VR) and augmented reality (AR) experiences
- Mobile applications
- Online forums and community boards
- Instant messaging apps (e.g., WhatsApp, Snapchat)

Supplementing and Enhancing Existing Instructional Materials

PRIMARY SOURCES

As learners' media literacy develops, you can supplement and enhance your existing instructional materials by incorporating primary sources. We often think of primary sources as being most relevant in social studies. As a high school US History and American Government instructor, they were invaluable to me. But when I taught elementary, I tended to rely less on primary sources and more on the textbooks.

Yet every subject has primary sources that may be integrated into instruction. Whatever content area you teach, the Library of Congress (www.loc.gov/programs/teachers/classroom-materials) and the Smithsonian Institution Archives (siarchives.si.edu/history/education) have a wealth of virtual primary sources that can be used without restriction. Check the associations for your content area. On my quest to find primary sources for math, I discovered the Mathematical Association of America and the National Council of Teachers of Mathematics are treasure troves of primary sources for math.

Don't let time or resource availability hinder your search for primary sources. Original documents and records that provide firsthand testimony or direct evidence might be your best friend when it comes to Equity Indicator 3, impartiality.

Primary sources are original documents or records that provide firsthand testimony or direct evidence of a topic, event, person, or period. They are unaltered records created at the time of the event or by someone who experienced the event firsthand. Examples include:

- Diaries or journals
- Letters or correspondence
- Speeches
- Photographs
- Audio recordings
- Video or film footage
- Newspaper articles from the time of an event
- Official documents (e.g., birth certificates, treaties)
- Artifacts (e.g., clothing, tools, furniture)
- Oral histories or interviews
- Artworks
- Laws and government documents

Primary sources provide supplemental content to your curricula to support impartiality and representation. Properly sourced and vetted, they provide a diverse range of perspectives on historical events. When supplementing with primary sources, keep these benefits and guidelines in mind:

- Primary sources complement secondary sources, your textbooks and anthologies, by offering firsthand accounts that enrich the secondary source's narrative. Choose sources from various cultural, ethnic, and social backgrounds to present a multifaceted view of the topic or subject area. This is particularly helpful if your materials contain a singular or dominant narrative that runs counter to the goal of impartiality.
- Have learners analyze primary sources. Create opportunities and assignments that encourage learners to think critically about the origin, purpose, and context of a primary source. This will assist them in distinguishing between different perspectives and biases.

- When you choose primary sources from marginalized or underrepresented groups, you can challenge existing stereotypes or misconceptions about those groups.
- Using primary sources, your learners will enhance their skills of critical reading, source evaluation, and evidence-based reasoning, all of which are essential for academic research and understanding the complex nature of social, scientific, and historical events. This applies equally to the arts, whether performance arts (such as music) or visual arts (such as paintings, architecture, furniture design, and so on).
- Letters and autobiographies such as *I Know Why the Caged Bird Sings* by Maya Angelou, or *Long Walk to Freedom* by Nelson Mandela, and contemporary diaries like Malala Yousafzai's BBC entries, *Diary of a Young Girl*, are primary sources that serve to humanize historical figures or events. They allow learners to make personal connections and empathize with people from different backgrounds and times.
- Learners can use primary sources for research as well as exemplars for projects. They can create their own newspapers, write diary entries, or reenact speeches. Leaning on primary source documents and artifacts, learners immerse themselves in diverse perspectives.
- Check out local primary sources (like town records or oral histories) to help learners explore the diverse histories within their own communities. Some cultures have a long tradition of oral history, so the elders serve as a primary source for information that may not be found in any other media. Local sources provide a connection to the community, making the past more immediate and relevant to your learners.
- Use primary sources to validate the histories of communities marginalized in your textbooks. These sources help to tell a complete and unbiased narrative and underscore the importance of marginalized peoples' contributions and experiences.

To successfully integrate primary sources from diverse perspectives in teaching, it's essential to continuously seek out repositories, libraries, or online databases that focus on diverse groups and experiences. It's also crucial to guide your learners in analyzing these sources with a critical eye, understanding the context, and recognizing biases or limitations inherent in any document. Remember, integrating media literacy into your instruction will help in this area.

In many places, discussions about controversial or sensitive topics are under attack. *The Diary of a Young Girl* is one of the thousands of books banned in several communities across the U.S. Know your community and be cautious. While some of you are ready to take on the book banners, others of you are not there yet. Find the approach to using primary source documents that will work for you in your context. By using primary sources, you can teach your learners how to be grounded in primary source evidence, allowing them to engage in informed debates and discussions, a valuable like skill!

Contemporary Commentary

Contemporary commentary refers to analyses, opinions, or reflections on current events, cultural shifts, societal issues, or trends that are produced during the same time period as the events or issues. This form of commentary provides insight into the prevailing views, beliefs, and attitudes of people living through those events. Examples of contemporary commentary include:

- Newspaper and magazine op-eds
- Blog posts
- Social media posts or trends
- Talk show discussions
- Podcast episodes
- Documentary films made about recent events
- Panel discussions or webinars
- Academic papers or conference presentations on current events
- Art or music reflecting current societal issues

As a blogger and podcaster, I am a huge fan of contemporary commentary. In addition to primary sources, consider contemporary commentary to supplement and enhance instructional materials. Many forms of contemporary commentary are not only widely available, but free.

Before introducing contemporary commentary, assess and develop your learners' media literacy using resources mentioned earlier. Media illiteracy can severely impact the results of teaching with contemporary commentary. Learners may continue to believe, for example, that social media content is truthful and reliable. Provide instruction so they have the tools to not just comprehend but to analyze and evaluate what they consume. In addition to implementing the strategies introduced in this chapter, check out the lessons in Appendix H.

With media-literate learners, you can use contemporary commentary as supplemental content to support teaching from diverse perspectives and support impartiality and representation. Commentary must be vetted—not all commentary is developmentally appropriate for all learners. So read, view, review, and listen carefully, before incorporating it into your instructional materials. While one episode from a podcast or post on a blog may be appropriate for your middle school learners, the next from the same source may not.

Contemporary commentary often varies widely based on the background, beliefs, and experiences of the commentator. Strive for balance. If you are looking to counter a skewed perspective in your text, find an opposing viewpoint or two. Present a range of commentaries to illustrate the breadth of perspectives on a given issue. Learners can develop skills in critically evaluating sources, identifying biases, and discerning the strength of arguments by analyzing contemporary commentaries.

With guidance and parameters, in a psychologically safe classroom, you can spark lively discussions, allowing learners to voice their opinions, challenge viewpoints, and defend their arguments. They can apply theoretical knowledge to real-world situations, using higher order thinking skills and making their learning more practical.

Use contemporary commentary to highlight underrepresented voices. When you select commentaries from marginalized groups, especially those reflective of your diverse learners, you acknowledge perspectives frequently overlooked in mainstream and secondary sources.

Engaging with personal narratives or reflections from individuals directly affected by an event can foster empathy and a deeper understanding of the human impact of societal issues. The best exemplar of this is the multicultural response to the public lynching of George Floyd. Black Lives Matter protests were multicultural events, with White allies showing up in significant numbers. When empathy is fostered, it overcomes stereotypes and supports unity based on humanity.

Finally, encourage learners to use contemporary commentaries as exemplars to produce their own. Go beyond the text by fostering a sense of contribution to ongoing societal debates. National Public Radio's Student Podcast Challenge for learners in grades 5 through 12 in 2019 garnered almost 6,000 entries. Check out dozens of winners at npr.org/series/662609200/npr-student-podcast-challenge for ideas that your learners can leverage for creating their own.

Remember, to successfully incorporate contemporary commentary into teaching, it's essential to curate a balanced set of sources representing various viewpoints. While contemporary commentaries offer valuable insights, they must always be used in conjunction with primary and secondary sources to develop a comprehensive understanding of a topic. Always guide your learners to approach contemporary commentary critically and teach them to consider the background and potential biases of the commentator.

Social Commentary

Social commentary is an element of a narrative. These narratives may use a variety of forms of expression, including poetic verse, to critique and offer insights into a society's cultures—their values, norms. It may address issues of society or social elements. Generally, social commentary does more than critique, as it most often advocates for change.

Social commentary provides avenues for engaging learners in contemporary events that connect to social studies, science, and literature content. Linking literary, historical, or theoretical lessons with contemporary events can make the content more relevant and engaging for learners. It also helps learners understand the societal and cultural context in which events occur, creating deeper comprehension that may be leveraged for analysis and evaluation.

USING SOCIAL COMMENTARY WITH LITERATURE

Take a look at the literature selections you're using. Social commentary is particularly relevant when studying works featuring marginalized people and communities of color. So, look for works that feature the story of a person of color or a member of a marginalized group as the protagonist.

Here are two examples of literature perfect for social commentary that can serve as a mirror, window, or door to middle school learners:

- *The House on Mango Street* by Sandra Cisneros (2004) is a series of vignettes illustrating the lived experience of Esperanza—a Latina growing up in a Latine neighborhood in Chicago. Learners can explore how her experiences reflect the current social issues faced by Latine communities. You might include a grand conversation to discuss the impact of low income or gender expectations on personal identity and community relationships. If you have Latine learners, give them space to share a perspective from their own broader community. This may open dialogue about the lived experiences of other immigrant children and the challenges they face in their daily lives.

- Jacqueline Woodson's autobiographical novel *Brown Girl Dreaming* (2014) tells the author's lived experience as young Black girl growing up in South Carolina and New York during the 1960s and 1970s. The book touches on the struggle for racial identity and racial equality during the Civil Rights Movement—a struggle that continues to this day. The book is written in verse, so you might include a lesson analyzing poetry by Amanda Gorman, National Youth Poet Laureate, focusing on works that tell the stories of other Black people in America. Grand conversations can be geared toward understanding the historical context of the Civil Rights Movement and its relationship to the Black Lives Matter movement and the contemporary struggle for racial justice.

USING SOCIAL COMMENTARY IN SCIENCE COURSES

You might be wondering about infusing social commentary into science instruction. It is a valuable way to engage learners in science while enhancing critical thinking, as well as leveraging their media literacy to increase awareness of how science connects to societal issues. Below are two middle school and two high school lesson ideas. The lesson ideas are followed by classroom activities and discussion points that can be adapted for these lessons and others. Think of them as models, an impetus for you to infuse social commentary throughout the year.

One of the core ideas of the Next Generation Science Standards (NGSS) standards for technology and society is that "technological advances can have a profound effect on society and the environment" (NGSS Appendix J, page 2). The standards are designed to increase learners understanding of the relationship between technology and society, and how technology can be used to solve problems—perfect for social commentary! Learners can investigate how technological advancements, like smartphones and internet access, have varied impact on different groups. They should consider factors such as the digital divide and access to equitable education.

In the life science and earth and space science dimension of the middle school NGSS lie developing understanding of the impact of human activities on the environment (NGSS Appendix J). Learners can study air and water pollution issues and their impact on diverse communities, focusing on the disparate impacts on communities of color and low wealth.

Similarly, in the high school earth and space science dimension, learners can focus on how climate change disproportionately affects marginalized communities worldwide. Learners should examine factors like geographic vulnerabilities, economic disparities—particularly in developing nations—and policy discussions.

And while not explicitly called out in the NGSS, a lesson on health disparities and biomedical ethics can be integrated through several of the key dimensions, including crosscutting concepts, science and engineering practices, and disciplinary core ideas. Learners can explore how social factors, such as race, socio-economic status, and access to healthcare, impact medical treatment and health outcomes of marginalized communities. Learners may delve into ethical questions in medical research and healthcare policies in the community, nation- or worldwide.

For topics such as these, and of course those of your own devise, you can create lessons that aim to bridge scientific concepts with real-world societal issues.

Research and Presentation

Learners conduct an in-depth evaluation of a specific issue related to the lesson. It could be a case study or recent research on the topic as it impacts a one or more communities. Learners examine how these issues reflect broader societal inequalities, particularly for marginalized peoples. Extend the learning to examine how governmental policies could address the inequalities.

Role-Playing Panel Discussion

Learners take on the roles of community members, scientists, businesses, and policymakers, to debate an issue related to the topic. For example, how each of those parties' view climate change and how it impacts their community or their work. The complexities of scientific and ethical decision-making from each perspective should be explored.

Data Analysis and Interpretation

Learners analyze real-world data related to the lesson topic and interpret what it suggests about social and scientific issues. In reflective dialogue circles, learners discuss the importance of data in understanding and addressing societal issues and the potential biases in data interpretation.

Community Engagement Project

Learners develop a project that involves community engagement, such as a local environmental survey or a digital literacy workshop. As a reflection piece, learners reflect on the importance of scientific literacy and engagement in addressing community issues.

Ethical Dilemmas and Decision-Making

Learners explore ethical dilemmas related to the lesson topic, for example, funding for health research or toxic waste disposal. In reflective dialogue circles, learners discuss the ethical dimensions of scientific decision-making and the balance between scientific advancement and societal good.

USING SOCIAL COMMENTARY IN SOCIAL STUDIES COURSES

Perhaps I'm biased, having been a political science major as an undergrad and assigned to teach American government and U.S. History right out of teachers' college. I can name that. But I also know from those early experiences that integrating social commentary into the social sciences is crucial for fostering critical thinking and awareness of social issues. And then, there's this from the National Curriculum Standards for Social Studies:

> The primary purpose of social studies is to help young people make informed and reasoned decisions for the public good as citizens of a culturally diverse, democratic society in an interdependent world (National Council for the Social Studies [NCSS], 2010, p. 3).

In this section, I present two middle school and two high school lesson ideas followed by five classroom activities and discussion points you can adapt for others of your own creation. Each of these crosses multiple themes of the National Curriculum Standards of Social Studies (NCSS, 2010). Since the subject area of social science is broad, and the focus of each grade level varies from state to state, use these as starters or prompts for extending your own focus area at your grade level. And just as with the science lessons, these examples do not suggest a one-and-done approach, but rather serve as inspiration for you to infuse social commentary throughout the year.

As you read, you'll notice that many of the lessons and activities for literature, science, and social studies have cross-disciplinary possibilities. If your instructional context allows for cross-departmental collaboration, discuss with your colleagues options for linking their content to yours. Our learners' lived experiences do not happen in subject-matter silos.

At the middle school level, a lesson on understanding immigration and cultural diversity would call on learners to study the history and contributions of various immigrant groups in the United States—both voluntary, such as those seeking a better life, and involuntary, those captured and brought here enslaved. Learners should discuss the challenges faced and cultural richness brought to the country. If your middle grades standards do not address U.S. history, modify this to address the geographical area under study.

A second middle school lesson would focus on geography, having learners understand the concept of linguistic diversity and its presence both in the U.S. and globally. Learners would work to recognize the challenges and opportunities that linguistic diversity presents in contemporary society and across time and place.

At the high school level, learners would explore systemic racism in U.S. history with a focus on historical events and policies that have contributed to systemic racism, such as redlining, segregation, and the criminal justice system.

A second high school lesson would examine globalization and its impact on Indigenous communities worldwide. Learners would focus on cultural, economic, and environmental impacts.

These lesson activities and discussion points will engage your learners in critical analysis of social issues, enhance their comprehension of societal dynamics, and continue to develop their skills in research, debate, and empathy. Lessons you create, following these examples, should serve the same purposes. When designing lessons, align them with your social studies standards and frameworks.

Documentary Viewing and Reflection

Learners watch a documentary related to the lesson topic and write a reflective piece or engage in a reflective dialogue circle. Discuss the main takeaways, how the documentary deepens their understanding of the issue, and its relevance to current societal challenges.

Case Study Analysis

Analyze a specific case study that exemplifies the lesson's theme, for example, human trafficking, the Southern border crisis in the United States, multilingual education, a landmark civil rights case, Indigenous sovereignty. Examine the historical and contemporary implications of the case study and its impact on current policy in contemporary society.

Role-Playing Panel Discussion

Learners can take on the roles of various interested parties to debate an issue related to the topic and simulate a meeting, negotiation, legislative hearing, or mock court. Learners should reflect on the challenges of addressing complex social issues from diverse perspectives and the importance of empathy and understanding.

Research and Presentation

Learners conduct an in-depth evaluation of a specific issue. It could be a landmark court case, a case study, or authentic research on the topic as it impacts one or more of their local marginalized communities. Learners should present their findings and discuss how these findings contribute to understanding broader societal issues. Extend the learning to examine how governmental policies could address any inequalities they've found.

Debate on Contemporary Issues

Organize a debate on a contemporary issue related to the lesson. Encourage learners to use evidence and critical thinking in their arguments. Learners should reflect on the complexities of the issue, diverse viewpoints, and the role of informed debate in democratic societies.

These activities not only deepen your learners' understanding of the course content, but also promote empathy, critical thinking, and awareness about the experiences of marginalized peoples. With media literacy skills, learners have the ability to go beyond the standards. They evaluate content through a lens of equity, identifying where bias lies, and creating their own critiques—or social commentary—through a variety of mediums.

Conclusion

In this chapter, you moved from evaluation, to solutions, to action. You began to address and offset the bias you found in your curriculum materials. You explored strategies for immediate implementation, including ways to supplement and enhance the materials.

In Chapter 8, we shift to academic assessment, the next step of the CARTI Framework. You'll examine your classroom assessments through all four equity indicators. You'll also look at how bias and racism play a role in assessment, both currently and historically.

This chapter has two reflect and act exercises focused on planning instruction based on what you've learned. You may want to open up your lesson planner along with your journal for these exercises. If you are completing this work as part of a book study or professional learning, they present a wonderful opportunity for departmental or cross-departmental collaborative planning.

Reflect and Act

Reflect on the three strategies for developing media literacy in your classroom (pages 122–125). Which of these will you implement first in your classroom? Do you anticipate any challenges? If so, how can you overcome them?

Reflect on your current use of primary sources, contemporary commentary, and social commentary in your instruction. Which of the tools from this chapter will you use to expand your practice? What forms of commentary are you most comfortable having your learners engage with? If you're uncomfortable with some forms, reflect on why and what you can do to overcome your discomfort.

●●● MY MINDSET METER

Complete the mindset meter as a self-assessment. Make connections building on what you've learned, your instructional setting, and your lived experience. Focus. Reflect. Analyze. Strategize.

Knowledge: This is the meaning of media literacy as I understand it from this chapter:

____

____

____

____

Comprehension: This is how I must address bias that presents in my instructional materials:

____

____

____

____

Application: This is how I will use reflective discussion circles to have my learners engage in social commentary:

____

____

____

____

Analysis: This is where my learners are lacking or demonstrating mastery in media literacy:

____

____

____

____

Synthesis: This is how I will integrate social commentary in the next unit I plan:

____

____

____

____

Evaluation: I used to think ______ but now I think ______.

____

____

____

____

THE FOUNDATIONS OF EQUITABLE ASSESSMENT

CHAPTER 8

The CARTI Framework, Step 4: Academic Assessment

In the previous chapters, we have focused on the first three steps of the CARTI Framework—cultural awareness, instructional methods, and curriculum content. In this chapter, we shift to the fourth step, academic assessment. We begin by improving our understanding of the benefits of assessment, as well as examining the dangers of improperly vetting, validating, and valuing assessment (see Figure 8.1).

What Is the Purpose of Assessment?

Whether your assignment is kindergarten or high school, foundational reading or AP calculus, assessment is an essential tool for establishing goals, driving instruction, and examining the effectiveness of our practices. Whenever we are assessing learners, we need to ask ourselves these questions:

Why are we collecting evidence of student learning?

What are we measuring?

Are we using the best tool for the job?

Figure 8.1

The CARTI Framework

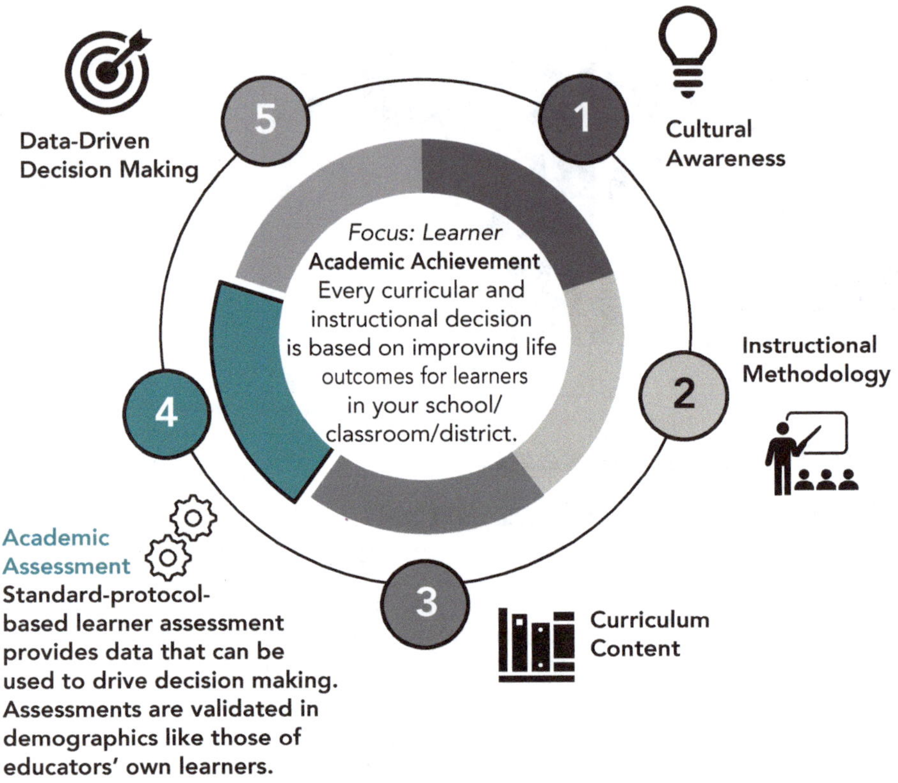

Focus: Learner **Academic Achievement** Every curricular and instructional decision is based on improving life outcomes for learners in your school/classroom/district.

1 Cultural Awareness

2 Instructional Methodology

3 Curriculum Content

4 Academic Assessment

Standard-protocol-based learner assessment provides data that can be used to drive decision making. Assessments are validated in demographics like those of educators' own learners.

5 Data-Driven Decision Making

As you examine the following six purposes for assessment, think of them as a thread that weaves through and guides your actions in the steps of the CARTI Framework. Assessment results indicate whether to change curriculum or adjust instructional methods. They inform whether to adjust group or class size, composition, or instructional time. Assessments act as a compass for educational direction and strategy.

> **The first purpose of assessment is identifying learner strengths and weaknesses, guiding differentiated instruction.** While universal tailored instruction is not yet a reality, assessments—ranging from written to hands-on tasks—can provide a comprehensive academic profile of a learner. Effective assessments should reveal not just

struggles, indicating a need for instructional improvement, but also excellence, suggesting a need for greater challenges. Recognizing natural abilities, like a learner's talent in poetry, can foster confidence and guide relevant, challenging tasks. Conversely, understanding weaknesses, particularly in foundational skills like reading and math, is crucial for targeted support. This foundational function of assessment underpins equity, ensuring meritocracy and the just treatment of marginalized learners.

What This Looks Like Across the Grades: Nip It in the Bud or Get at the Root

Assessments that guide instruction ensure meritocracy and the just treatment of learners. Ideally, learners never need intervention because they receive instruction that meets their needs from the very beginning. Building foundational skills through the lens of the four equity indicators should eliminate the need for intervention later on (see Chapter 1). However, every K–12 school system has learners who may have missed some foundational skills mastery. The more years they complete with unfinished learning, the further and further they fall behind.

That doesn't mean it's too late to fix. Small bits of unfinished learning, caught early, can be addressed before they grow larger. If you have high-quality curriculum, the needed tools may be found in the teacher's guide.

For those learners who've gone multiple years with unfinished learning, the challenge is greater. Let's look at two examples: math and reading comprehension.

Let's say you have a learner who struggles with simplifying fractions, or in algebra, with polynomials. Remediation after remediation just doesn't seem to be helping. Meanwhile, math instruction moves forward, and the learner continues to struggle. Let's say the root cause of the struggle is not fractions. It's long division. Without addressing the root, the learner will continue to fall behind as long division is a fundamental skill essential for many higher math topics.

Or perhaps you have a learner who struggles with reading comprehension when reading independently. Even though you model and apply strategies during shared reading, and strategy posters are on display, the learner still struggles on their own. And let's assume that the literature is culturally relevant, so there's no cultural disconnect. The root cause of the struggle is not comprehension, it could be reading fluency, which may have roots all the way down at the phonics and blending level. Once again, without intervening at the root, the learner will continue to struggle with grade-level reading. This is a struggle that will impact the learner across multiple subjects. This is addressed in more detail in my book, *Effecting Change for Culturally and Linguistically Diverse Learners, Second Edition* (Berry, 2023).

A second purpose of assessment is to provide feedback. Feedback, as a fundamental function of assessment, is essential for informing learners, parents, caregivers, and educators about academic progress and areas for growth. It facilitates understanding, supports metacognition, and encourages self-improvement. Effective feedback highlights both strengths and weaknesses, fostering confidence and a growth mindset. For parents and caregivers, it provides insight into their child's progress and how to support their learning at home. Between educators, feedback aids in making informed instructional decisions, ideally maintaining a positive balance even in challenging situations. It should be specific, timely, and culturally sensitive. And it should evolve with the learners' progression to continually guide and improve the learning experience.

Tracking learner progress, the third function of assessment, is pivotal in shaping curriculum and instruction. By using formative assessments, such as screeners and diagnostics, educators establish baselines and identify specific unmet needs in the learners' skills or knowledge. This process, guided by equity, informs necessary adjustments in instruction to ensure all learners succeed. Continuous monitoring, even informally, must account for cultural and environmental factors, avoiding bias. Outcomes-based measures further track progress, with frequent assessment allowing timely instructional pivots. This cyclical tracking process aids in creating a culturally responsive and inclusive learning environment.

Six Purposes of Assessment

1. Identify learner strengths and weaknesses, guiding differentiation.
2. Provide feedback.
3. Track learner progress to shape curriculum and instruction.
4. Inform administrative and policy decisions.
5. Form the cornerstone of the grading process.
6. Prepare learners for future assessment.

The data we glean from assessment is a key measure of educational performance, informing administrative decisions and policy at various levels. It provides insights into school effectiveness, resource allocation, and instructor efficacy. When used ethically and in context, assessment data upholds educational standards and promotes equity. However, it must be interpreted responsibly, considering cultural biases and other factors that affect learner performance, to prevent unfair impacts on the educational community.

Furthermore, assessments form the cornerstone of the grading process. They provide a quantitative measure of a learner's understanding and performance against what should be a valid benchmark. We'll dive deeply into the function and purpose of grades in Chapters 10 and 11.

Finally, assessments should serve to prepare our learners for future assessments. Wait. What? Yes! Think about it. Assessment doesn't end when we leave formal instruction. Regular assessment acclimatizes the learner to the process of being tested. It prepares them for the global economy and world of work they will enter when they graduate or exit high school. We live in a world were evaluation, feedback, and continuous improvement are integral parts of personal and professional growth.

Examining Classroom Assessment Practices Through the Lens of Equity

Now, consider all six of the purposes of assessment discussed above and let's look at them through the lens of our four equity indicators. I've touched on this in several of the individual functions, so, let's take a big picture look here.

MERITOCRACY, ASSESSMENT, AND DIVERSE LEARNERS

Remember that meritocracy is the idea that power is held by people based on their ability. That is the equitable use of meritocracy. When we talk about meritocracy and assessment, we ask the same questions:

- *Who has the power?*
- *Are we using power for the good of the marginalized in our school community?*

There's a simple answer to the question *Who has the power?* In your classrooms, when it comes to assessment, typically it's you. You have the power. The question is,

- *If our system of assessment is equitable, do those holding the power have the ability, the desire and the commitment to use that power for good?*

Are we, as classroom educators, using our power of testing for the good of learners who are culturally and linguistically diverse, without bias against those who are not?

Of course, we are going to focus this discussion on assessment within your span of control, what you can change or influence. So, think about your assessment practices. Consider what you assess, when you assess, and how you assess. Ask yourself if the way that you assess or test in your classroom may adversely affect learners from diverse backgrounds. Take a moment to journal your response.

STANDARDS, ASSESSMENT, AND DIVERSE LEARNERS

Remember that standards are the metrics against which we measure academic performance and upon which we craft and deliver instruction. And standards are the metrics against which learners demonstrate their mastery. The two essential questions here are:

- *Who has mastery?*
- *Are we taking action to result in learners demonstrating ongoing mastery year over year?*

When assessment practices are equitable, the standards are not the high bar, but the minimum proficiency. What we assess and how we do so should accurately and equitably demonstrate learners' levels of proficiency. When we think about accuracy and equity, think about what will best show what a learner knows. In chemistry, should we use a five-paragraph essay or a lab demonstration solving a given problem? Is it equitable to use the same mode of demonstration for two different learners—one who is an emergent level multilingual learner and a second child who is proficient in School English? What actions will you take after receiving results to support learners increasing proficiency from the current assessment to the next? From the current school year to the next?

IMPARTIALITY, BIAS, AND RACISM AND ASSESSMENT

You'll recall that impartiality is another term for fairness or being without bias. Here we ask these two essential questions:

- *Who has representation?*
- *Are we accurately and appropriately considering the cultures of all those affected, or are we acting from a middle class, White-European, Western cultural bias?*

When we look for impartiality in our assessments, we want to ensure that we are not harming learners by administering tests that are culturally biased; that we are not seeking responses that must be framed in a White-European, Western mindset. The terminology, concepts, and frameworks used must be those which were taught to mastery during instruction.

Cultural bias in assessment has been a topic of educational research and debate for decades. In my work reviewing prepublication curriculum, I have identified cultural bias several times. Whether evidenced in cultural references or language and linguistics, items that put Black, Latine, Indigenous, and other learners of color or linguistic diversity at a disadvantage, not for their ability to learn, but to see and interpret the world through a White-European lens is partial, biased, and potentially racist.

We should remain mindful of the second indicator of equity—impartiality—as we develop our own assessments and review commercial ones. At all times, we must ask those two essential questions. We must remember to consider our own cultural viewpoint and the cultures of the learners in our classrooms.

ASSET ALLOCATION, ASSESSMENT, AND DIVERSE LEARNERS

Recall asset allocation is about creating constructive inequality to remedy the historical oppression of marginalized learners (see Chapter 1). We ask these two essential questions:

- *Is there positive structural inequality?*
- *Are we choosing and allocating assets to create opportunity and excellence for all involved?*

When it comes to assessment, these questions cannot be fully addressed by considering which test you choose or how you choose to administer assessment. The idea of positive structural inequality may be addressed by offering multiple modes of the same assessment. For example, if your emergent multilingual learners perform better in their primary language, and a primary language assessment is available, great! Give it to them. But what about those who do not have that option?

Consider that some learners may come from collectivist cultures, where working together to solve problems is the norm. If, in your development of cultural competence, you learn this is a norm for some of your learners, can you structure the assessment as a collective assignment? Of course, this raises the question of grading, which we'll consider in Chapter 10.

Time is another variable. Will additional time for completing an assessment support equity for your historically marginalized learners?

As we evaluate our assessment systems for equity, we find that asset allocation to eliminate inequity is a bit of a conundrum. Yes, the idea of positive structural inequality means giving more to those who have less. But we must work within the policies and legal constraints of our school systems.

Addressing Bias and Racism in Assessments and Assessment Practices

At this point, I will ask you: *Why should we address bias and racism in assessment and assessment practices?* What are your concerns? What do you see? Take a minute and jot down your thoughts based on your experiences as an instructor and as a learner. In your journal create a two-column chart with "as an instructor" in one column and "as a learner" in the other. What have your experiences been?

Now I'll give you my top ten reasons we must address bias and racism—structural and institutional—in assessment. We'll dig deeper into what you can do to address biased and racist assessment practices in the next chapter. For now, let's see where we connect.

My number one reason: promoting educational equity. Ensuring that all learners receive the resources and educational opportunities they need to succeed is the reason I write, educate, speak, blog, and podcast, why I produce contemporary and social commentary content. Biased assessments perpetuate inequalities. They hinder marginalized and culturally and linguistically diverse learners from accessing the same quality of education and opportunities as their non-marginalized peers.

Second, because representation matters. Because of impartiality, our second equity indicator. How many of you wrote something in your "as a learner" column that had to do with not seeing yourself and your lived experiences in assessments? Assessments that exclude or marginalize CLDL groups' experiences or knowledge send a message that their perspectives are less valuable or worse: irrelevant. Addressing biases ensures that diverse voices and experiences are acknowledged and valued.

Coming in at number three is cultural responsiveness in curriculum and instruction. Biased assessments can guide educators to make incorrect instructional decisions. An educator may perceive a learner's low performance on a biased test as a deficiency in understanding, rather than recognizing the bias in the assessment. This reinforces stereotypes and reduces the implementation of culturally responsive instructional practices.

My fourth reason lies in our ethical and legal responsibilities. Sure, many countries have laws and policies in place to ensure that education is accessible and equitable for all, regardless of race, ethnicity, or language. And at a time when laws are being put in place in the United States to deny access to information that is inclusive of all peoples and cultures, there is certainly much work to be done. But in classrooms, where you can make an ethical decision, using biased assessments violates the principles of equity and inclusivity. Remember, our CARTI framework lies in the overlap of learning science and what is ethically right for learners. For those who wish to be change agents, work to ensure that laws support what is ethically right.

Naturally, supporting linguistic diversity has a spot in my top ten. Language is closely tied to culture, and our multilingual learners from culturally diverse backgrounds speak many languages other than School English. Addressing assessment biases ensures that multilingual learners who are still acquiring School English proficiency are assessed on their knowledge and skills, not their language abilities.

Reason number six: we must eliminate, or at the very least mitigate, both **social identity threat** and **stereotype threat**. Research informs us about this danger (Steele et al., 2002). We know that when learners from marginalized groups are exposed to negative stereotypes about their abilities, their performance can decline. So, we must actively confront and remove bias. This helps reduce the effects of social identity and stereotype threat. It allows our learners to perform to their actual capabilities, rather than to lowered expectations informed by implicit and explicit bias or racism.

Ranking these last four items is difficult for me. There's little difference in just how important each is. For position number seven, though, I'll say it is the broader societal implications of assessments. Assessments shape our learners' trajectories in terms of college admissions, scholarship opportunities, and even future careers. Biased assessments can systematically deny opportunities to marginalized learners, reinforcing societal inequalities.

Reason number eight, we must prepare our learners for a diverse world. Not just our culturally and linguistically diverse learners, all our learners. The global landscape is diverse. Unless they live off the grid in a remote region of the world, our learners are going to interact with people from different backgrounds and cultures in their educational, personal, and professional lives for the remainder of their lives. Assessments that promote equity and cultural responsiveness help prepare our learners for this diverse world. This equips learners with a more comprehensive understanding and appreciation of global perspectives. And it prepares them for the opportunity to work in a global organization where a White-European lived experience may not be the norm.

I've put strengthening community relations and trust at number nine, only because of the recency effect. As educators, we don't simply serve children. We serve communities. And those communities, especially more marginalized communities, are more likely to trust and support schools when they believe that the assessments given are fair, unbiased, and equitable. Building positive school-community relationships requires this trust. Fostering parental and caregiver involvement and ensuring successful collaborations between educators and families requires this trust. If you address bias and racism in assessments, you enhance this trust.

Finally, there's the educators' community. So, my reason number 10: enhancing the professional integrity of you, the educator. Remember, you are charged with the responsibility of nurturing and guiding all learners. Using or relying on biased assessments undermines your professional integrity and commitment to serving all learners equitably. It violates the Hippocratic Oath of Educators you (hopefully) took in Chapter 1. When you address bias in assessment, you uphold the core values of our profession. You ensure that every learner is seen, valued, affirmed, and supported in their academic journey.

That's my top ten. And my big why: Because the impact of bias and racism in assessments is not just an educational concern but a societal imperative. It intertwines with the broader goals of promoting equity, justice, and inclusivity in all facets of society. By ensuring that assessments are free from biases, educators, policymakers, schools, and districts take a significant step toward creating an equitable and just educational landscape.

How many of my top ten connect to your lived experience? Did reading my list spark any additional memories? If so, what will you do with that information?

social identity threat—the fear individuals feel when they believe they'll be judged or stereotyped based on their group membership, potentially leading to underperformance or stress.

stereotype threat—the anxiety or distress a person feels when at risk of confirming negative stereotypes about their social group, affecting performance and behavior.

Stereotype Threat, Self-Worth, and Self-Esteem

As I reflect on my experiences as an educator and as a learner, particularly in my master's and doctoral programs, I cannot recall a single course or even assignment that addressed the issue of stereotype threat. And stereotype threat can have such a profound effect on learner performance!

I think about the thousands of children who passed through my classroom and wonder if I perpetuated it? Especially during my first few years in the classroom. What might the impact have been? I know now.

I know that stereotype threat can consume significant cognitive resources (Davis & Martin, 2018). It might have left my learners with fewer resources available for task performance. It would have been mental overhead cost that impeded their ability to process information, solve problems, and recall relevant knowledge.

I know that stereotype threat decreases motivation and effort (Totonchi et al., 2021). If my learners were confronted with a negative stereotype about their abilities, they may have become demotivated or disengaged. My learners' rationales might have been, "If Ms. B's expectations are that I will underperform, then exerting effort will be an exercise in futility."

I know that stereotype threat causes both emotional and physiological distress (Baker et al., 2020). I think about the learners that always had a stomachache on the day of an important assessment. Stereotype threat triggers stress responses. It increases heart rate and cortisol levels. And this physiological stress would disrupt their focus and concentration, further diminishing performance on assessment or learning tasks.

And I know that I suffered from stereotype threat as a learner, both as a child and as an adult. I was constantly told by my colleagues that my expectations for my learners was ridiculously high, that I should take a "chill pill," that "these kids..." well, you know. I can breathe a sigh of relief and relish in a clear conscious. Maybe it was intrinsic, based in my own lived experiences. But somehow, I knew the damage an improper or biased assessment could have on my learners' self-perceptions, self-worth, and self-esteem.

Bias, implicit or explicit, conscious or unconscious, manifests in attitudes and behaviors in individuals, in structures, and in institutions. Perhaps the implicit bias comes from the way data about learners is disaggregated and the persistent underperformance of Black, Indigenous, and Latine learners remains part of the educational dialogue. Consider how those messages creep into your psyche as an educator. Consider how learners, their parents, and caregivers consume the media proclaiming achievement outcomes.

Stereotype threat is situational. It is a predicament a person, a learner, may find themselves in. Having an awareness of being judged or treated a certain way because of their identity causes learners to become anxious, potentially negatively affecting their performance and confirming the negative sterotype.

If learners don't perform well due to being under threat, their poor performance confirms and reinforces the negative stereotypes held by biased people in power. This perpetuates a cycle of bias and stereotype threat. In addition, it impacts the individuals' physical health. Does your heart race when you have to take a high-stakes test? Or when you are put into a position where you know everyone is judging you and your performance has life-long implications? Addressing bias in general—and in assessment in particular—is essential to reducing instances of stereotype threat and fostering equity.

From my own experience I know that exposure to biased assessments can lead learners from marginalized groups to internalize the negative stereotypes about their abilities. And whether these manifest as self-doubt or a diminished sense of intellectual capability, they may remain with us for many years.

I think about my own relationship with certain content that was part of my graduate studies. Fortunately, by then I had developed enough awareness about how things worked to work around it. To recognize the bias for what it was and answer from the lens the instructors were looking for. Our preadolescent and adolescent learners may not have these lenses.

When learners must repeatedly confront bias in assessments, it may lead them to question their competencies. It may erode or diminish their confidence in their academic abilities and potential to succeed in future endeavors. Just imagine if the prompts or answers given don't connect to anything in your lived experiences. You might question not only your competency, but your value as a person, your life as something worthy.

And as one's self-worth is questioned, they may begin to avoid challenges or advanced opportunities, believing they are either incapable or that the achievement is beyond their reach. Instead of recognizing that a biased assessment doesn't fairly measure their capabilities, learners might attribute their underperformance to an inherent lack of ability, fueling feelings of inadequacy.

Think about the alienation and disengagement some learners may feel when confronted with a culturally biased assessment. Have you ever had a student who simply sat, or threw up their hands, or uttered an expletive as they pushed away an assessment? What you may have perceived as anger or disrespect is merely a coping mechanism for the hopelessness and alienation they feel. Habitually and persistently devalued, sometimes the outburst is all they can muster.

Conclusion

In this chapter, you shifted to the next step of the CARTI Framework: academic assessment, viewing classroom assessments through the four equity indicators. You examined the role bias and racism play in assessment, and explored sterotype threat and its impact on learners' self-esteem and self-worth.

In Chapter 9, we'll turn our attention to how we align equitable assessment practices with the culturally relevant instructional practices we've discussed thus far. I'll break down what that looks like across the four broad grade spans. You'll get some examples of what it looks like to have culturally *in*competent conversations about assessment with your learners' parents and caregivers—and help correcting those incompetencies.

This chapter has one reflect and act exercise: a reflection, a bit of a self-assessment. As you perform that reflection, think in terms of what you might want on hand if you were to engage in reflective dialogue circle. If you are completing this work as part of a book study or professional learning, conduct that circle.

Reflect and Act

Look back at your notes regarding your experiences as an instructor and as a learner. If I now ask you why we should address bias and racism in assessment and assessment practices, what are your concerns? What do you see? Have your concerns changed over the course of the chapter?

●●● MY MINDSET METER

Complete the mindset meter as a self-assessment. Make connections building on what you've learned, your instructional setting, and your lived experience. Focus. Reflect. Analyze. Strategize.

Knowledge: The meaning of equitable assessment as I understand it from this chapter:

____

____

____

____

Comprehension: The purpose of assessment in the classroom as I understand it from this chapter:

____

____

____

____

Application: This is how I will use assessment in my classroom:

____

____

____

____

Analysis: I will examine my assessment practices through this lens:

____

____

____

____

Synthesis: This is how I will reduce stereotype threat for my learners:

____

____

____

____

Evaluation: I used to think ______ but now I think ______.

____

____

____

____

CHAPTER 9

ALIGNING EQUITABLE ASSESSMENT WITH CULTURALLY RELEVANT INSTRUCTIONAL PRACTICES

In this chapter, we explore principles and strategies for creating equitable assessments and implementing equitable assessment practices. Just as in Chapter 8, we maintain the premise that equity requires understanding, affirming, validating, and respecting every child that walks into our schools. Our work in this chapter continues step 4 of the CARTI Framework—academic assessment (see Figure 9.1).

Integrating equitable assessment practices with culturally relevant pedagogy is crucial for fostering the inclusive classroom environment you're working to create, nurture, and sustain. That alignment and integration requires making adjustments to your assessment practices. I call these adjustments "Can-Do Practices." As you reflect upon each of the eleven Can-Dos that follow, think about where each one aligns to one or more steps of the CARTI framework. Devise a plan to begin implementing them into your practice, keeping in mind what you've learned about steps 1 through 4 of the CARTI Framework.

Figure 9.1

The CARTI Framework

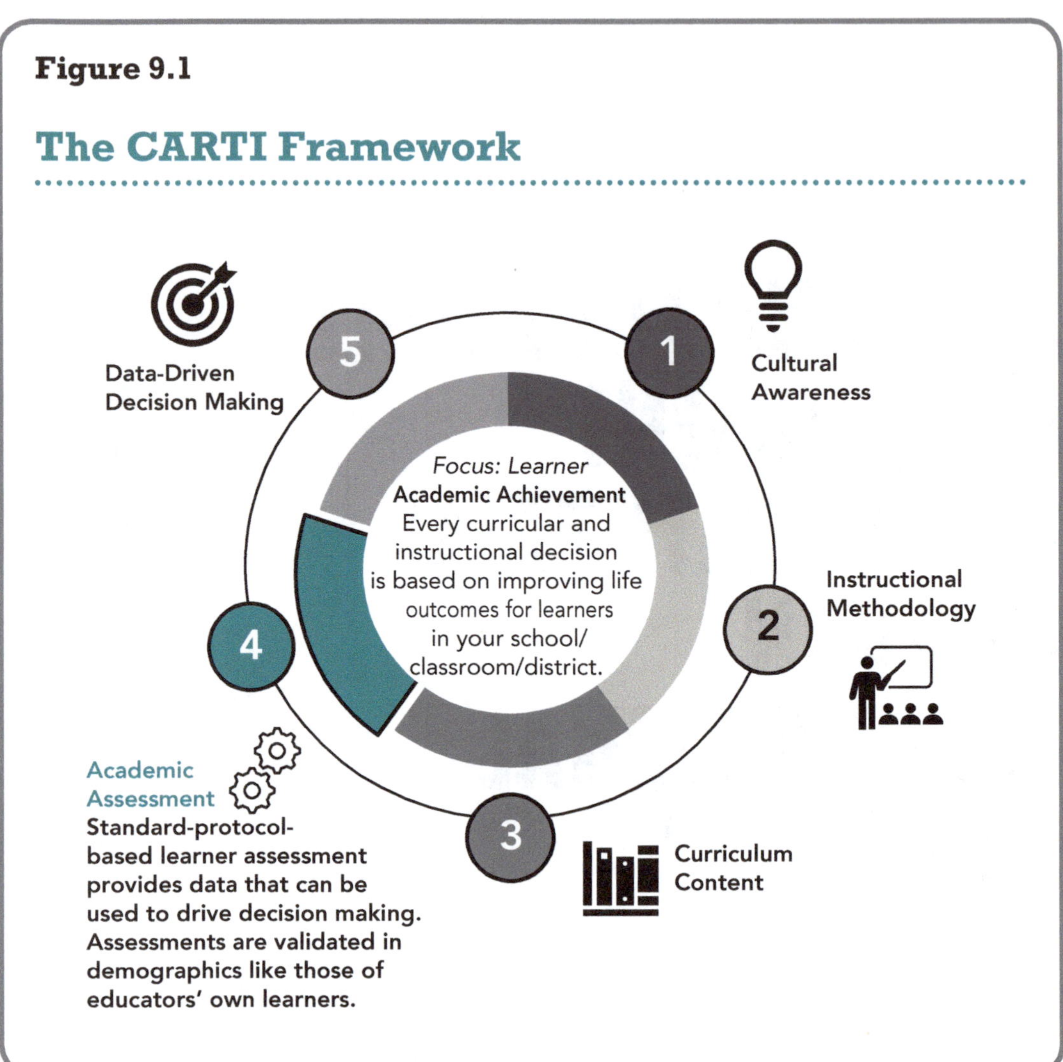

Eleven Things You "Can Do" for Equity Alignment

CAN-DO #1: SELF-REFLECT TO CHALLENGE BIASES.

Make it a point to regularly engage in ongoing self-reflection as well as professional development. We must all continue to work on identifying our own biases and understanding how these biases can be reflected in instructor-created and commercial assessments. When we acknowledge systemic inequities—at the classroom, district, or higher level—we are better positioned to challenge those inequities.

CAN-DO #2: REDUCE THE COGNITIVE LOAD ASSOCIATED WITH SPECIFIC TYPES OF ASSESSMENTS THAT MIGHT TRIGGER STEREOTYPE THREATS.

Look for a range of formative and summative assessments you can use to gauge learner understanding. Consider project-based assessments (Widiana et al., 2022), portfolios, reflective and interactive journals, and performance-based assessments alongside traditional paper-pencil or online exams. Provide multiple avenues for learners to demonstrate their knowledge and skills.

You may wonder about the validity of some of these tools, like project-based assessments and journals. After all, the CARTI Framework calls for assessments that have been validated in demographics like your own. And yes, these assessment items are more qualitative in nature. Keep in mind that the six different functions or purposes of assessment discussed in Chapter 8. Developing your equity lens helps hone your skills in choosing assessments that support the purpose you have identified.

CAN-DO #3: ASSESS THE CONTEXTUAL RELEVANCE OF AUTHENTIC ASSESSMENTS.

Authentic assessments require learners to apply their understanding in a context that is relevant to them (Tawil et al., 2023). Work to ensure that assessment scenarios are culturally appropriate (Oliveri & Lawless, 2018). Learners should readily connect to the prompts and scenarios and be able to bring their lived experiences into the assessment process.

CAN-DO #4: VALIDATE LEARNERS LIVED EXPERIENCES THROUGH LOCALIZED AUTHENTIC ASSESSMENTS.

In creating your own assessments, especially project-based and other authentic tools, incorporate local issues, histories, and values. This makes the assessment more relatable and less alienating (Oliveri & Lawless, 2018) for learners from marginalized communities.

CAN-DO #5: COMBAT DEMOTIVATION WHILE CREATING BUY-IN.

Co-create assessment criteria with learners at the middle and high school levels. Involve them in the creation of rubrics and assessment criteria. This democratizes the assessment process and can alleviate some of the anxieties associated with assessment, as learners have a clearer understanding of what is expected of them. Learners, like all of us, feel empowered and motivated when we have voice and agency.

CAN-DO #6: CULTIVATE METACOGNITIVE SKILLS TO REDUCE MENTAL OVERLOAD.

Encourage learners to reflect on their thought processes and strategies. This not only gives you another dimension to assess but also helps to mitigate the impact of stereotype threat by refocusing learners' attention on their problem-solving tactics rather than their perceived innate ability.

CAN-DO #7: REDUCE ANXIETY AND INCREASE ENGAGEMENT BY SCAFFOLDING ASSESSMENTS.

Scaffold assessments just as you scaffold instruction for struggling learners! Break down assessments into smaller, manageable tasks. Think about your environment, your learners, and their span of attention. Each task should be designed to gradually develop and measure the skills and knowledge that are necessary for learners to succeed in the overall assessment.

If you measure and ensure mastery daily, the "big" test becomes a mere formality. Your learners already know they know. Scaffolding makes assessments more accessible for all learners, including those from marginalized backgrounds (Santos et al., 2015).

CAN-DO #8: INCORPORATE PEER- AND SELF-ASSESSMENT

Engaging learners in the assessment process makes them active participants in their learning journey. Peer and self-assessments potentially bring out different perspectives (Tawil et al., 2023) and reduce the influence of instructor bias, especially if your lived experience does not mirror the learners', or you are in the early stages of developing your cultural competence with their cultures and communities. Peer- and self-assessment helps combat internalized stereotypes and allows learners to view their abilities through a variety of perspectives.

CAN-DO #9: CREATE A CONTINUOUS FEEDBACK LOOP, PROVIDING CONSTRUCTIVE FEEDBACK THAT MITIGATES FEELINGS OF FUTILITY.

As discussed in Chapter 8, you need a continuous feedback loop with each learner. Make sure that the feedback provided is timely, specific, actionable, and affirming. Frame feedback in a way that encourages a growth mindset and reassures your learners that skills and intelligence can be developed (Bryant & Carless, 2010).

CAN-DO #10: ENGAGE PARENTS, CAREGIVERS, AND COMMUNITIES WHOSE ALTERNATIVE LENSES CAN HELP YOU SEE MORE CLEARLY.

Establish communication channels between your classroom and learners' homes. Open two-way communication gives families agency (NASP, 2012). Parents and caregivers can offer valuable insights into the learners' cultural context. This information comes in handy when designing authentic assessments.

CAN-DO #11: ADVOCATE FOR POLICY CHANGE TO ADDRESS SYSTEMIC INEQUITIES OUTSIDE THOSE YOU CAN CHANGE IN YOUR CLASSROOM.

Your classroom is one system. The first 10 "Can-Dos" support combating systemic inequities in your classroom that are (depending on your context) within your control. Start there. Then, when you're ready for more, take on bigger systems. When you're further along the Pathway to Cultural Competence—consciously and unconsciously competent—engage in more challenging proactive and transformative behaviors. Work at the school, district, or higher level to reform assessment policies. This may mean lobbying school leaders and policymakers (such as local and state board members) to recognize the flaws in standardized testing and invest in equitable assessment forms.

When you align equitable assessment practices with culturally relevant pedagogy, you foster an inclusive learning environment that not only recognizes but also celebrates the cultural capital that each learner brings into your classroom. Taking this holistic approach contributes to mitigating the harmful impacts of biased assessments, stereotype threats, and systemic inequities, ultimately leading to better academic outcomes for all learners.

Culturally Relevant Assessment Across the Grades

In Chapter 8, we considered the six purposes of assessment—why we measure learning. And you now have 11 things you can do to make your assessments more equitable. Now, let's examine what equitable assessment looks like in practice across grade levels. Culturally relevant assessments are free from bias. They foster learner agency. To achieve this, assessments must be continually evaluated using the Four Equity Indicators of meritocracy, standards, impartiality, and asset allocation.

For learners in grades PK–2, culturally relevant assessments prioritize tangible, sensory-based tasks. They aim to be inclusive by respecting familial and cultural practices, focusing on the whole child.

In grades 3–5, culturally relevant assessments start to incorporate learners' emerging literacy and numeracy skills. Their ability to read to learn provides an opportunity for introducing more contextually relevant materials and offering choices in how they demonstrate higher order comprehension.

In the middle grades, culturally relevant assessments increasingly emphasize critical thinking and more complex cognitive tasks. We ask learners to integrate real-world problems that resonate with their various cultural perspectives.

Finally, at the high school level, culturally relevant assessments engage learners in more abstract, complex tasks that involve critical analysis. They must offer multiple avenues for expression and focus on real-world applicability.

Let's look at each of these in greater detail, considering the various assessments you currently use, or would like to develop. And don't just read your grade span, see what's suggested above and below. You might gain some ideas you can share with colleagues.

ASSESSING EARLY LEARNERS (PK–GRADE 2)

Culturally relevant assessments used for our youngest learners in grades PK–2 should be age-appropriate and rooted in their lived experiences, cultures, and linguistic backgrounds. Here are nine principles to align with:

1. **Incorporate cultural references.** Support learners in making connections from their world to the content. Use real-world scenarios, characters, or realia that are familiar to learners' own cultural backgrounds in questions and tasks.
2. **When learners' primary language skills are more advanced than their School English, use linguistic adaptations.** Offer assessments in the primary language where possible and appropriate. Employ translanguaging and code-switching techniques to make assessments more accessible. Always accept translanguaging and code-switching in learner responses. If the goal is to find out what they know, it shouldn't matter in what language they can best explain it. That is, unless the subject matter is School English: grammar, usage, mechanics, and composition.
3. **Remember that a picture is worth a thousand words!** So, use diverse visual representations and inclusive images that resonate with the cultural, racial, and ethnic identities of all learners.
4. **Include assessments that allow learners to show their understanding through varied modalities like drawing, acting, or verbal explanation, to honor diverse communicative styles.**
5. **Engage family and community members in creating and even sometimes in administering assessments.** Much can be learned from members of the community (Widiana et al., 2022). Their wisdom—regarding their culture, their histories, their lived experiences, their language—can support you in making assessments that are both more relevant and less intimidating for learners.
6. **Think of the various aspects of learners that enable them to complete assessments, then evaluate those assessments holistically.** Reflect on the multiple facets of a learner's abilities. Consider social, emotional, and cultural competencies alongside academic ones.
7. **Use formative techniques to guide instruction and seek nontraditional opportunities for using them.** Weave formative assessments such as observations, portfolios, and anecdotal records into everyday activities and play.

8. **Aim for language and content impartiality—avoiding bias.** Ensure that the language, scenarios, and questions used in any assessment are free of stereotypes and biases. This includes bias of omission. Remember the third equity indicator question? *Who has representation?*

9. **Any rubrics you use to evaluate these youngest learners should be culturally sensitive.** This may be their first encounter with a classroom setting and any form of assessment. Evaluation criteria must recognize and value diverse skills and ways of knowing, rather than solely White Western European cultural norms, and even sometimes our own state standards.

When you align these nine principles with culturally relevant instructional practices, you ensure that assessments serve as empowering, rather than alienating, experiences for young learners.

ASSESSING MIDDLE CHILDHOOD LEARNERS (GRADES 3–5)

Learners in grades 3–5 are capable of more complex tasks and reasoning. Even so, the principles of cultural relevance remain crucial. Below are ten culturally relevant assessment principles for this age group.

1. **Start by constructing contextualized questions.** Make sure that questions and prompts are rooted in contexts that are familiar to your learners' social and cultural backgrounds. For example, if a math word problem involves buying items from a store, consider using items that are actually found in the stores frequented by learners in their community. If an exemplar text or prompt involves taking a trip, make sure that the destination and mode of transportation is familiar to learners.

2. **As for earlier grades, when learners primary language skills are more advanced than their School English, use linguistic adaptations.** Wherever possible and appropriate, offer assessments in the primary language. Employ translanguaging and code-switching techniques to make assessments more accessible. Accept translanguaging and code-switching in learner responses. In addition, use language that is inclusive and avoid idiomatic expressions that may not be universally understood.

Idioms? Put 'Em on the Back Burner

We use idioms all the time—often without even thinking about the cultural nuances they carry. For multilingual learners, idioms are especially problematic. You likely understand the meaning of such idioms as "piece of cake," "kick the bucket," and "let the cat out of the bag." But think about how a child with limited English proficiency and cultural context might interpret them.

Even those of us who are fully proficient in School English might struggle with idioms steeped in the culture of an unfamiliar region of the United States. Southern idioms like "bless your heart" carry a tremendous amount of nuance. While on the surface it seems like an expression of sympathy, depending on the context, it can be anything but.

Now, add language on top of culture and consider these Spanish language idioms:

"Echar los perros," which translates to "throwing the dogs"; "estar en la luna de Ponce," which translates to "to be on the moon of Ponce"; "Dar una vaina," which means "to give a pod." Unless you are culturally connected to El Salvador, Puerto Rico, or Dominican Republic (in that order), the literal translation of the phrase does nothing to provide understanding of the phrase.

And while those who speak just a little Spanish might be able to comprehend the simple words, "no es fácil," which translate to "it's not easy," it is in the Cuban cultural context that one understands the phrase expresses the complexities and challenges of daily life in Cuba. This simple phrase might be a commentary on economic hardship, bureaucratic obstacles, or personal struggles.

3. **Keeping in mind Equity Indicator 3, provide representational equity.** Ensure that there is visual as well as textual content in the assessment material that represents a variety of races, genders, and cultural backgrounds. Make sure your learners' cultural backgrounds are represented.
4. **Diversify learners' options for responding.** Go beyond multiple-choice and short-answer questions. Include opportunities for learners to demonstrate their understanding in various ways such as oral presentations, projects, or portfolio submissions. Providing diversity of response modes honors different cultural forms of expression and communication.
5. **Assess in multiple dimensions, thinking beyond pure academic competency.** These are formative years for the development of identity and self-concept. Use assessments that gauge both academic and social-emotional competencies, as the two are interrelated (Setemen et al., 2023).

6. **Foster critical thinking through the use of culturally rich and culturally connected texts.** This is an opportunity to engage learners in higher-order thinking while also affirming their cultural identities. Integrate questions that involve analysis of culturally relevant literature, historical events, or social scenarios. These provide additional opportunities for assessing learners' social emotional competencies.
7. **Engage family and community in the assessment process.** The knowledge that community members bring into your classroom can support your efforts in making assessment more relevant and less intimidating. At this grade span, you may wish to incorporate community-based projects or real-world applications of learning as forms of assessment.
8. **After the assessment provide feedback to support learner engagement (Tawil et al., 2023).** Administer formative assessments so that you may provide ongoing, culturally responsive feedback that encourages learners to see mistakes as opportunities for growth rather than as failures.
9. **Construct culturally sensitive rubrics.** Assessment criteria must be transparent and reflect diverse cultural values and modes of learning. Criteria cannot be solely conventional, mainstream metrics of success based on White Western European cultural norms and even sometimes our own state standards.
10. **Audit for equity by routinely reviewing the assessment outcomes.** Look for patterns of bias or inequality by race, gender, language, socioeconomic status, or any of your students' other identities (see Chapter 3). Adjust your assessment strategies accordingly and use the data to inform your needs for professional learning.

The goal at this grade span is to ensure that assessment tools and practices are culturally validating, while also rigorous enough to foster higher-order thinking skills. When you integrate these elements into assessment design and administration, you align with the broader goals of culturally relevant pedagogy that reflects the four Equity Indicators.

ASSESSING ADOLESCENT LEARNERS (GRADES 6–8)

Culturally relevant assessment for adolescent learners in grades 6–8 involves a more nuanced approach. Learners at this stage are becoming more self-aware. They have an increasing capacity for abstract thought. And they are more socially and emotionally complex. Building and expanding on the principles introduced for grades PK–5, here are eleven culturally relevant assessment principles for this age group:

1. **Start by using inclusive content.** At this level, assessment materials should feature a variety of perspectives, histories, and cultures, especially those represented in the classroom. Topics should be relevant to the experiences and interests of your learners. Seeing their lived experiences in the materials will increase engagement and make the assessment more meaningful.
2. **Second, be authentic.** Support content-to-self connections. Incorporate real-world tasks that make the skills and knowledge being assessed relevant to your learners' lives. For example, social studies assessments could involve current events relevant to their diverse communities and lived experiences. Literature assessments can ask learners to make text-to-self and text-to-world connections wherever possible.
3. **Maintain a sensitivity to language.** Hopefully, at this level, newcomer emergent multilingual learners are receiving specialized instruction. However, those supports are not always available. So, where feasible and practical, offer assessments in the learner's primary language (Ahmed Abdel-Al Ibrahim et al., 2023). Employ translanguaging and code-switching techniques to make assessments more accessible. Accept translanguaging and code-switching in learner responses. And continue to use language that is inclusive, avoiding idiomatic expressions that may not be universally understood.
4. **Being mindful of the impact of stereotype threat and the adolescent learner's greater level of awareness of stereotypes.** you'll want to mitigate stereotypes. Always be aware of the many ways—in content, evaluation, feedback—that assessments can reinforce stereotypes. Then, work to neutralize such impacts. Make sure questions are framed in ways that do not activate stereotype threats for learners. Make sure that evaluation and feedback, both to the individual learner and to whole groups, have no stereotype creep.
5. **You'll want to provide learner agency (a recurring theme in practices at this level).** At this level, it's not enough for you to simply diversify the response modes in an assessment. Adolescents have greater capacity and desire to act independently and make choices about their own learning experience. Providing agency means various modes of assessment not only support different ability levels and cultural backgrounds, but learners can choose their response mode. For instance, a learner could choose between writing an essay, creating a presentation, or doing a community project to demonstrate understanding.

6. **Consider offering collaborative assessments.** If your learners come from collectivist cultures, where working together to solve problems is the norm, consider structuring some assessments as collaborative projects. Group problem-solving and co-construction of knowledge is the norm in much of the world of work. Think about it, is professional development most effective on your own? No. We collaborate, we exchange thoughts, ideas, challenges, leaning on our collective intelligence to improve our own practices. Providing opportunities for learners to do the same at this level supports their acculturation into careers after high school or college.
7. **Lean into communities.** Involve learners in creating assessment criteria. Include self-assessment and peer-assessment methods that empower them to take ownership of their learning and support their own agency. Incorporate more community-based projects and real-world applications of learning as forms of assessment.
8. **Provide formative feedback to support learner engagement.** Just as for the lower grades, use low-stakes formative assessments to guide instruction. But go deeper by using that data to provide ongoing, culturally responsive feedback that provides learners with insights into their learning process and encourages them to see mistakes as opportunities for growth rather than as failures. Make sure that your feedback is culturally relevant in content and form.
9. **Use culturally sensitive rubrics.** Assessment criteria must be transparent. It must reflect diverse cultural values and modes of learning. At this level, you can use rubrics and evaluation methods that account for cultural variability in expression, reasoning, and problem-solving. Continue to remain clear of criteria that are solely conventional, mainstream metrics of success based on White Western European cultural norms and even sometimes our own state standards.
10. **Providing greater agency gives you an opening to have learners to lean into self.** Encourage your learners to reflect on their own thought processes and learning preferences, promoting metacognitive skills. Self-assessments are perfect opportunities for learners to evaluate their work according to a set of criteria. Make sure the criteria maps to the components of cultural relevance addressed throughout this book.
11. **Interpret data to drive instruction and learning.** Continuously analyze your assessment data to identify any biases or disparities in outcomes based on race, gender, language, socioeconomic status, or other student identities (Chapter 3). Adjust instruction and assessment

methods accordingly. Use the data to inform your needs for professional learning as well.

The goal at this grade span is to create an assessment environment where every learner has agency, sees themselves reflected and valued. Such an environment gives them an equitable opportunity to demonstrate their abilities. When you create this environment, assessments become tools not just for measurement, but for empowerment.

ASSESSING YOUNG ADULT LEARNERS (GRADES 9–12)

Culturally relevant assessment for young adult learners in grades 9–12 requires a look at the complexities of identity and self-awareness that become even more pronounced at this stage (Azizi & Farid Khafaga, 2023). This makes the need for culturally relevant assessment even more critical. As older adolescents grapple with more abstract concepts and become increasingly independent, understanding and demanding agency, the assessments we use should reflect their growing cognitive and emotional capacities.

Here are twelve culturally relevant assessment principles for this age group.

1. **Start by stimulating critical engagement.** Young adult assessments should challenge learners to think critically about complex social and cultural issues, drawing from a range of interdisciplinary resources and a variety of perspectives. Don't just offer an avenue for learners to see the real-world application of the concepts they are studying, dare them to confront the issues. This is particularly important for engagement and deep understanding.

Exemplars

As exemplars for grades 9–12, consider these two subject-matter assessments.

Social Studies: Ask learners to recontextualize historical events through a podcast or video presentation incorporating primary sources from diverse viewpoints and conclude with a reflection on how different narratives shape our understanding of history and contemporary social issues.

Environmental Science: Consider an environmental justice case study. Assessment could involve a research project where learners identify an existing environmental justice issue, analyze the scientific and social factors contributing to it, and propose evidence-based solutions. The learners can present their findings in a paper, presentation, or as part of a panel discussion.

2. **Challenge critical thinking through authenticity.** Assessments should be rooted in real-world scenarios (see Exemplars on page 167). However, at this stage, the complexity and nuance can be increased. Create opportunities for learners to analyze the social justice and other implications of current events or scientific developments.
3. **Look for ethical and social responsibility in assessment probes and responses.** Assess learners not just on academic content, but also on their ability to engage ethically and responsibly with the material, especially when discussing cultural, social, scientific, and historical issues.
4. **As always, maintain a sensitivity to diverse languages.** Be mindful of language differences, particularly for multilingual (especially emergent level) and sociocultural language learners. Employ translanguaging and code-switching techniques to make assessments more accessible. Accept translanguaging and code-switching in learner responses. And continue to use language that is inclusive, avoiding idiomatic expressions that may not be universally understood.
5. **Ensuring that assessments don't unintentionally confirm stereotypes is crucial.** Actively counteract stereotypes and stereotype threat by being hypervigilant in your assessment practices. To support young adult learners' success in the classroom and into adult life, it is crucial you frame questions in a manner that doesn't perpetuate biases. Learners at this level will call you on it, should they spot it.
6. **Provide even greater agency.** Offer multiple pathways for assessment to support different learning abilities and cultural backgrounds. Whether that means written essays, oral presentations, creative projects, or community engagement, give learners agency. Providing choice accommodates different cultural expressions of knowledge and skill (Widiana et al., 2022). It also supports learners' growing awareness of the ways they may respond as they enter the world beyond high school.
7. **Consider collaborative assessments.** If your learners are rooted in collectivist cultures where collaboration is highly valued, think about framing some evaluations as team-based projects. These learners are close to entering the world of college, careers, or the military, and in many professional settings, teamwork and shared knowledge creation are standard practices. Offering collaborative assessment experiences at this stage aids in preparing them for their post-secondary education and future careers.

8. **Provide formative feedback to support learner engagement.** Offer frequent, constructive, and individualized feedback that guides learners toward improvement. Even at this level, feedback should encourage them to see mistakes as opportunities for growth rather than as failures. Monitor your feedback for sensitivity to cultural nuances in how you communicate that feedback and how it is received.

9. **Leaning into self should be routine at this level.** Go beyond simply encouraging your learners to engage in reflective practices that challenge their own thought processes, biases, and assumptions. Make it mandatory. Challenge them to do so. This is especially relevant for young adult learners who are forming more concrete worldviews. As in middle grades, include self-assessments where learners evaluate their own work according to a given set of criteria. Make sure that criteria maps to the components of cultural relevance.

10. **Just as you ask learners to engage in self-assessment, ask them to be involved in creating assessment criteria.** Engage learners in co-constructing the assessment benchmarks and criterion. This makes them active participants in the evaluation process (Tawil et al., 2023), and lends the assessment greater cultural relevance.

11. **Attend to digital literacy as well as media literacy.** Include assessments that evaluate a learner's ability to effectively find, use, evaluate, create, and communicate information using digital technologies. Create assessments that encompass skills required for navigating content in the digital world, including the use of computers, smartphones, and other devices. Create probes that require learners to evaluate the reliability and credibility of digital content. Be mindful that while technology is a cultural force that impacts all learners, it may not be equally accessible to everyone.

12. **Finally, audit for equity keeping in mind the CARTI Framework.** Review assessment outcomes routinely, after every assessment and at least once or twice a month. Continuously analyze outcomes to identify patterns of disparity based on race, gender, language, socioeconomic status, or student's other identities (see Chapter 3). Make ongoing adjustments in instruction, assessment design, and implementation to address those disparities.

The goal at this grade span is to foster an inclusive environment that allows learners from all backgrounds to showcase their capabilities effectively and fairly. Equitably. Creating this environment and tailoring assessments to be more culturally relevant supports young adults in their transition to their post-secondary education and future careers.

Communicating With Parents and Caregivers

Think back to Chapter 3 and the work on developing cultural awareness. Recall one of the components of cultural awareness: adaptability. Communicating and interacting effectively with parents and caregivers of diverse cultural backgrounds may involve adapting your behavior to respect other cultures.

It is critical to engage in open and effective dialogue with our learners' families concerning assessments. This communication is fundamental to fostering equitable educational experiences. Make it a point to transparently share assessment insights, as it demonstrates that you recognize the value of establishing a collaborative partnership with your families.

The home-school partnerships you create and nurture not only support learners' holistic development but also ensure that education reflects the diverse backgrounds and experiences of every child. Work to develop mutual trust, inclusivity, and understanding. Together, educators and families can collaboratively create learning environments that champion academic achievements and personal enrichment for each learner.

Talking about assessment results is not always easy. However, if you first build a mutually respectful and trusting partnership, you create a climate where those conversations work to bolster outcomes and support positive academic experiences for every child. Sharing assessment insights with families provides them with a clear understanding of their child's academic journey, strengths, and areas needing attention. Let families know that you desire and value their feedback. This is a bridge of collaboration, where both home and school communities actively invest in the learner's holistic development.

Think about these conversations through the lens of equity and the four equity indicators. It is essential to share assessment data transparently and inclusively. This means using language that is free of educational jargon and ensuring that feedback resonates with the diverse backgrounds of families. In other words, don't talk to them using the language I am using with you.

Moreover, demonstrating empathy and cultural sensitivity when discussing assessment outcomes cultivates an atmosphere of mutual trust and inclusivity.

Throughout the year, keep the dialogue open. This is essential for fostering equitable communication—especially in communities where talking to educators or coming to the school might be considered disrespectful. You may need to constantly reassure, even instruct, your families to voice their queries, seek deeper understanding, and share their cultural and personal insights.

Engaging in these two-way conversations offers you a broader perspective on a learner's experiences outside the classroom and paves the way for instruction that is truly respectful of learners' diverse backgrounds.

Empower your families with a clear understanding of all assessment results. Make the connection between standardized results that may reflect a cultural bias, and your culturally relevant assessments. If a child shines in one format and not another, explain to families why that might be so, and the implications of the disconnect, if any. Equip parents and caregivers with the necessary knowledge and resources to support and improve their child's learning experiences at home.

Take a collaborative approach to solidify the belief that education, particularly in a diverse society, is a communal endeavor. Together, you and your families can create a learning environment that champions both academic achievement and personal enrichment for every learner.

What This Looks Like in the Classroom

Remember the work on implicit and explicit bias in Chapter 2? Think about that as you read through the following three scenarios. Each of these is a hypothetical conversation between an instructor who lacks cultural competence and a parent or caregiver. Each of these conversations bears great resemblance to conversations I had with teachers during meetings about 504 plans for my biracial son.

After reading each scenario, get out your pen and mark up the instructor's portion of the script to correct all that is wrong with it. Think about the type of language used: words, tone, and sensitivity. After you've finished, look in Appendix I for my un/consciously competent revisions.

SCENARIO 1

Instructor: "Hello, Mrs. Rodriguez. I wanted to discuss Juan's recent reading assessment results with you. His scores are far below average compared to some of his peers, and I'm concerned about his progress."

Mrs. Rodriguez: "I'm sorry, I don't understand. He's been doing his homework and reading every evening. We check his backpack and the papers he brings home."

Instructor: "I've also noticed he tends to answer questions related to familiar situations incorrectly. Maybe it's due to a language barrier or something. Has Juan been here his whole life? You know, some things might just not resonate with kids from backgrounds like Juan's."

Mrs. Rodriguez: (Taken aback.) "Juan was born in this country as was I, his father, and our parents. We speak English at home. His grandparents speak Spanish to him to make sure he knows both languages. What do you mean by 'familiar situations'? Can you show me examples of what you're talking about?"

Instructor: "Well, there was this one question about a family's Thanksgiving dinner. Maybe Juan isn't familiar with that tradition?"

Mrs. Rodriguez: "We've celebrated Thanksgiving every year. Just because we don't eat the same food as you doesn't mean Juan doesn't understand the holiday."

Instructor: "I apologize, I just thought it might be a cultural thing."

SCENARIO 2

Instructor: "Hello, Mr. and Mrs. Jackson. It is Mr. and Mrs. Jackson, right? I wanted to discuss Malik's progress in English with you. He's making a lot of grammatical errors in his writing assessments, and it's impacting his grades."

Mr. Jackson: "Can you give me an example?"

Instructor: "Sure, in last week's written exam, Malik wrote, 'He ain't done nothing,' instead of 'He hasn't done anything.' I've also noticed he frequently mispronounces words, especially the 't-h' sound. I'm concerned he might have dyslexia or some type of speech or processing disorder."

Mrs. Jackson (Who happens to be a English professor at the local university, unbeknownst to the instructor): "Malik doesn't need an IEP referral. He's bilingual. He speaks School English and African American English. African American English is a legitimate language variety with its own grammatical rules. It's an important part of our culture."

Instructor: "Well, in school we only use standard English. Maybe if he read more books and watched shows that use proper English, he'd improve?"

Mrs. Jackson: "Malik reads extensively and is exposed to a variety of English styles. In fact, his favorite authors are Langston Hughes and James Baldwin. Authors I've noticed are not in your syllabus. As for his use of AAVE as opposed to School English, perhaps specifying in the assignment that no languages other than School English will be accepted would provide some clarity."

Instructor: "I didn't mean to stereotype . . ."

SCENARIO 3

Instructor: "Hello, Mr. Nguyen. I wanted to discuss your son, Tuân's, math performance. I've noticed he's struggling a bit, especially on his timed tests, which surprises me. Most of the boys like him I've had in the past excel in mathematics."

Mr. Nguyen: "Tuân is his own person. I don't think it's appropriate to compare him to other students based on him being Asian. Each child has unique strengths and challenges."

Instructor: "I didn't mean to stereotype, but I just thought, given the trend, he might have an easier time with math."

Mr. Nguyen: "Tuân enjoys reading, music, and art. We're working on improving his math skills, it's just never been his strongest subject."

Instructor: "Hmm... I didn't know that."

Progress Monitoring in the Content Areas With a PLC

To work toward educational equity, monitoring learner progress in understanding the big ideas of science and social studies is an imperative. Here is a PLC collaborative strategy flow you can adopt in your school or district for this purpose.

Subject-area teams should first engage in curriculum mapping to identify key "big ideas" and milestones that learners are expected to achieve not only in, but across, grade levels. Your

(Continued)

(Continued)

state standards and frameworks are a good place for guidance there. Make sure that your curriculum maps are "living" documents. Update them periodically to reflect new pedagogical understandings or societal changes.

Interdisciplinary teams composed of science, social studies, English, and other relevant disciplines can facilitate a more comprehensive view of big ideas that often span multiple subjects.

Subject-area experts should create, and interdisciplinary teams co-create, formative and summative assessments that focus on these cross-disciplinary big ideas. These assessments should be culturally responsive and linguistically accessible to ensure they are equitable measures of understanding for all learners, especially those from marginalized communities.

Consider conducting peer classroom observations and sharing constructive feedback. This can be a powerful tool for professional learning. Peer observations can help to identify gaps or biases in instructional techniques, aiding in the equitable comprehension of those big ideas (Homayouni, 2022).

At the same time, create a shared database where educators can input and analyze data to help track learner progress. When you take this approach and disaggregate data by variables such as race, socioeconomic status, and language proficiency, you can work to pinpoint and address inequities. (Grades, which we get to in the next chapter, are subject to extreme implicit and explicit bias.)

If the school faculty does not reflect the demographic of your marginalized learners, consider involving community leaders, parents, and caregivers in the conversation, with a focus on involving those representing marginalized groups. Host listening sessions or invite parents, caregivers, and community leaders to join a development committee. Their perspectives can offer valuable insights into how the curricular "big ideas" are resonating with different communities. Taking an inclusive approach on the front end can lead to more equitable outcome on the back end.

Provide ongoing professional development that focuses on both subject matter expertise and culturally responsive pedagogy. This is essential. Support sharing resources, research findings, and strategies to improve instructional practice in a way that is equitable and just.

For those further along the cultural competency pathway, there's policy advocacy. Educator-leaders can use the data and experiences from these collaborative practices to advocate for systemic changes. This could involve lobbying for more equitable funding, assessments, and resources, which would benefit learners from diverse backgrounds.

By taking a collaborative, interdisciplinary, and equity-focused approach, PLCs can more effectively monitor learner progress in understanding the big ideas of science and social studies. Set a goal to drive instructional changes that are tailored to meet the needs of all learners, particularly your culturally and linguistically diverse learners and those from other marginalized communities.

Commercial Assessment Review and Analysis

When using commercial curriculum or other assessments developed by a third party, review and analyze them for impartiality. Consider:

The Test Development Process: Was the assessment developed by a diverse group of educators, experts, and stakeholders?

Stereotype Threat: Does the assessment contain negative stereotypes of marginalized learners? Research has shown that when learners are reminded of stereotypes about their group's abilities, their performance declines (Steele et al., 2002).

Validity and Reliability: When test items are culturally biased, it questions the validity of the test, that is, whether the test is measuring what it claims to measure. Was the assessment normed or validated against a culturally and linguistically diverse population of learners?

Conclusion

In this chapter, you looked at aligning equitable assessment practices with the culturally relevant instructional practices you learned in earlier chapters. You read about strategies for equitable assessment specific to the grade span you work with, and considered a few scenarios showing culturally *in*competent conversations with learners' parents and caregivers. You then referenced Appendix I to see models of appropriate conversations.

You're now ready for the next step on the CARTI Framework: data-driven decision making, with the focus on equitable grading. We start Chapter 10 by examining the purpose of grades and their roles in various aspects of your learners' academic careers. We then examine grading practices through each of the four equity indicators. We wrap up with a look at equitable grading in a standards-based grading system.

This chapter has only one reflect and act exercise: a deep reflection and self-assessment. As you perform this reflection, think about the conversations you've had with parents and caregivers.

Reflect and Act

Reflecting on the scenarios of communication with parents and caregivers, what damage might have been done by the instructor's words? How might the instructor have prepared for those conversations? How might the parent have responded to more culturally competent language? Does this cause you to think about the conversations you've had—or will have—with your parents and caregivers?

●●● MY MINDSET METER

Complete the mindset meter as a self-assessment. Make connections building on what you've learned, your instructional setting, and your lived experience. Analyze. Strategize. Integrate.

Knowledge: Three to five big ideas about equitable assessment that I learned in this chapter:

____

____

____

____

Comprehension: The goal of culturally relevant assessment for my grade span as I understand it from this chapter:

____

____

____

____

Application: This is how I can use the assessment strategies I learned in this chapter:

____

____

____

____

Analysis: I can identify the following motives and causes for equitable assessment in my classroom:

____

____

____

____

Synthesis: This is how I will create culturally relevant assessments for my learners:

____

____

____

____

Evaluation: I used to think ______ but now I think ______.

____

____

____

____

THE FOUNDATIONS OF EQUITABLE GRADING

CHAPTER 10

In Chapter 8 we examined the foundations of equitable assessment. We looked at the various forms and functions of assessment, and what is required to select, develop, and administer assessment through the lenses of the four equity indicators. In this chapter, we mirror that work, focusing on equitable grading. Our work is grounded in step 5 of the CARTI Framework: data-driven decision making (see Figure 10.1). Here we focus specifically on decisions about grading.

Data-driven decision making involves six sub-phases: act, analyze, plan, implement, monitor, and assess. These phases are cyclical, never-ending, and best visualized as a 360-degree feedback loop (see Figure 10.2). As we explore equitable grading, looking at grading practices through the lens of equity, keep in mind this feedback loop.

The Role of Grades in Evaluating Learner Knowledge and Skills

In education, grades serve as communication of a learner's understanding of a subject. At least that is what we are told and what we assume. As performance indicators, grades should represent a child's mastery of course content. A higher grade is generally understood as an indicator that a learner has comprehended and retained a larger amount of the subject matter.

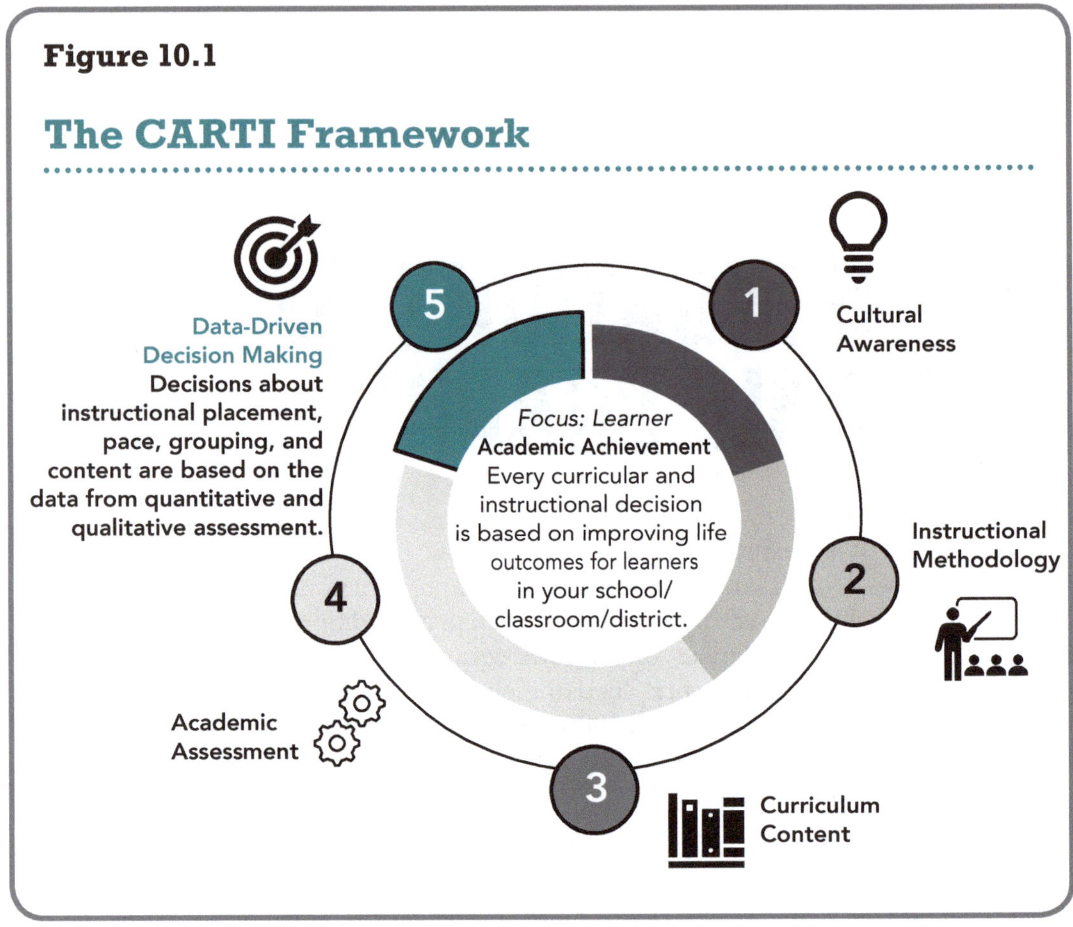

As benchmarks, grades should provide a way to compare a learner's performance against a standard or across a cohort of other learners. This type of comparison can help us identify where a learner excels or where they might need additional support.

Grades should also allow us to track a learner's progress. Improvements in grades over time can be a positive reinforcement for a learner, letting them know that their understanding is increasing.

Depending on the subject or course and the type of assignments given, grades can help to identify a learner's strengths and weaknesses. They can help pinpoint where learners need support. You might have a learner who excels at written assignments but struggles when it comes time to take a test. They may suffer from difficulty with recall under pressure. Perhaps they suffer from stereotype threat. Or perhaps they simply need to learn test taking strategies.

Figure 10.2

Feedback Loop for Data-Based Decision Making

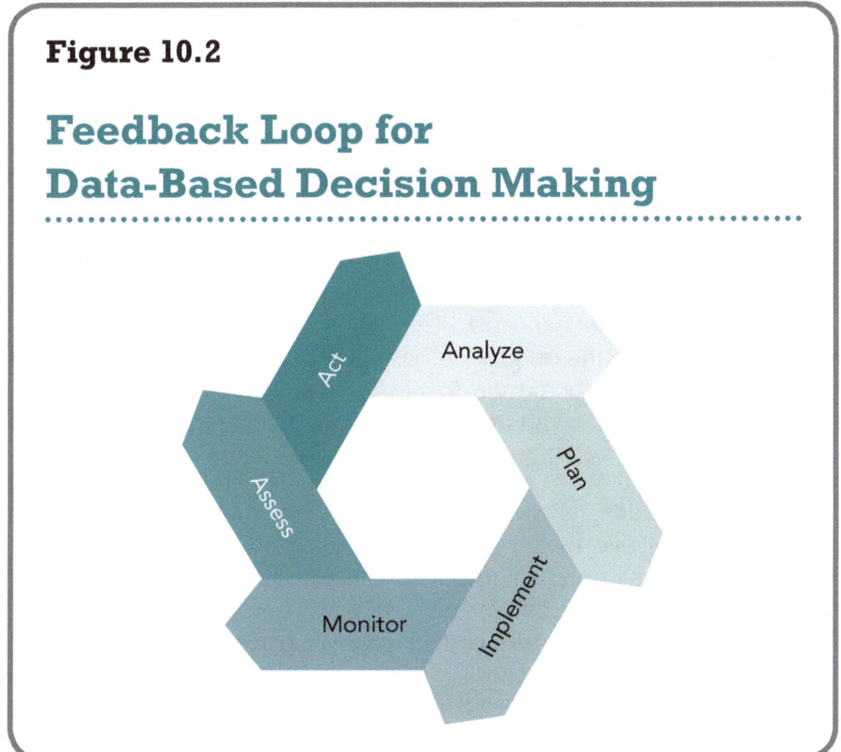

However, grades may fall short as accurate measures of a learner's ability or understanding. Their accuracy as performance indicators depends on whether or not the instructor averages grades over time or assigns a final grade based on the highest grade in each category being measured.

As a benchmark against a standard, grades provide solid information about where a learner excels or needs support. However, if you are comparing learners across a cohort of other learners, we must consider differences in learner backgrounds, languages and home environments, as well as their prior instruction and the quality of instruction.

When it comes to identifying a learner's strengths and weaknesses, a variety of assignments and assessments are required to determine where a learner may excel or need support. This requires an educator who allows learners to demonstrate their knowledge in a variety of ways and through a variety of products. We've addressed these principles throughout this book.

The Role of Grades in Motivating Learners

A second role of grades is to provide motivation to study and engage with the content. This is relevant for some, not all, learners. For some learners, grades are a tangible reward for effort and understanding. Grades hold them accountable for their learning. However, whether grades are seen as a motivational reward depends on the learner and often the culture from which they come. It also depends on grades being truly reflective of a learner's knowledge and performance in class. This, in turn, depends on classroom educators who are free of implicit bias, particularly bias against culturally or linguistically diverse learners.

The role of grades as motivators varies from one learner to the next. Learners are under a tremendous amount of social pressure and stress, both in and out of school. Grades may carry negative effects, such as undue stress, either from home, or the learner's social circle. When a learner is intrinsically motivated to attain high grades, they may put pressure on themselves to do well. That pressure may be acceptable and navigable, or it may be debilitating.

An excessive focus on grades can detract from intrinsic motivation to learn for the sake of learning. It may detract from a learner gaining deeper understanding and being able to apply the knowledge that they've attained. As educators, it's important for us to balance our use of grades with other forms of feedback and motivation. It is in this manner that we can support all learners effectively.

The Role of Grades in College Admissions

Finally, grades impact a learner's opportunities for higher education and career prospects. A learner's high school GPA and the rigor of their course load are two of the most important factors considered during the college admissions process, especially where admissions testing has been eliminated. Grades signal to college admissions teams that candidates have academic aptitude, consistency, and ability to handle challenging coursework (Zinshteyn, 2021). Learners with a strong academic record are often more competitive during the application process.

Examining Grading Practices Through the Lens of Equity

When examining grading practices through a lens of equity, there are three things that we must consider: (1) traditional grading systems and how they impact culturally diverse learners' motivation and learning, (2) alignment of grading practices with equitable learning goals, and (3) culturally relevant feedback in the grading process. We return to the four indicators of equity as a tool to examine our practices.

Meritocracy and the Impact of Traditional Grading Practices

Remember that meritocracy is the idea that power is held by people based on their ability. That is the equitable use of meritocracy. When we talk about meritocracy and grading, we ask the same questions:

- *Who has the power?*
- *Are we using power for the good of the marginalized in our school community?*

In our classrooms, when it comes to grading, typically the instructor has the power. The question is, "If our system is equitable, are those holding the power the ones who have the ability, the desire and the commitment to use that power for good?" Are we, as classroom instructors, using our power of grades for the good of marginalized learners without bias against those who are not? This doesn't mean grading learners of color or linguistically diverse learners differently. It means using your power to create a grading system that adopts the indicators of standards and impartiality.

Think about the traditional grading practices you use: norm reference grading, grade averages, deduction-based or zero-based grading. Ask yourself if the way you grade may disproportionately affect marginalized learners.

If you use norm reference grading, have those norms been built upon demographics that match the learners in your classroom? If you use grade averages, do you consider the trajectory of learning?

Are the averages weighted? And if so, might the weighted items have a disproportionate impact on certain learners? Particularly, for example, linguistically diverse learners in a subject that is language heavy?

If you use zero-based grading systems where learners start with zero points at the beginning of the course and earn points for demonstrating their competency or their mastery, what criteria do you use to assign points? Is that criteria culturally and linguistically unbiased? Or are there learners who may be privileged by such a system while others are disadvantaged?

Similarly, if you use a deduction-based system where your learners start with 100% and then lose points for mistakes or missed assignments, what criteria do you use to deduct points? Are the criteria culturally and linguistically unbiased? Are there learners who may be privileged by such a system while others are disadvantaged?

In both deduction-based and zero-based systems, the key factor is the criteria you use to assign or deduct points. The effectiveness of any grading system depends on how accurately it assesses learners' understanding, competency, and mastery of criteria; and if it provides clear and immediate feedback so learners have an opportunity to improve.

Standards and the Principles of Equitable Grading Practices

Remember that standards are the metrics that we use to craft and deliver instruction and to measure academic performance. Learners demonstrate their mastery of standards. Again, the two essential questions here are:

- *Who is demonstrating mastery?*
- *Are we taking action to result in learners demonstrating ongoing mastery year over year?*

When grading practices are equitable, the standards are not the high bar, but the minimum proficiency. What we provide instruction in, and how we provide it, should ensure that children meet that minimum level of proficiency. When we think about grading on an A to F scale, is minimum proficiency represented by an A? Or does an A represent mastery? And exactly what do we mean when we say *proficient*?

I define **proficiency** as having the knowledge and skills to meet the standard. The learner understands the core concepts and can complete basic tasks without significant difficulty. A learner who is proficient has knowledge, comprehension, and application skills, but does not necessarily have deep or comprehensive understanding of the subject matter.

I define **mastery** as a level beyond proficiency. Mastery indicates a higher, more comprehensive level of understanding or skill. A learner who has mastery can apply their knowledge and skills in complex, novel, or in-depth ways. Not only do they understand core concepts, but they can analyze, synthesize, and evaluate information within and across subject areas.

I often say that content mastery is like knowing your name or the days of the week. It's just there. There is no stress, difficulty, or cognitive challenge retrieving the information and analyzing, synthesizing, or evaluating it. When we have mastery, we have a level of comfort that allows for creative problem solving and independent thought.

proficiency: A high degree of competence or skill; expertise. Demonstrates knowledge, comprehension, and application skills.

mastery: Comprehensive knowledge or skill in a subject. Able to engage in analysis, synthesis, and evaluation.

We must make grading more transparent and consistent. All learners benefit when all of their instructors use clear and transparent grading policies. All learners should understand how their work will be evaluated. As educators, most of us are evaluated on our performance at least once a year. Imagine if every time an administrator observed you, they changed the standards. Or didn't tell you the standards you were being evaluated on. Imagine if your evaluation was conducted by three administrators who each had different policies that they did not share with you. In settings where learners have, for example, seven different instructors with seven different grading policies and seven different grading schemes, grading is not transparent but rather opaque.

We must have consistency in our grading schemes, with practices and policies where all learners are held to mastery of a specific standard and are not assessed on their behavior. This is crucial for several reasons. The first is a matter of fairness. Consistent grading procedures ensure that all learners are evaluated by the same criteria. Think about our definition of equity: "without bias against or favoritism for." Arbitrary or biased grading can lead to learner discouragement and disengagement.

Another reason for consistency is a matter of clarity of expectations. You might be familiar with this advice: "Tell them what you're going to tell them. Tell them. Then tell them what you told them." We can adjust that to express clear expectations: "Here's what you must know. Here's the instruction on what you must know. Here's what you should have learned." When learners understand what they are expected to master, rather than how they are expected to behave, they can then focus on acquiring knowledge and developing skills.

Additionally, grading consistency promotes learning. What is the standard of learning in our classrooms? When we focus on mastery, learners are incentivized to reach those higher levels of thinking, rather than simply act in ways they think will lead to a higher grade. When I eliminated letter grades while providing reading intervention and focused learners on mastery of content, they worked harder in each lesson. They understood what it meant to master the content, and they focused less on how that would translate to a letter grade.

Yet another reason for consistency is accurate assessment, which we covered thoroughly in Chapters 8 and 9.

And the final reason is that consistency is about equity. More specifically, it's about asset allocation. We want to make sure that every learner, regardless of their background or personal circumstance, is not only evaluated using an unbiased standard, but is given assets such as time, tools, and additional supports needed for their success. Leveling the playing field may not be enough, but it is a beginning. This doesn't mean using a different standard when grading learners of color or linguistic diversity. It means examining the standards for cultural or linguistic bias, using your power to consider how learners' diversity impacts their mastery of the standards, and then developing or modifying the grading scheme to accommodate the difference.

Just as an example, consider your policy on late assignments. If you penalize learners for turning in late work, why? What is the penalty? What change do you aim to get because of that penalty?

Punctuality is a cultural concept. In some cultures, monochronic cultures, it's highly valued and considered a sign of respect. In polychronic cultures, punctuality is not adhered to because the focus is on relationships and completion of tasks rather than sticking to a rigid schedule (Ursu & Ciortescu, 2021). Monochronic cultures view time in the linear fashion, and they prioritize schedules and deadlines. The most notable monochronic cultures are also Western European (Germany, Scandinavia, and the

United Kingdom) and the United States (Ursu & Ciortescu, 2021). Polychronic cultures, those rooted in Latin America, Africa, and South Asian cultures, do not view time the same way. In those cultures, interpersonal relationships are valued over punctuality and time-consciousness (Kurian, 2013b). This doesn't mean all learners whose ethnic origins are in polychronic cultures require accommodation here. It means learners may be at varying levels in their ability to conform, or desire to adapt to a monochronic classroom culture or grading norm.

Now think about penalty for late work again. Is the goal of your instruction, and hence your penalty for late work about punctuality? That would be a cultural-based behavioral goal rooted in a White Western European cultural norm: a monochronic cultural norm. Or is your goal mastery of content, an academic goal? Where do you meet the asset allocation indicator, in this case "time," to support equity? Which state academic standards support submission of homework "on time"? If an additional hour, day, or even a few days makes the difference between a learner demonstrating a lack of proficiency and mastery, shouldn't we be more accommodating of the later work? I firmly believe we should.

Table 10.1 describes what equitable grading schemes look like and what to avoid.

Table 10.1

What Equitable Grading Schemes Look Like in the Classroom

EXEMPLARY CLASSROOMS LOOK LIKE THIS	EXEMPLARY CLASSROOMS *DO NOT* LOOK LIKE THIS
Norm-Reference Grading	
Norms are built on a national representation of culturally and linguistically diverse learners that reflect your learner demographic.	No information is provided about the learner demographic on which the norms are based, or they are based on primarily White learners.
Grade Averaging	
Categorical averaging is used, e.g., tests, homework, in-class work, group work, written.	No categories are used, or categories may include areas that are subjective or discriminatory, such as participation, decorum, or neatness.

(Continued)

(Continued)

EXEMPLARY CLASSROOMS LOOK LIKE THIS	EXEMPLARY CLASSROOMS *DO NOT* LOOK LIKE THIS
Averages are weighted to prevent disproportionate impact of a single category, e.g., homework 25%, in-class work 25%, group work 25%, tests 25%.	No distinction is made to consider the learner's ability to demonstrate proficiency in one area over another.
Deduction-Based Grading	
Clear and consistent rubrics are used and shared with learners well in advance. Rubrics are unbiased and culturally responsive, respective of learners' lived experiences.	Criteria is inconsistent, subjective, behavior-based, or discriminatory, e.g., participation, decorum, timeliness, or neatness.
Zero-Based Grading	
Clear and consistent rubrics are used and shared with learners well in advance. Rubrics are unbiased and culturally responsive, respective of learners' lived experiences.	Criteria is inconsistent, subjective, behavior-based, or discriminatory, e.g., participation, decorum, timeliness, or neatness.
All Grading Schemes	
Grading is based solely on assessment of proficiency: understanding, competency, mastery of criteria.	Learners are awarded points based on behaviors such as participation, decorum, timeliness, or neatness.
Feedback is clear and immediate.	Feedback is not given, or is vague, subjective, or delayed.
Learners have an opportunity to revise and resubmit without penalty.	Learners are not given the opportunity to improve on their submitted work based on feedback.

Impartiality, Bias, and Racism in Grading Practices

In Chapter 1, we defined impartiality as "fairness or without bias." Here we ask these two essential questions:

- *Who has representation?*
- *Are we accurately and appropriately considering the cultures of all those affected, or are we acting from a middle class, White Western European cultural bias?*

When we look for impartiality in our grading systems, we want to ensure that we are not harming learners by subliminally grading them against their lived experiences, their race, their culture, or their language.

The third indicator of equity, impartiality, can greatly influence our grading practices and help to ensure an equitable learning environment. At all times, we must continue to ask ourselves those two essential questions. We must consider our own cultural viewpoint and the cultures of the learners in our classrooms. Let's look at ways impartiality affects grading.

I imagine we all assume that our grading is a fair assessment. When grading is impartial, we want to make sure we are focusing on the quality of a learner's work, not any personal characteristics like their race, gender, or socioeconomic status. We want to make sure that we're not considering a learner's behavioral tendencies when we assign a grade. These are things to consider as we develop our own grading practices. We must be absolutely certain that each and every learner has an equal opportunity to get a high grade based on their academic performance and nothing else.

One goal of impartial grading is to reduce bias. Whether that bias is explicit or conscious or implicit or unconscious, we must be aware of what the bias is. Bias has a way of surreptitiously creeping into our thought processes. Be mindful that bias can be positive as well as a negative. We may tend to see certain people or certain cultures favorably. Favorable biases can lead to grade inflation. We may be blind to our own biases, but our learners are not. Have you ever heard learners say that you favor a particular child? Or that another instructor always favors particular types of learners? Our learners see biases that we are unaware of.

Being mindful of our learners' lived experiences helps create an environment where grades reflect a learner's effort and understanding rather than personal factors. Consider the role of language in your classroom and in your grading scheme. If you instruct on a subject where language is critical to demonstrating mastery and have learners who have not mastered School English, then you must consider the learner's language experience, their mother tongue (including sociocultural languages), and their attempts at mastery, as well as whether they have actually mastered the content.

The feedback we provide to our learners must be accurate as well as impartial. If it is not, how will our learners understand where they need to improve? Feedback should be based on clearly defined criteria that are applied equally to all learners. If we do not provide clear and consistent feedback, our learners will not understand their strengths and weaknesses. And, we must provide opportunities for learners to show what they learned based on feedback they were given. When we are consistent in our feedback, we can ensure that all learners are graded on the same scale, reducing the likelihood of grade inflation or grade deflation.

Impartiality is our goal, our ideal. Unfortunately, we all suffer from some bias, whether implicit or explicit, and these biases can significantly influence our grading. Remember that explicit bias refers to attitudes and stereotypes that affect our understanding, our actions, and our decisions in an intentional or conscious manner. These are the things that we can name and that we act on, perhaps even knowing that they are wrong. In terms of our grading practices, we might have explicit bias based on a learner's background, behavior, socioeconomic status, gender, race, ethnicity, or even a sibling that you taught previously.

Let's say, for example, that you have learners who are newcomers. If you consciously believe newcomers are less intelligent, then you might grade them more harshly, even though you know that they do not yet speak School English. Consider, how brilliantly would you shine if thrown into a school in the newcomers' country of origin, not speaking their language? Though you might know the content, you would be unable to express it in a linguistically proficient manner. Would you want to be graded on your language ability? By the same token, favoritism based on a shared language or shared culture or personality characteristics is similarly biased. That favoritism must be avoided.

Remember also that implicit or unconscious bias refers to attitudes and stereotypes that affect understanding, actions, and decisions in ways one is not aware of. These are those thoughts that are deep down at the bottom of our icebergs (see page 29). It is generally difficult for us to either understand or control our implicit biases. This makes them that much more insidious. If you have implicit bias based on being from a middle class, White Western European culture, you may unconsciously give higher grades to learners whose names are familiar or who have a White-European origin. That same unconscious bias might be reflected as you read certain styles of writing or arguments or perspectives. Those that resonate with your own cultural experiences or belief systems may potentially lead to unfair grading practices. Implicit biases about gender might also be reflected in your grading, especially in subjects that are stereotypically associated with a specific gender.

Practitioner's Perspective

Going through school in the 1960s and 1970s with the name *Almitra* was never a walk in the park. I don't remember ever having an instructor who correctly pronounced my name on the first attempt, even though it is phonetically regular. When I became an educator, I made a concerted effort to make sure I could say each child's name as their parents intended. When I noticed that a child of ethnicity had an anglicized nickname, I would ask them privately if that was the name that they preferred to be called.

Many learners confessed that they would prefer to be called by the name that their parents gave them, however teachers routinely mispronounced it. I would ask them to teach me how to say their name properly and to hold me accountable to do so. Some names were easy. Others took more time and certainly more effort on my part. But the smile that came across their faces when I did it properly, when I called them what they preferred to be called, was heartwarming.

Even now, when I provide professional learning sessions, I come across names that are a little more difficult for me. I still ask those educators what they prefer to be called and to teach me how to say their names properly. Many times, I'm told stories of how they came to have a nickname that did not reflect their preference. And often, these are scars that are worn into their adulthood.

It only takes a moment to learn someone's name. But the impact lasts a lifetime.

Whether conscious or unconscious, explicit or implicit bias in our grading leads to a lack of fairness and equity in our classrooms. It negatively impacts learners who are disadvantaged by these biases and creates an environment that is not conducive to learning or to growth.

In Chapter 2, you learned about the four-tiered model of racism. Let's review the four tiers and then look at how each impacts grading practices.

Remember that tier one racism is structural. These are the laws and policies instituted by national, state, and regional departments of education that give unfair advantage to some learners, and result in unfair or harmful treatment to learners of color because of their race. Tier two racism is institutional. These are the rules and policies instituted by your school or school district that disproportionately impact learners of color.

While tier one and tier two racism may not be in your sphere of influence, tiers three and four certainly are. Tier three happens in your classroom through jokes, harassment, threats, and microaggressions. This is interpersonal racism, and it happens routinely during instruction. Sometimes it comes across in the way that we talk about the content. It may be an under the breath comment. It may be the sigh of disgust. Or annoyance. Little phrases like, "you people," or "those people." These are all constant and coded reminders to learners of color that they are lesser than, that they are not appreciated, that they are not respected.

Tier three racism happens between your learners as well. As the classroom leader, if you fail to interrupt interpersonal racism that is occurring between learners you are equally guilty of the racism. Those same sighs of disgust, the annoyances, the coded words and phrases spoken by learners should be interrupted.

Finally, tier four racism is personal. While I can't imagine that anyone reading this far in this book holds racism in their heart and acts on that racism in their own classroom, it is possible that you know someone who does so. Far too many times we have seen examples of tier four racism on social media when a learner has recorded a teacher engaged in a racist rant.

Both tier three (interpersonal) and tier four (personal) racism are highly visible. They impact our learners directly and daily. They impact the way our learners learn and the comfort that they feel in the classroom environment. They fuel stereotype threat. It is hard to imagine that they do not also creep into the grading practices of the classroom teacher. So, let's look at two ways that this occurs.

The first way is a lowered expectation. Whether implicitly or explicitly, instructors may hold lower academic expectations for learners of certain races. These different levels of expectations may also be due to stereotypes or biased beliefs. When we expect less from learners due to their race, we don't provide the same level of feedback, support, or opportunities for challenging assignments. This affects the grades and opportunities for learning that these learners receive.

The second way is biased evaluation. Racism may provide a channel for teachers to be tougher on learners from certain racial and ethnic backgrounds. These learners are marked down more severely for mistakes, particularly grammatical ones on written assignments. These learners are less likely to be given the benefit of the doubt in ambiguous situations. And they are less likely to be given opportunities to turn in late work or missed assignments, especially when racism supports beliefs that learners of color are lazy or have no respect for time.

Examining the role of impartiality, bias, and racism in grading practices is not complete without considering the impact of stereotype threat, first discussed in Chapter 8. Stereotype threat is not a practice that instructors impose on learners, however many learners of color suffer from it. You must be cognizant of it as you examine and adjust your grading practices.

Learners who are suffering from stereotype threat, increased anxiety, and stress as they attempt to disprove the negative stereotypes about their identity groups may become disengaged from instruction. They may not submit assignments or participate in class discussion and activities. They may seek ways to escape the classroom to avoid confirming the negative stereotype. While it may not seem logical, the behaviors that result from stereotype threat can cause a self-fulfilling prophecy (Aronson et al., 2002).

Asset Allocation and Promoting Equity in Grading

The last equity indicator, asset allocation, is about creating constructive inequality to remedy the historical oppression of marginalized learners. Remember our essential questions here are:

- *Is there positive structural inequality?*
- *Are we choosing and allocating assets to create opportunity and excellence for all involved?*

As we promote equity in grading, we use asset allocation to eliminate grading disproportionality and achievement gaps. The idea of positive structural inequality means giving more to those who have less. This doesn't mean grade inflation for marginalized learners! Here's an example of what it does mean:

Let's say I have learners who have access to Wi-Fi, computers, and parents with college educations and the means to provide support at home. In the same classroom I have learners with no access to Wi-Fi, no computers at home, and parents who may not have graduated from high school. If I assign all learners a paper that requires work outside the classroom, the use of internet searches, and submission as a word-processed document, I must consider the unequal resources of my learners.

Positive structural inequality means that I either allow more time, or dedicate more in-class resources to learners who do not have access to those resources outside the classroom. Positive structural inequality might also mean that I offer tutoring sessions after school for learners who do not have support at home. However, if those same learners lack transportation, or have after-school jobs or other home-based responsibilities, after-school support will not meet their needs. Its unequal accessibility creates another provision gap, an inequity.

While we might initially think that these additional supports are not fair, the goal is to eliminate gaps and disproportionality. Assets and resources are committed in a targeted way to provide what is needed for those who need it. At the same time, I am ensuring that I do no harm to my learners who have sufficient access to resources outside the classroom.

Reflect back to my experience with my sixth-grade learners (page 93). Providing multiple ways for learners to demonstrate their knowledge is just one way to provide positive structural inequality. Another method is to provide multiple opportunities for revision and improvement, particularly for learners who are multilingual, including those who speak African American English, Chicano English, Hawaiian Creole, Jamaican Patois, or other sociocultural languages.

EQUITABLE GRADING IN A STANDARDS-BASED SYSTEM

Up to this point, I have addressed four common grading schemes—ones many of us grew up with or have used in our own classrooms (see Table 10.2). However some districts are using a newer model: a standards-based grading (SBG) system. If you're using an SBG system, perhaps mandated by state law, you may have been wondering, "How can I reflect grading with equity in our SBG system?" If your SBG is grounded in the work of Robert Marzano (2006), you're likely well on your way. The specifics of how SBG is unlike the grading schemes discussed thus far are shown in Table 10.2.

> Standards-based grading is a method of assigning grades that ties student achievement to specific topics within each subject area. It allows teachers, students, and parents to clearly communicate about specific areas of strength and need. Ultimately, standards-based grading gives a clear and concise answer to the student's question, "What do I need to do to improve?" (Heflebower & Hoegh, 2014, pp. xiii–xiv)

SBG is a grading scheme that requires clearly articulated learning goals, proficiency scales to measure those goals against, assessments that determine the learner's proficiency status against each of those goals, and a method of reporting and communicating the learner's status to the learner, their parents and caregivers, other educators, and institutions—such as colleges and universities.

On initial review, SBG seems pretty well grounded in meritocracy and standards. And it is! However, it completely ignores the impact of personal bias on grades—even when grading in a standards-based system.

In an SBG, you must integrate the emphasis on clarity, fairness, and specificity aligned with specific learning objectives (standards) called for in SBG systems with the mindset of eliminating implicit and explicit bias called for in equitable grading. Like all schemes, there is a human element that is not delineated in the structure. Equitable change occurs only when you arrive at the grade without favoritism for or bias against a learner or group of learners.

Reporting equitable grades in an SBG system means considering *how you provide instruction* and *what you provide instruction on* (covered previously in this book), through the lens of equity.

To think about this, it's useful to look at some standards and find places where equity might be infused. In Table 10.2, you'll find a selection of ELA and History/Social Science standards. (You can conduct this exercise using any standards for your grade level and subject matter.) Think about the four equity indicators as you examine each standard. Where might equity be lacking? What might it look like to integrate equity when assessing students' mastery of the standard?

Table 10.2

Applying an Equity Lens to Standards

STANDARD	LACKING EQUITY	WITH EQUITY
Grades K–5		
Distinguish between similarly spelled words by identifying the sounds of the letters that differ.	Educators grade learners who speak a language other than School English, including sociocultural languages like African American English or Chicano English, who have a phonetic map that does not match School English without consideration of the linguistic difference.	Educators consider *the learner's home language and that language's map to School English in evaluating proficiency.* Equity Indicator: *Impartiality: You consider the linguistic culture of the learner.*
Describe the connection between two individuals, events, ideas, or pieces of information in a [an informational] text.	Educators grade learners . . . __________ __________ __________ __________	Educators consider . . . __________ __________ __________ __________

(Continued)

(Continued)

STANDARD	LACKING EQUITY	WITH EQUITY
		Equity Indicator: __________ __________ __________ __________
Recount stories, including fables and folktales from diverse cultures, and determine their central message, lesson, or moral.	Educators grade culturally diverse learners who have difficulty connecting to the content of stories on their inability to comprehend a central message or moral that is profoundly different from their lived experience or cultural norm.	Educators consider *the learners' lived experiences and use rubrics that provide guidance for the learner to continue to grow and improve.* Equity Indicators: *Standards and Impartiality: You use a rubric to support growth and mastery over time and you consider the cultural norms of the learner.*
Describe the relationship between a series of historical events, scientific ideas or concepts, or steps in technical procedures in a text, using language that pertains to time, sequence, and cause/effect.	Educators grade culturally and linguistically diverse learners without regard to cultural differences in terms or norms, concepts, or ways of thinking.	Educators *respect and accept the influence of learners' cultures and lived experiences in their interpretation of a text.* Equity Indicator: __________ __________ __________ __________
Write opinion pieces on topics or texts, supporting a point of view with reasons and information. Introduce a topic or text clearly, state an opinion, and create an organizational structure in which related ideas are grouped to support the writer's purpose. Provide reasons that are supported by facts and details. Link opinion and reasons using words and phrases (e.g., for instance, in order to, in addition).	Educators grade culturally and linguistically diverse learners based on reasoning that aligns with the educator's world view, even though the guidelines, including structure, information, and reasoning support the standard.	Educators . . . __________ __________ __________ __________ Equity Indicator: __________ __________ __________ __________

STANDARD	LACKING EQUITY	WITH EQUITY
Provide a concluding statement or section related to the opinion presented.		
Report on a topic or text or present an opinion, sequencing ideas logically and using appropriate facts and relevant, descriptive details to support main ideas or themes; speak clearly at an understandable pace.	Educators grade . . . __________ __________ __________ __________	Educators . . . __________ __________ __________ __________ Equity Indicator: __________ __________ __________ __________
Grades 6–8		
Compare and contrast texts in different forms or genres (e.g., stories and poems; historical novels and fantasy stories) in terms of their approaches to similar themes and topics.	Educators grade on an insufficient variety of genre that may not reflect literature from diverse cultures, where learners' stores of knowledge from their own cultural literature may not connect with the chosen texts.	Educators grade *based on texts from across time, space, and cultures taking particular care to allow learners to reflect on texts that reflect a broad range of racial and cultural diversities.* Equity Indicator: *Impartiality: You consider the cultural lived experience of the learner.*
Use knowledge of language and its conventions when writing, speaking, reading, or listening. A. Choose language that expresses ideas precisely and concisely, recognizing and eliminating wordiness and redundancy.	Educators grade linguistically diverse learners, including those who speak African American English or Chicano English, based on School English conventions without consideration of the conventions of the learner's mother tongue.	Educators consider *the conventions of the learner's home language, including expressive language that conveys meaning in a manner consistent with the home language.* Equity Indicator: *Impartiality: You . . .* __________ __________ __________ __________

(Continued)

(Continued)

STANDARD	LACKING EQUITY	WITH EQUITY
Write informative/ explanatory texts to examine a topic and convey ideas, concepts, and information through the selection, organization, and analysis of relevant content.	Educators grade learners . . . __________ __________ __________ __________	As an educator, I consider . . . __________ __________ __________ __________ Equity Indicator: __________ __________ __________ __________
Identify aspects of a text that reveal an author's point of view or purpose (e.g., loaded language, inclusion or avoidance of particular facts).	Educators grade learners based on the author's point of view as given in the teacher's guidance in the text or the teacher's own perspective.	As an educator, I consider . . . Equity Indicator:
Grades 9–12		
Cite strong and thorough textual evidence to support analysis of what the text says explicitly as well as inferences drawn from the text.	Educators grade culturally diverse learners who may not analyze or draw inferences through the White Western European norm promoted in schools, through that narrow lens. Educators do not allow for inferences that may not match their own expectations.	Educators *accept the inferences drawn by learners, provided learners can make a connection to their culture or lived experience to support their inference.* Equity Indicator: *Impartiality: You consider the diversity of learners' lived experiences to support an alternative viewpoint from which to infer.*
Apply knowledge of language to understand how language functions in different contexts, to make effective choices for meaning or style, and to comprehend more fully when reading or listening.	Educators grade linguistically diverse learners, including those who speak African American English or Chicano English, based on School English conventions without consideration of the functions of language, including their culture's linguistic style and the use of code-switching and translanguaging.	Educators . . . __________ __________ __________ __________

STANDARD	LACKING EQUITY	WITH EQUITY
		Equity Indicator: __________ __________ __________ __________
Analyze the author's purpose in providing an explanation, describing a procedure, or discussing an experiment in a text, identifying important issues that remain unresolved.	Educators grade learners . . . __________ __________ __________ __________	Educators grade learners . . . __________ __________ __________ __________ Equity Indicator: __________ __________ __________ __________
Evaluate an author's premises, claims, and evidence by corroborating or challenging them with other information.	Educators grade learners . . . __________ __________ __________ __________	Educators grade learners . . . __________ __________ __________ __________ Equity Indicator: __________ __________ __________ __________

I've given you a few examples across the elementary, middle, and high school grades, then provided stems or left items blank, for you to conduct the exercise yourself.

SBG With Equity in the Classroom

Properly used, SBG can provide educators, learners, and families a clearer understanding of what learners know and can do. It can pinpoint areas of strength. It can assist us in determining areas requiring additional support and providing it.

Importantly, SBG promotes a growth mindset. When we concentrate on learners developing mastery over time, it fosters an asset-oriented classroom culture. Early mistakes are seen as learning opportunities, not permanent deficits. Learners are given agency, encouraged to view challenges as part of the learning process, leading to increased resilience and motivation.

Finally, SBG should remove many subjective factors discussed in this resource, such as participation, effort, and behavior. It should make the grading process more equitable when combined with an explicit focus on the four equity indicators. When we create this level of clarity, we can reduce ambiguities and potential biases, ensuring that standards-based grades are a true reflection of a learner's proficiency in a subject.

Conclusion

In this chapter, we began our work on equitable grading aligned to step 5 of the CARTI Framework: data-driven decision making. We considered the purpose of grades and the roles they play in various aspects of your learners' academic careers. We examined grading practices through each of the four equity indicators, and looked at equitable grading in a standards-based grading system.

In Chapter 11, we extend the theoretical from this chapter to action: communicating grading. I'll provide you with strategies to communicate with learners at each of the grade spans, as well as with parents and caregivers. You'll get a model for creating a culturally responsive syllabus and guidelines for extending the work through your PLC.

This chapter's reflect and act exercises are designed not only for your personal reflection, but for discussion and collaboration with your colleagues. If you have grade level or departmental sessions to support aligning grading policies, use these prompts to support an open and equity-focused conversation.

Reflect and Act

What is the role of grading in your school or classroom? Is it an assessment of knowledge and skills? Does it motivate your learners? Is there any potential for grade inflation based on the practices and policies you have in place? What adjustments, if any, could you make to make it purely evaluative of learner's knowledge and skills and serve as a motivator?

Reflect on your own grading policies and practices. Consider the elements within them that might be culturally connected more to a White Western European mindset rather than the culturally diverse learners in your classroom. What adjustments could you make to more appropriately connect to the children that you serve?

What are some of the ways that you can provide positive structural inequality in assignments and assessments?

••• MY MINDSET METER

Complete the mindset meter as a self-assessment. Make connections building on what you've learned, your instructional setting, and your lived experience. Analyze. Strategize. Prioritize. Integrate.

Knowledge: The purpose of grading as I understand it from this chapter:

____

____

____

____

Comprehension: The use of standards-based grading with equity as I understand it from this chapter:

____

____

____

____

Application: This is how I can examine my grading practices based on what I learned in this chapter:

____

____

____

____

Analysis: I will prioritize these things in my grading practices:

____

____

____

____

Synthesis: This is how I will use or support equitable grading in my context:

____

____

____

____

Evaluation: I used to think ______ but now I think ______.

____

____

____

____

CHAPTER 11

COMMUNICATING GRADING POLICIES AND PRACTICES WITH PARENTS AND CAREGIVERS

In Chapter 10, we laid the foundation for equitable grading practices. Now, we'll extend that learning to how we communicate grading information to learners, parents, and caregivers. We move from step 5 of the CARTI Framework—data-driven decision making—back to step 1, connecting to cultural awareness (see Figure 11.1). As we go through the cycle of the CARTI framework and its 360-degree feedback loop, continuously examining our practices and our work, we become incrementally better at serving our learners.

Communicating Grading Policies and Practices

Once we've completed a deep examination of our grading policies and practices and made the revisions that are necessary to support our goals of equity, we must communicate our policies and practices effectively to all stakeholders. This communication varies by grade span. So, let's look at how we communicate with learners

Figure 11.1

The CARTI Framework

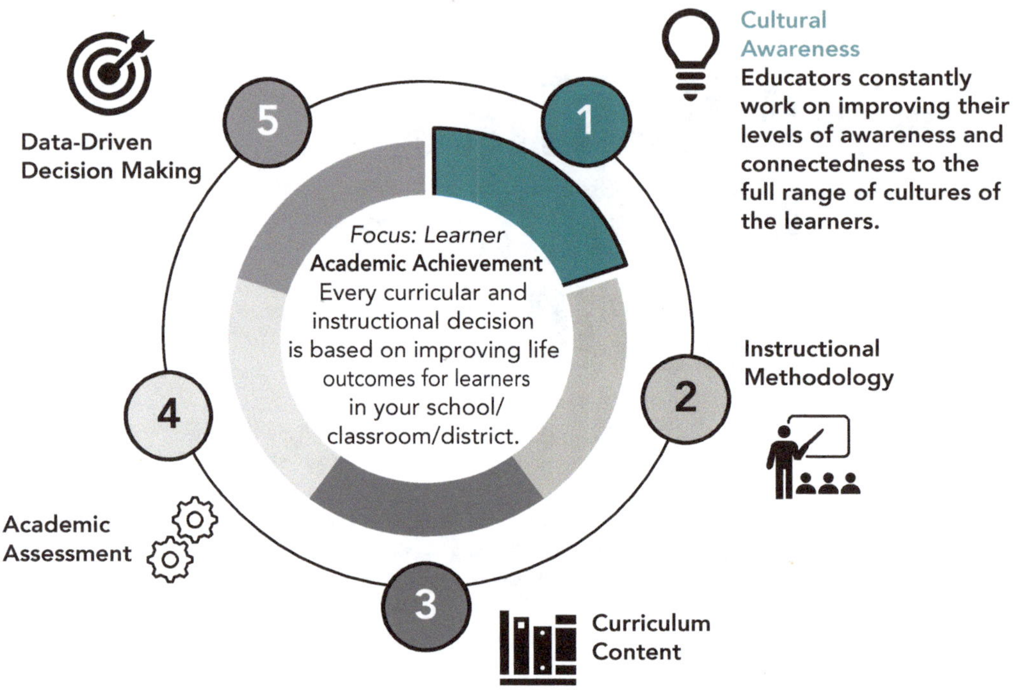

Cultural Awareness
Educators constantly work on improving their levels of awareness and connectedness to the full range of cultures of the learners.

1

Instructional Methodology

2

3

Curriculum Content

4

Academic Assessment

5

Data-Driven Decision Making

Focus: Learner
Academic Achievement
Every curricular and instructional decision is based on improving life outcomes for learners in your school/classroom/district.

in four grade spans, as well as how we might communicate with families and caregivers.

COMMUNICATING WITH EARLY LEARNERS (PK–GRADE 2)

Communicating grading policies and practices to early learners requires using simple concepts and age-appropriate language and examples. Here are several practices for your classroom communication.

First, we want to make sure that we use simple and clear language. Avoid using educational jargon; young children do not come into prekindergarten or kindergarten understanding grades or how they are determined. Most are happy with a smiley face on their paper. But in instances and systems where a letter grade is required, consider telling your learners that a grade is like a special note that shows how well they are understanding what they are learning. Connect it to a game that you play in the classroom or out at recess where the grade that you give is like finding out how well we did in the game. Whether you use letter grades or other symbols such as check marks or plus signs, you need to show children the marks that indicate they have learned the material or skills and did a good job. We also need to explain symbols we use to indicate that children need to practice skills to do better. Tell them that it's OK to not get the best marks all the time, and that the most important thing about grades is that they are trying their best and that they are learning and having fun.

We want to use visuals. Young learners understand visual representation better than verbal explanation. Use charts, posters, and other visual aids to show what the marks mean. For example, you might use a color-coded chart that shows levels of progress and achievement.

Next, you'll want to make connections to concrete examples that children already know. While behavior should never be reflected in grades, we provide instruction for young learners on how to behave in the classroom, for example, cleaning up after an activity. If stickers are awarded for completing that task, you can equate a high grade to the sticker that students receive for good behaviors.

Make sure that your early learners understand the difference between effort and improvement and that they are both important. Young learners are developing agency and self-efficacy. Teach them that making mistakes is part of the learning process and that trying their best is very important. Model how to respond to a mistake. When you make a mistake, call it out, and correct it, making the connection of you correcting your error to them correcting their work. You can even make an error on purpose as an example and wait for your students to identify your error. Make a production of how to correct your mistake.

Discuss the purpose of grading with your early learners. Talk about how grades help everyone—you, children, parents, and caregivers—know their areas of growth and what they need to work on. Make sure your early learners understand that grades are not about comparing them to their classmates. Let them know that grades are for their own information about what to work on.

Early learners can be sensitive to criticism. Negative feedback can harm their self-esteem. Reinforce the idea that grades are not a measure of their worth or their value, but a tool to help them learn and grow, just like a pencil is a tool for them to write on paper.

Remember, it's OK if young learners do not fully understand the concept of grades. At this age, especially at the pre-kindergarten and kindergarten levels, we want to focus on fostering a love of learning, rather than emphasize performance and outcomes.

COMMUNICATING WITH MIDDLE CHILDHOOD LEARNERS (GRADES 3–5)

Communicating your grading policies with middle childhood learners requires a clear and straightforward approach. At this age and stage, learners are typically able to understand more complex concepts. They can take greater responsibility for their learning, and you can facilitate that by doing the following.

In the first days of the school year, have a discussion about grades. Ask your learners what they think grades are and why they think that they're important. Use their responses as a starting point to clarify misconceptions and to introduce your grading policy.

As with young learners, you'll want to use clear, age-appropriate language that is suitable for learners' comprehension level. Even at grade 5, avoid using education jargon. Explain key terms clearly, and check for understanding.

Whether you're using letter grades, numerical grades, rubrics, or some other system, clearly define the grading scale and what each grade represents. Explain what you will be grading and how you will grade it. For example, tests, homework, projects, and so on. Give learners clear, concrete examples of what constitutes acceptable and undeveloped work. Remember that class participation is culturally sensitive. Think carefully and clearly about whether you will grade class participation. If you do grade class participation, be aware of the cultural differences in your classroom and create a culture that supports participation.

Highlight the importance of effort and progress for these learners. Make sure they understand that grades are just one measure, not the only measure of success. Students are still building agency and a belief in themselves. Emphasize the value of consistent effort, improvement, and learning from mistakes. Along those lines, consider developing a policy for correcting and resubmitting work for a grade.

Consider using charts or posters showing your grading policy. Make sure that they are clearly visible in your classroom. Depending on the age of learners, you can provide handouts with the grading policy.

Create an environment where students are encouraged to ask questions to clarify points they don't understand during class discussions or while completing assignments. Keep channels for feedback open and regularly check to make sure your learners understand the grading process and policies.

In the first days of school, send home information explaining your grading policy to parents and caregivers. Offer suggestions for how they can talk about grades with their children. And on back-to-school night, be prepared to provide information to your parents and caregivers again. Make sure that in those first few weeks of school, parents and caregivers have received feedback on their children's work and have had an opportunity to see your policy in action, especially for learners who may have needed to revise and resubmit work.

Finally, revisit and explain grading policies at regular intervals throughout the year. As learners complete, revise, and resubmit one or more assignments, they may have questions or require clarification on grading. Address any questions or concerns that your learners may have developed over time. Creating a supportive and transparent grading environment contributes to better learning outcomes and reduced anxiety related to grades. Aim to use grades as a tool for growth and development for learners, not just an assessment of knowledge.

COMMUNICATING WITH ADOLESCENT LEARNERS (GRADES 6–8)

Adolescent learners are typically transitioning to more independent learning. Communicating the grading policy is crucial. Adolescent learners should have key terms defined, the grading scale explained, and know exactly what work will be graded. In a departmentalized middle school where learners may see six to eight instructors in any day, a syllabus is helpful. This is particularly true if the school does not have a universal grading policy.

If you use a syllabus, spend time going through it with learners. Discuss your expectations and criteria as they are spelled out in your syllabus. Explain how you will grade assignments, projects, tests, participation, and so on. Students may benefit from exemplars that show A-level work compared to C-level work. If you use rubrics, provide them to students and review them using exemplars so students have a clear understanding of how their work will be graded against the rubrics. Keep in mind that participation grades are culturally sensitive.

These students have likely had sufficient experiences with grades to have a sense of their purpose. However, explain the purpose of grades in your classroom. Make sure that your grades and your explanation of them reflect the learner's understanding and mastery of the content. Remind learners that grades are not a measure of their worth, but rather a tool to help them to learn and grow.

At this level, students typically see grades as something important. You'll want to stress the importance of the learning process, continuous effort, and improvement. Discuss your policy about learning from mistakes, and revising and resubmitting work without penalty.

Adolescent learners may be starting to think about high school, college, and career. This is a good opportunity for you to discuss how their grades in middle school set the stage for their future academic achievement. At the same time, you'll want to reassure them that one low grade is not a determinant of their future. This is a time for them to develop behaviors that will carry them through their high school career.

Even if you provide a syllabus, consider using additional tools, visual aids, verbal explanations, and written policies. Keep extra copies of the syllabus available so that students may retrieve one at any time. Though we might wish students would keep an informational packet throughout the entire semester, the reality is that things get misplaced. Be considerate of your students' home experiences and provide opportunities for them to retrieve information as needed.

Adolescents are capable of deep understanding and often have more complex questions. Create a classroom environment, a culture, that encourages your learners to ask questions, voice concerns, and even give feedback on your grading policy. Though parent and caregiver engagement tend to wane during these grades, send home your syllabus and your grading policy, and discuss it during parent meetings and back-to-school night. Your policy should be posted on the class web page or online system used to communicate with parents. Make sure parents and caregivers are informed and can support their child's understanding at home.

To ensure understanding and compliance, regularly revisit your grading policies during class meetings or other opportunities, addressing any confusion or concerns. Transparency, fairness, and understanding are key when you're discussing grading policies with adolescent learners. You have a tremendous opportunity to lead them to increased accountability, motivation, and academic success.

COMMUNICATING WITH YOUNG ADULT LEARNERS (GRADES 9–12)

Communicating grading policies with young adult learners requires a clear and thorough approach. This is a time of increased academic demands with potential implications for college, military, and careers beyond high school. At this level, a syllabus is typically used. It should include a comprehensive explanation of your grading policy. On the first day of school, discuss types of assignments, your grading scale, and the grading scheme. Be prepared to explain your use of norm-referenced grading, grade averages, or zero-based grading. Remember that some types of grading schemes disproportionately affect students of cultural and linguistic diversity. And keep in mind that at this age, some students must work in order to survive. If your attendance policy impacts learners' grades, students who must work may disengage from your class because of that policy. It is equally important to consider your policy on class participation, and on late and resubmitted work.

Your syllabus should discuss criteria and expectations and should explain the purpose of grades in your class. Throughout the semester, clearly state the expectations for each assignment or assessment. Where it's possible use rubrics, and provide exemplars of high-quality and low-quality work. Routinely check for comprehension of your policy toward revised and resubmitted work. If the purpose of grades is to reflect students' understanding, progress, and areas for improvement, then revision and resubmission should not be penalized. Create a class culture that highlights the importance of consistent effort and learning. Explain that future employers will not necessarily expect perfection, but they will expect students to give their best effort, to improve over time, and to always be learning.

You also have the opportunity to discuss how grades in high school impact students' future opportunities such as college admissions, scholarships, entry into the military, or job prospects. And in a world where young adults are often given adult responsibilities, and where peer pressure and social media too frequently drive students to self-harm, you cannot emphasize enough that grades are not the sole determinants of their future success.

If you use a syllabus, consider using additional tools, visual aids, verbal explanations, and written policies. Post the syllabus in the classroom, so that students may refer to it at any time. Keep extras on hand for those who may need an additional printed copy. Be considerate of your learners' lived experiences by providing opportunities for them to retrieve information as needed.

Regularly revisit your grading policies to ensure understanding and compliance. Encourage questions and have conversations. Allow your learners to voice any concerns or confusion regarding your grading policy. Don't think of this as criticism, but instead as learners taking agency in their education. Address concerns that may arise.

And while high school students are more independent, and many parents and caregivers seem to have less involvement, it is your responsibility to keep them in the loop. Post the syllabus and grading policy to your classroom web page or make them available for download to ensure parents and caregivers have access to the information. We may be skeptical as to whether copies sent home will ever make it; send them anyway. Then, plan to discuss your grading policy during back-to-school night and parent meetings.

At this last stage of their compulsory education, learners should be encouraged to take ownership of their performance. Understanding your policies and practices can help them to strategize their efforts, and lead to better performance and reduce stress.

Communicating With Families and Caregivers

Communicating your grading policies with parents and caregivers from culturally diverse communities can be challenging due to cultural differences and language barriers. It may be that the learners themselves are serving as translators. It could be that parents' educational expectations or unfamiliarity with the educational environment in the United States create a new and unique barrier. Still, ensuring equitable access means it is critical for parents and caregivers to receive information about your policies.

We cannot make assumptions about the academic knowledge of parents and caregivers. So when explaining grading policies, avoid educational jargon. Use language that is easy for the layperson to understand. Make sure that your policy details are concise, direct, and straightforward.

If your school is in a community where diversity of languages is common, providing translated versions of your policies is helpful. If your school does not provide resources for translation, use an online translation service. While it may not be perfect, the gist of your policy and procedure should still be conveyed. But do not assume that parents can read the languages that they speak. If you send home a policy translated from English, also send the English version.

Visual aids often transcend language barriers. Consider using diagrams, charts, or other visual aids to explain how grades are determined in your school or classroom.

If you are a school leader, consider holding information sessions. Arrange meetings or workshops where instructors can explain the grading system in your school. Have interpreters available. Allow time for socialization so that parents and caregivers can speak with others from in the community, and also provide an opportunity to ask questions and gain a better understanding of the educational system.

As a school leader, you can also connect with cultural community groups. Create partnerships to help bridge the gap between your school and its diverse families. Community groups can often provide insight into cultural nuances, and support more effective communication with different cultural groups. For some, written communication may be preferred. With others, digital communication such as emails or website updates are best. Some cultures value face-to-face communication over print or digital.

And whether you are a school leader or classroom educator, always empower parents and caregivers. Do your best to provide resources and tools to help them assist their children and understand your policies and expectations (see Table 11.1). When parents and caregivers understand the system, they are better equipped to support their child's learning. And then in all communication, be respectful of cultural differences. Be patient. The goal is to ensure that all parents and caregivers, regardless of their cultural backgrounds, can support their child's academic journey effectively.

Table 11.1

What Communication Should Look Like

COMMUNICATION LOOKS LIKE THIS . . .	IT *DOES NOT* LOOK LIKE THIS . . .
Language is age-appropriate.	Language is overly academic or uses acronyms not readily understood by the population at large.
Language is simple, clear, and consistent. *Excellent work showing how well you understand fractions!*	Language is complex, vague, or inconsistent: *Your prodigious endeavor in delineating the intricacies of fractional concepts manifestly elucidates an advanced epistemological grasp, redolent of nuanced pedagogical assimilation.*

(Continued)

(Continued)

COMMUNICATION LOOKS LIKE THIS . . .	IT *DOES NOT* LOOK LIKE THIS . . .
To support emergent bilingual learners, parents, and caregivers who may not have high levels of School English literacy, diagrams, charts, or other visual aids are used to explain how grades are determined in your school or classroom.	Communication is text-heavy and relies on complex text.
Grading scales and schemes are clearly defined, presented, and available for examination by students, parents, and caregivers.	Grading scales and schemes vary depending on the assignments. Learners, parents, and caregivers do not have ready access to information about scales and schemes or are not afforded an overview and instruction on your process or rationale.
Grading policies are reviewed on a regular basis throughout the year.	Grading is not open for discussion, nor reviewed at the request of learners, parents, or caregivers.
Syllabi are used beginning at the middle grades and continuing through high school. See the model syllabus outline that follows.	Syllabi are not used or are vague.

Model Syllabus Outline

A syllabus is a crucial document that outlines the structure, content, and expectations of your course or class (if self-contained). While the specific details of a syllabus vary based on the level and subject, the following elements are usually included:

SECTION 1—Course Information

- Course title, grade level
- Instructor's name and contact information (email, phone, text)
- Classroom location
- Semester or term dates

SECTION 2—Course Description

- A brief overview of the course content, goals, and objectives
- Prerequisites, if applicable

SECTION 3—Learning Outcomes

- Clear and measurable objectives that describe what students are expected to learn and achieve by the end of the course

SECTION 4—Required Texts and Materials

- List of required texts, readings, and any other necessary materials
- Access information for online resources such as learning management system and third-party websites
- Access and availability information for any additional out-of-classroom resources (computer lab, library, etc.)

SECTION 5—Course Schedule

- Weekly breakdown of topics, chapters, or units to be covered
- Important dates for quizzes, tests, projects, and assignments
- Important dates for field trips, guest speakers, or special events

SECTION 6—Assessment and Grading

- Explanation of how students will be assessed and how grades will be determined
- Breakdown of grading components or categories (homework, quizzes, exams, projects, etc.)
- Weight of categories or assignments, exams, projects, participation, etc.
- Grading scale and criteria for each grade (e.g., A, B, C)
- Information about late submissions, post-feedback revisions, and other grading policies

SECTION 7—Assignments and Projects

- Detailed descriptions of assignments, projects, papers, or presentations
- Instructions, resources, rubrics, and due dates
- Guidelines for formatting, citations, submission procedures

SECTION 8—Class Policies

- Attendance expectations and policies
- Late work and make-up policies and procedures
- Academic integrity and plagiarism policy
- Use of electronic devices during class
- Classroom behavior and etiquette expectations
- Policy on disruptive behavior

SECTION 9—Communication

- Methods of communication (email, school messaging platform, etc.)
- Response time for student or parent/caregiver inquiries (how soon they need to request support, how quickly you will respond)
- How and when parents or caregivers will receive progress reports

(Continued)

(Continued)

SECTION 10—Resources and Support

- Information about available resources, such as tutoring services, library services, computer labs, writing centers, and online platforms
- Your availability for additional support (before- or after-school office hours)
- Any additional support for struggling learners or those with learning exceptionalities

SECTION 11—Course-Specific Policies

- Any policies unique to the subject matter or class format (e.g., lab safety, art supply care)

SECTION 12—Expectations for Growth and Improvement

- Guidance on how students can seek improvement throughout the course
- Suggestions for effective study habits and time management

SECTION 13—Disclaimers

- A statement indicating that the syllabus is subject to change based on class needs and unforeseen circumstances
- A statement indicating that the syllabus information does not supersede any school or district policy as outlined in the student handbook or code of conduct

It's important to make certain that your syllabus is clear, organized, and easy to understand. A well-constructed syllabus sets the tone for the course, supports the culture of your classroom, helps manage student expectations, and provides a roadmap for successful learning!

Conclusion

In this chapter, we returned to step 1 of the CARTI framework—cultural awareness—and applied it to the process of communicating our grading policies and practices to learners, parents, and caregivers. We explored action steps for communication at different grade spans, and considered what culturally responsive communication of grading practices does and does not look like.

In Chapter 12, we once again move from theory to practice, from foundation to action. You'll be working through nine tasks, step-by-step, to implement equitable grading in your context. So, make sure you've got plenty of pages in your journal, and gather your sticky notes, colored flags, markers, and highlighters!

But first, take the time to complete this chapter's reflect and act exercises and the mindset meter.

Reflect and Act

Reflect on your past communications with parents and caregivers. How will your future communication shift based on your learning here?

Reflect on your grading practices over the past few years. What percentage of a student's grade has been based on something that might be cultural? Consider items like timeliness, neatness, perspective, and viewpoint.

If you are a middle or high school educator, consider using the outline in this chapter to revise your course syllabus. Or, if you have not previously used a course syllabus, create one for a course you teach. Use the outline provided as a starting point.

●●● MY MINDSET METER

Complete the mindset meter as a self-assessment. Make connections building on what you've learned, your instructional setting, and your lived experience. Analyze. Strategize. Prioritize. Integrate.

Knowledge: The purpose of communicating with parents and caregivers about grading as I understand it from this chapter:

____

____

____

____

Comprehension: This is why it is important to explain grading policies to learners in the grades I work with:

____

____

____

____

Application: This is how I will communicate my grading practices based on new learning from this chapter:

Analysis: I will examine my communication practices through this lens:

Synthesis: This is how I will modify my syllabus or parent/caregiver grading policies letter:

Evaluation: I used to think ______ but now I think ______.

IMPLEMENTING EQUITABLE GRADING

CHAPTER 12

In Chapter 10 we established the foundations of equitable grading, examining grading practices through the lenses of the four equity indicators. In Chapter 11, we focused on communicating our practices and policies with learners, parents, and caregivers.

In this chapter we work toward implementing equitable grading in your classroom, for your grade, your subject matter, and your learners. We move from foundation to implementation, from understanding to action. It's time to take all that we've been learning and put it into practice in your setting.

This chapter guides you through nine specific tasks. You'll begin by identifying where you are now in terms of the purpose of grades in your setting. From there you'll continue through the remaining tasks from identification, to implementation, to assessment, where you'll refine the baseline rubrics I've developed to reflect your own needs and context.

This chapter invites you into participatory, task-oriented work. So, gather your journal, pencils, pens, highlighters, and sticky notes—real or digital—and let's get started!

Shifting From My Old Way to an Equitable Way

To move from where you are to an equitable, or more equitable, grading system, you first need to define precisely where you are. For simplicity's sake, I use the term *setting*. Your setting may be your classroom, your subject-area department, your grade-level cohort, your school, your district, your county, or state. Focus on your setting. Here is our mantra for this work: *"Don't worry about the things you cannot change. Change the things you can no longer accept."*

The tasks are designed so you can work on them independently or with a group. If you are working with a group, ensure that you have created a psychologically safe space. Refer to Chapter 2 if you need a refresher (refer to the heading: From the First Day of School Forward: Establishing and Maintaining a Safe and Inclusive Classroom Culture). Psychological safety is necessary to do this work with your peers in a PLC. Everyone in the group must feel safe to contribute and to challenge.

Whether you're working solo or with a group: Be brutally honest. Speak your truth. Challenge the status quo.

For each of these elements, think independently. What do *you* believe? Then, if you are working with a group, discuss it. Come to a consensus and develop a response that honors the most brutal of all responses.

TASK 1. IDENTIFYING THE CURRENT PURPOSE OF GRADES IN YOUR SETTING

A. In your setting, what is the current role of grades in evaluating learners' knowledge and skills?

B. In your setting, what is the current role of grades in motivating learners?

C. In your setting, what roles are grades serving in college admission? Is this true for culturally diverse and marginalized learners as well?

TASK 2. IDENTIFYING THE DESIRED PURPOSE OF GRADES IN YOUR SETTING

A. In your setting, what is the desired role of grades in equitably evaluating learners' knowledge and skills?

B. In your setting, what is the desired role of grades in equitably motivating learners?

C. In your setting, what is the desired role of grades in college admissions, particularly for the culturally diverse and most marginalized learners?

TASK 3. IDENTIFYING THE NECESSARY SHIFTS

Now that you've identified where you are and where you'd like to be, let's identify the changes, or shifts, that must occur to get to your desired state of equity.

For each of the items in task 2, complete this sentence frame:

- *To/For ______ to ______, ______ must ______.*

Here's an example:

- *To have grades equitably motivate my underperforming learners of color, I must develop among those learners a higher awareness of opportunities that will be available to them because of higher grades. The opportunities must resonate with those learners.*

You may have only one shift per item. You may have ten. Write them in your journal. This all depends on your setting, your current state, and your desired state. You may identify items that you feel are beyond your span of control. Write them anyway. Even if you cannot control those shifts, it is important to recognize them.

These shifts are *who* and *what* items. *Who* needs to shift? *What* needs to shift?

TASK 4. PRIORITIZE YOUR NEEDS

Now that you have identified the needed shifts, let's work toward the *how*. How do you turn needed shifts into action items? First, you prioritize.

But much like the proverb about eating an elephant, the only way to tackle the number of shifts you identified may be one at a time. It will take time. And it is likely that all shifts are not of equal importance, nor can they feasibly be addressed all at the same time. So, let's begin our first sub-task, simplification.

Simplify

I refer to this task of simplification as *naming the thing*; really, it's a simple matter of settling on an abbreviated term, a big bucket, for one or more similar shifts. Let's say you have three or four shifts that all have to do with developing higher awareness among various groups of marginalized learners. You might not need to work on the four separately. Put them all in one bucket. You might name this bucket *creating awareness among learners.* This is a *big shift.*

Naming the thing helps to create one clear, concise descriptor of several very closely related shifts. Just make sure that it will be easily understood by all who will be impacted by this work, or anyone you may share the work with.

You may also find that some shifts fit into more than one bucket. That's okay! Don't worry about everything being nice and tidy. Sometimes, this work gets messy.

What are your things?

Once you've created your big buckets, put each on a separate piece of paper (hard copy or digital) before moving on to the next step (Figure 12.1). Then, arrange you work so that you can see everything all at the same time as you continue to the next step. Digital apps such as Padlet and Trello might make this simpler, and facilitate collaboration. Do what works best for you.

Figure 12.1

Creating Buckets

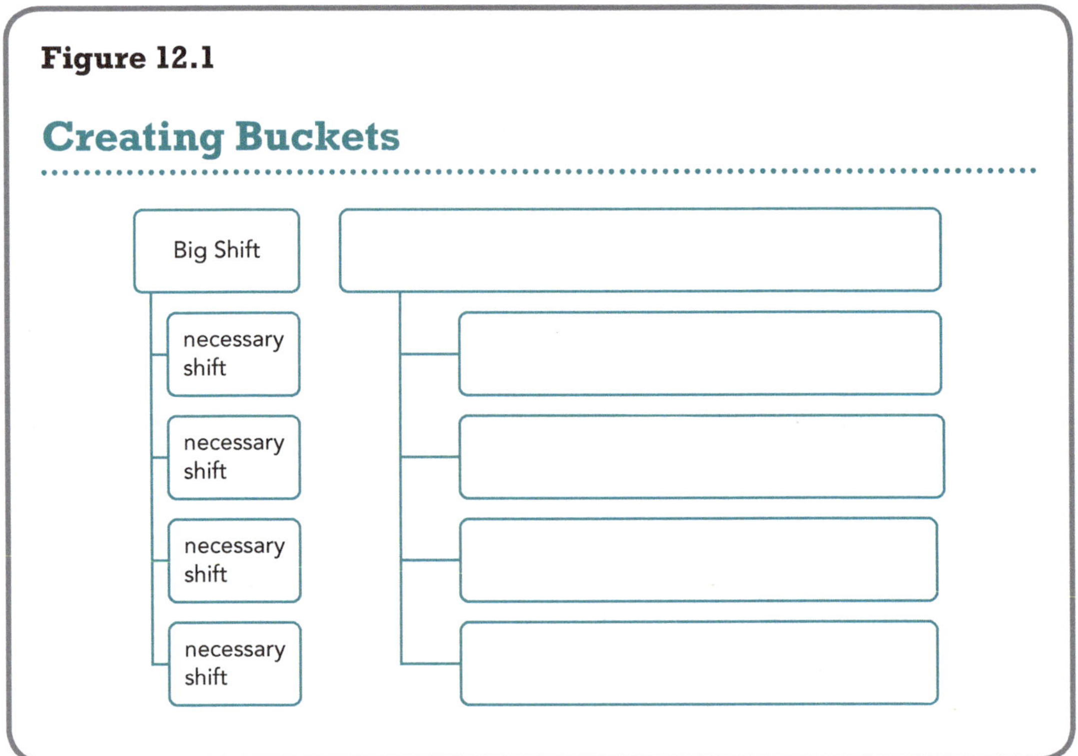

I recognize this may seem to be a bit of an arduous task. But if I were in the room with you, conducting this as a live workshop, this is precisely how we'd do it. There is a reason for this. So, take your time. It's more important to get it right than to finish it fast.

Analyze

The second task is to analyze each item to determine which will have the most significant positive impact on learner achievement and equity. You'll do this by asking and answering four questions for each of the buckets you've named (see Figure 12.2). If you are working with a group, it's best to do this in "gallery walk" format, going from one item to the next, asking each of the impact questions and making notations directly on the charts. Discuss each and mark up your charts as you go.

Figure 12.2

Sample Big Bucket Chart After Simplifying

CREATING AWARENESS
AMONG LEARNERS

Shift 1: To have grades equitable motivate our underperforming learners of color, we must develop a higher awareness among those learners to opportunities that will be made available to them because of higher grades. Those opportunities must resonate with those learners.

Shift 2: Your second necessary shift

Shift 3: Your third necessary shift

These are the questions you'll ask and answer.

1. To what extent will working on this contribute to equity within the next year? Over the next 2–3 years? Longer?
2. Does this require immediate attention, or will it be resolved over time and with the implementation of higher priority action items?
3. How big is the gap between my current state and my desired state?
4. To what extent would prioritizing this shift have a positive impact in other areas?

Those four questions focus on the impact of addressing each big shift. That is, how much each change in policy, practice, or mindset will move the needle toward implementing truly equitable grading.

What are your unanswered questions or concerns? What thoughts are you having that trouble you?

Evaluate

Our third sub-task is to evaluate the feasibility, or probability, of successfully making the shifts you've identified as your big buckets (see Figure 12.3). Just as above, work on one item at a time. Discuss these questions for each big shift. Remember our mantra, "Don't worry about the things you cannot change. Change the things you can no longer accept."

Figure 12.3

Sample Big Bucket Chart After Analyzing

CREATING AWARENESS AMONG LEARNERS

Shift 1: To have grades equitable motivate our underperforming learners of color, we must develop a higher awareness among those learners to opportunities that will be made available to them because of higher grades. Those opportunities must resonate with those learners.

Shift 2: Your second necessary shift

Shift 3: Your third necessary shift

ANALYZE

1. A lot for next year! Especially if we start this spring.
2. Immediate attention.
3. The gap is biggest for our students coming from the housing project and our newcomers who are refugees.
4. Should increase engagement in school. Should help with building relationships and understanding between students and faculty.

Next, consider:

- *Is it likely that focusing on this shift will contribute to reducing or eliminating the inequity I intend to address?*
- *Is it likely that the people in or connected to my setting will support and embrace this shift?*

Prioritizing your shifts in this manner helps to determine which items have achievable action steps based on the current climate surrounding your setting. When you consider the feasibility of each shift, you'll also likely determine what work on shifting mindsets will be needed to move forward effectively (see Figure 12.4). Do you have colleagues, supervisors, learners, or parents and caregivers who will need convincing that this shift is beneficial to your learners' life outcomes?

Figure 12.4

Sample Big Bucket Chart After Evaluating

CREATING AWARENESS AMONG LEARNERS

Shift 1: To have grades equitable motivate our underperforming learners of color, we must develop a higher awareness among those learners to opportunities that will be made available to them because of higher grades. Those opportunities must resonate with those learners.

Shift 2: Your second necessary shift

Shift 3: Your third necessary shift

ANALYZE

1. A lot for next year! Especially if we start this spring.
2. Immediate attention
3. The gap is biggest for our students coming from the housing project and our newcomers who are refugees.
4. Should increase engagement in school. Should help with building relationships and understanding between students and faculty.

EVALUATE

1. YES!!!
2. Not sure. Faculty curmudgeons

Score

The fourth task of this screening process is to examine each of your named items through the lens of four equity indicators (see Figure 12.5). For the four indicators, give each priority a numeric score of one to five. See Figure 12.6 for descriptions of each numeric score.

Figure 12.5

Sample Big Bucket Chart With Scoring Chart

CREATING AWARENESS AMONG LEARNERS

Shift 1: To have grades equitable motivate our underperforming learners of color, we must develop a higher awareness among those learners to opportunities that will be made available to them because of higher grades. Those opportunities must resonate with those learners.

Shift 2: Your second necessary shift

Shift 3: Your third necessary shift

ANALYZE

1. A lot for next year! Especially if we start this spring.
2. Immediate attention
3. The gap is biggest for our students coming from the housing project and our newcomers who are refugees.
4. Should increase engagement in school. Should help with building relationships and understanding between students and faculty.

EVALUATE

1. YES!!!
2. Not sure. Faculty curmudgeons

SCORE

Meritocracy	Standards	Impartiality	Asset Allocation	Total

The most efficient way to do this is to evaluate all big shifts on just one indicator at a time. For example, evaluate all shifts on meritocracy. Using the exemplar we've been working with, I'd ask the question:

- *How well does "creating awareness among learners" address who has the power in terms of grading, and will the power then be used for the good of the marginalized in our school community?*

You may need to refer to Chapter 10 (beginning at the Examining Grading Practices Through the Lens of Equity section) to review the four equity indicators as applied to grading and the questions to ask of each.

Scoring requires some deep thinking. Give yourself time to reflect on each indicator and genuinely assess how each of your big shifts potentially addresses that indicator. Once you've settled on an appropriate score, write that number in your score chart (Table 12.1).

Table 12.1

Scoring Rubric

NUMERIC SCORE	DESCRIPTION
1	It is extremely improbable that this big shift will support this indicator, as there are significant barriers and obstacles in place.
2	While there is a chance that this big shift may support this indicator to some extent, it faces significant challenges and limitations.
3	There is a moderate likelihood that this big shift will support this indicator, with potential for success if appropriate strategies and resources are applied.
4	There is a good chance that this big shift will effectively support this indicator, with a strong potential for success if implemented with care and commitment.
5	It is very probable that this big shift will effectively support this indicator, as it can be well-designed and supported by robust strategies and resources.

Once you've scored the four indicators, total the amount for each big shift. You will have a numeric value between four and twenty. This is the fun part, or at least the clarity point. Place your "big shift" pages in order from highest to lowest value. If you're using a digital tool or app, number the screens. This will show your ranked priorities. Now record the big shifts in priority order in your journal.

Review your results. Start with your most highly scored shift and work your way down. You may have several tie scores you need to break.

TASK 5. DEVELOPING YOUR EQUITABLE GRADING POLICY

Can't I just draft a policy and implement?

You could, but there's a chance that your implementation may fail. And we don't want that to happen. While your setting may provide you tremendous autonomy, the work you do every day impacts others in and outside of your professional space.

Thinking about the human connections to your setting helps frame the culture that must be put into place to support an equitable grading system. For this task, we'll examine your current grading policy through the lens of the four equity indicators, then craft a new policy that is reflective of a transformative setting, one that is consciously competent, and compliments the culture that you seek. Record your responses to the questions below in your journal.

Let's start with where you currently are. What is the policy around grades and grading that impact your setting? If there is no policy, write that down.

Does the policy meet the criteria of meritocracy? Does the policy ensure that those holding the power over grades and grading are accountable for using that power for the good of all, and particularly the marginalized, without bias against those who may not be marginalized? Explain how it does or does not.

Does the policy meet the criteria of standards? When it comes to grading practices, does the policy ensure that there is a universal standard that clearly defines both the high bar and the minimum proficiency? Does it ensure that what is taught and how it is taught is determined by what is required for each learner to meet that minimum level of proficiency? Does it ensure that there is transparency and consistency across all classrooms? Explain how it does or does not.

Does the policy meet the criteria of impartiality? When it comes to grades and grading, does the policy ensure that educators are not harming learners by subliminally grading them against their lived experiences, their race, their culture, or their language? Explain how it does or does not.

Does the policy meet the criteria of asset allocation? When it comes to grades and grading, does the policy ensure that positive structural inequality exists to eliminate grading disproportionality and achievement gaps?

Reflect on your responses. Your next task is to develop a policy, a practice, of equitable grading. You might begin with the template in Figure 12.6. It contains eight sections that should appear in

Figure 12.6

Grading Policy Template Working Draft

SECTION	MERITOCRACY	STANDARDS	IMPARTIALITY	ASSET ALLOCATION
Grading Scale				
Category Weights				
Late Work				
Redos and Retakes				
Academic Integrity				
Extra Credit				
Feedback and Communication				
Special Accommodations				

your final document. You may add others that are specific to your setting. For each section, write what you want your policy or practice to say to meet the criteria of each equity indicator.

For example, what do you want to say to meet the criteria of standards in the section on grading scale? What will ensure there is a standard that clearly defines both the high bar and the minimum proficiency? What will ensure that there is transparency and consistency in your setting? As you work through the template, consider where and whether to consider the elements in Figure 12.7.

Figure 12.7

Additional Elements for the Policy Template

ELEMENT	CONSIDER OR EXCLUDE?	SECTION IT BELONGS IN	NOTES
Mastery-based assessment			
Formative vs. summative assessments *Will these be factored differently How?*			
Grade Floor *e.g., No grade below 50%*			
Zeros *Can a zero be a final grade or will incompletes be assigned to allow for a make-up?*			
Group Work *How will individuals be graded on group assignments?*			

ELEMENT	CONSIDER OR EXCLUDE?	SECTION IT BELONGS IN	NOTES
Participation *How will participation be assessed? What weight will it carry?*			
Extra Support *What opportunities will there be for learners to receive additional support or tutoring?*			
Homework *What is the purpose of homework and its weight in an overall grade?*			
Grading Periods *What is the cut-off date for submitting assignments in each term?*			
Process for Disputing Grades *Offer a clear, consistent process for learners or parents/caregivers to appeal a grade.*			
Accessibility *Identify the formats and languages in which the policy will be made available.*			

This is another heavy lift. Take your time. Again, it is better to get it right than to finish it quickly.

Now that you've determined what equity looks like for your grading policy, let's distill the information down to a single sentence or two for each component. Consider your audience as your write. The language should be accessible to your colleagues, parents, caregivers, and depending on the grade levels you are working with, the learners. I recommend writing a version for your colleagues first; then create a simplified version for your learners, or for those of you working in lower grades, a version for their families (Figure 12.8).

Figure 12.8

Grading Policy Template for Learners, Parents, and Caregivers

SECTION	
Grading Scale	
Category Weights	
Late Work	
Redos and Retakes	
Academic Integrity	
Extra Credit	

SECTION	
Feedback and Communication	
Special Accommodations	

Now, let's turn to the next three tasks. These will give you the strategies needed to ensure your plans are carried out and your goals are met.

TASK 6. MEASURE YOUR PROGRESS

You've identified your shifts. You've named "the thing," and you've set priorities. If it's been some time since you completed the first part of this chapter, you may want to take a moment or two to review, reflect, and make sure that your shifts are in alignment with your policies. Make any needed adjustments.

To measure progress, you'll find your baseline and determine what interval assessments will help you measure whether you are on track or not.

The essential questions here are:

- *Where am I now?*
- *Where do I need to end up?*
- *When do I need to get there?*
- *What do I need in order to arrive on time?*

The answers to those questions will help you develop your SMART goal and key performance indicator(s) (KPIs). Remember to consider how will you measure for progress. What is your KPI? How frequently will you measure? (Refer to Chapter 3 if you need a refresher.) You may have more than one SMART goal. Write your SMART goal(s) in your journal.

TASK 7. SELF-ASSESS

Many of the strategies used in the classroom for learners to self-assess their progress can be tailored to serve the purpose of self-assessing your implementation.

Self-Assessment Rubric

Regular self-evaluation using a well-designed rubric can pinpoint areas of strength as well as those requiring further attention. These are your "glows" and your "grows." The rubric can serve as a tool to assess your adherence to your equity-based grading implementation.

The rubric template in Figure 12.9 aligns with the Pathway to Cultural Competence you studied in Chapter 3. Since adoption of the practices and the shifts you desire is rooted in behavior, you must look at each criterion through a behavioral framework. The information from honest self-assessment will help you identify supports and resources you may need to achieve your equitable grading goals.

Unlike a grading rubric, the idea here is to determine where one lies along the Pathway and develop a plan to shift further toward, or stay in, the growth zone. Complete the sentence stems with an eye toward supports and resources. Refer to the culturally relevant rubrics in Appendix J to help frame your thinking. As you complete your rubric, think about additional criteria you might want to assess and include those in the first column.

Figure 12.9

Self-Assessment Rubric for Educators

	THE FEAR ZONE		THE LEARNING ZONE	THE GROWTH ZONE
	Unconsciously Incompetent Ignorant of the value of cultural diversity, enjoying of privilege, engaging in destructive behaviors (demonization, oppression)	**Unconsciously Competent** Aware of your cultural ignorance and incompetence, but may be open to professional learning and personal development	**Consciously Incompetent** Aware of cultural differences and learning to respectfully navigate multiple diverse cultural settings; recognize what you don't know	**Consciously Competent** Respect, value, and affirm cultural differences; welcomed in culturally diverse spaces; can communicate your knowledge and instruct others
Bias Awareness and Mitigation Understanding the extent to which my own personal biases (implicit or explicit) influence grading; taking the steps to mitigate these biases when grading.	**To improve my practice** __________ __________ __________ __________ __________ __________	**To become more aware** __________ __________ __________ __________ __________ __________	**To further excel** __________ __________ __________ __________ __________ __________	**To help others grow** __________ __________ __________ __________ __________ __________
Cultural Relevance and Responsiveness The degree to which grading policies and practices honor and value the diverse cultural,	**To improve my practice** __________ __________ __________ __________	**To become more aware** __________ __________ __________ __________	**To further excel** __________ __________ __________ __________	**To help others grow** __________ __________ __________ __________

(Continued)

(Continued)

	THE FEAR ZONE		THE LEARNING ZONE	THE GROWTH ZONE
linguistic, and socio-economic backgrounds of learners, ensuring that grades do not penalize cultural differences.	________ ________ ________ ________	________ ________ ________ ________	________ ________ ________ ________	________ ________ ________ ________
Feedback Quality Feedback given to learners is clear, specific, and constructive. Feedback is tailored to individual needs, promoting growth and understanding rather than mere compliance.	**To improve my practice** ________ ________ ________ ________ ________ ________ ________	**To become more aware** ________ ________ ________ ________ ________ ________ ________	**To further excel** ________ ________ ________ ________ ________ ________ ________	**To help others grow** ________ ________ ________ ________ ________ ________ ________
Flexibility and Adaptability The willingness and ability to adjust my grading criteria, model, or methods based on equity—the unique needs and circumstances of learners; ensuring that the grading system is not rigid but adaptable to serve all learners equitably.	**To improve my practice** ________ ________ ________ ________ ________ ________ ________ ________ ________	**To become more aware** ________ ________ ________ ________ ________ ________ ________ ________ ________	**To further excel** ________ ________ ________ ________ ________ ________ ________ ________ ________	**To help others grow** ________ ________ ________ ________ ________ ________ ________ ________ ________

	THE FEAR ZONE		THE LEARNING ZONE	THE GROWTH ZONE
Transparency and Collaboration The extent to which grading criteria, model, methods, and results are transparently communicated to learners and their families. The degree to which I actively seek feedback from learners, parents, and caregivers to refine and improve grading practices.	**To improve my practice**	**To become more aware**	**To further excel**	**To help others grow**

Reflective Journals

Throughout this book, you've been keeping a journal where you've been responding to prompts and documenting your experiences, challenges, and successes related to grading with equity. Reflecting is an opportunity for introspection. It allows us to express our emotions and thoughts in the moment and track our growth over time. As educators we are all in the camp of older learners! Our worldviews may have hardened more than we like to admit. Reflective journaling challenges your thought processes, biases, and assumptions. It's the first criterion on the self-assessment rubric. When journaling, keep the Pathway to Cultural Competence front of mind.

Data Analysis

Data analysis aligns with step 5 on the CARTI Framework, data-driven decision making. Spend some time analyzing grade distributions disaggregated by race and other indicators of marginalization.

You identified yours in Chapter 3. Start with a benchmark of the grading period ending just prior to, or at the very beginning of, your implementation.

Analyze your data at the end of each semester. Put the results in writing! If students' grades are or become more consistent across diverse groups, it might indicate that your equity-based grading policy is having the desired effect. If they are not, review your self-assessments and other indicators to determine what additional resources and supports are needed. What is your struggle? What's missing? What's not working?

Seek Opportunities for Professional Learning

Regularly participating in professional learning sessions or workshops on equity-based grading can serve as a checkpoint. As part of a PLC, you can compare your current practices to the evolving standards and research in the field, refining your methods accordingly. If your district or organization does not offer those opportunities, check online. Many educational content and professional learning providers offer free online webinars are other resources to support this work. (And be sure to subscribe to my *Educational Equity Emancipation* podcast!)

These four strategies support your continuous improvement and commitment to equity in grading. But strategies have their own inherent challenges. Consider each one and how it might work for you. Use the planner template in Figure 12.10 to work through the pros and cons of each. I've given you the whys above. I've inserted one downside for each in the challenges and concerns column. As much as I like each and each is supported as a best practice, nothing is ever always sunshine and roses.

TASK 8. SEEK FEEDBACK

Feedback is a gift. And just as with self-assessment, many of the strategies used in the classroom for peer assessment can be tailored to serve a purpose here. Let's consider one strategy to solicit feedback from learners and two to request feedback from peers.

Learner Feedback Sessions and Surveys

No one is more greatly impacted by grades than learners. Especially at the middle and high school levels, giving learners voice and agency is the work of an educator who is in the learning and growing zones of the Pathway to Cultural Competence.

Offering regular feedback sessions or anonymous surveys for learners provides invaluable insights. By asking targeted questions about the grading policy, you can gather perceptions about

Figure 12.10

Planner for Self-Assessment Strategies

STRATEGY	HOW FREQUENTLY WILL YOU DO THIS?	HOW WILL YOU CHECK YOUR WORK?	ARE THERE ANY ANTICIPATED CHALLENGES OR CONCERNS?
Self-Assessment Rubric	________ ________ ________ ________	________ ________ ________ ________	*Self-assessment can sometimes lead to either overconfidence or underestimating my skills. I may miss my own gaps in performance.*
Reflective Journals	________ ________ ________ ________	________ ________ ________ ________	*Subjective and dependent on the awareness and willingness to confront my personal biases. Without guidance, I might not recognize or address deep-seated biases.*
Data Analysis	________ ________ ________ ________	________ ________ ________ ________	*This assumes that all other variables remain constant, which might not be the case. Multiple external factors might influence grading data.*
Seek Opportunities for Professional Learning	________ ________ ________ ________	________ ________ ________ ________	*The efficacy of professional learning varies. Without proper follow-up or continued support, my learning from the session/s might fade.*

the fairness and effectiveness of your grading practices from those on the receiving end. If you work with learners in lower grades, request feedback from and offer surveys to their parents and caregivers.

Peer Portfolio Review

Compile a portfolio of graded assignments. Your portfolio should contain a variety of assignments and assessments. Showcase a range of learners and backgrounds. Solicit a trusted peer or supervisor to assess your portfolio using the self-assessment rubric you designed earlier, or some other tool. Doing this periodically may help you gauge bias in your grading. And if it is biased, identify what needs to improve over time.

Peer Observations

Invite a colleague to observe your instruction and then, in reviewing learners' graded work, provide feedback. Classroom instruction so often happens in isolation. Fostering a culture of collaborative support can offer a fresh perspective and create opportunities to share best practices within your professional community.

These three strategies support continuous improvement and a commitment to equity in grading. They also have their own inherent challenges. So, consider each one and how each might work for you in your context. Use the planner template in Figure 12.11 to work through their pros and cons. I've provide one downside for each in the challenges and concerns column.

Just as we differentiate for our learners, it's equitable to differentiate for yourself. Choose a combination of strategies. Thinking holistically and taking a multifaceted approach, use both quantitative and qualitative assessments to monitor your progress when implementing equity-based grading.

TASK 9. COMMUNICATING WITH ALL CONSTITUENCIES

Your most important communication work begins here. The work you've done throughout this text, and the planning you're engaging in now, are critical components of a successful implementation launched and supported with transparency and accountability.

Throughout your implementation, use clear and consistent communication tools. Materials you share with learners, parents, and caregivers must be user-friendly and easy for everyone to use and understand. Your colleagues, learners, parents, and caregivers have a diversity of language and comprehension abilities. Be cognizant of that. Plan appropriately.

Figure 12.11

Planner for Incorporating Learner and Peer Feedback Strategies

STRATEGY	HOW FREQUENTLY WILL YOU DO THIS?	HOW WILL YOU INTRODUCE IT?	HOW WILL YOU SUPPORT IT?	ARE THERE ANY ANTICIPATED CHALLENGES OR CONCERNS?
Learner Feedback Sessions and Surveys				Naïve or immature learners might not always provide constructive feedback. Without anonymity, learners, especially those who are or feel marginalized, are often hesitant to provide honest feedback due to fear of retribution.
Peer Portfolio Review				Creating, maintaining, and regularly updating portfolios can be hard work. There's also a risk of confirmation bias if you only select items that confirm your belief in your equitable grading.
Peer Observations				This requires a psychologically safe environment. It requires a peer observer who is in the growth zone on the pathway to avoid bringing their bias into the feedback, potentially leading to misunderstandings or conflicts.

Consider infographics, videos, and FAQ documents that clearly explain your equitable grading practices. Develop these tools in the languages needed to reach everyone in your community. If needed, work with your local community to find resources and volunteers to assist with translations.

Conclusion

In this chapter, you've worked through nine tasks to shift to an equitable grading system, step-by-step. Congratulations! The hardest part of the work is now done. Remember: *Take your time! It is better to get it right, than to finish it quickly.*

There's no reflect and act in this chapter, nor mindset meter, because you'll spend the next chapter reflecting on the big ideas in this book. You'll set yourself up to not only do the right things, but to do them well, and do enough of the right things well to effect change.

Do take a moment and respond to the following evaluation prompt in your journal:

I used to think ______ but now I know ______.

____

____

____

____

CHAPTER 13

ESSENTIAL REFLECTIONS

Reflecting on the Big Ideas of This Book

In the opening chapter of this book, I asked you:

- *Have you ever wondered, when you sit in the quiet of your own thinking and reflecting space, "Am I really doing what is equitable? Am I providing instruction or leading or speaking with an equity mindset? Am I looking through the lens of equity? And how do I know?"*

Now, I'll ask you those questions again. This time, think about them:

1. Through the lens of the four equity indicators you've learned to use as your metric, and
2. Along a spectrum, the Pathway to Cultural Competence (see Table 3.1).

Take some time to think, to reflect. Then, respond to these prompts in your journal.

- Am I really doing what is equitable?
- Am I instructing or leading or speaking with an equity mindset?
- Am I looking through the lens of equity?
- How do I know?

The Four Equity Indicators

Meritocracy: Am I using my power for the good of the marginalized in my school community?

Asset Allocation: Am I choosing and allocating resources to create opportunity and excellence for all involved?

Standards: Am I taking action that results in students demonstrating ongoing mastery year over year?

Imprtiality: Are we accurately and appropriately considering the cultures of all those affected, or are we acting from a middle-class, White-European, Western cultural bias?

When it comes to effecting change, to shifting or moving along the Pathway to Cultural Competence, there are three questions I always ask educators to keep in mind as a quick self-assessment. Those three questions are:

1. Am I doing the right thing?
2. Am I doing the right thing well?
3. Am I doing enough of the right thing well?

Do the Right Thing

First, remember our oath:

> I will apply pedagogic measures for the benefit of all children according to my ability and judgment; I will keep them from illiteracy and innumeracy. I will neither use an inappropriate method, nor will I make a suggestion to this effect. I will not teach to a test. I will teach for the benefit of children, remaining free of all intentional injustice, of all mischief, and in particular, of low expectations for children who come to learn. (Berry, 2023)

Reflect on what it looks like for you (and your organization) to do the right things at each of the five steps of the CARTI Framework. Use the Four Equity Indicators and the Pathway to Cultural

Competence as your framework for reflection. Respond to the questions below in your journal using your reflections in the Mindset Meters at the end of each chapter as your baseline.

STEP 1. CULTURAL AWARENESS

I commit to constantly working on improving my levels of awareness and connectedness to the full range of cultures of my learners (Chapter 3, page 61).

- What is/was your baseline?
- What is your goal?
- Where are you now?

STEP 2. INSTRUCTIONAL METHODOLOGY

I commit to instructing for equality of outcomes by using methods that are effective enough for every learner to end each year at or above grade level (Chapter 5, page 100).

- What is/was your baseline?
- What is your goal?
- Where are you now?

STEP 3. CURRICULUM CONTENT

I commit to selecting and using instructional materials that are culturally appropriate so that every learner can see themselves in the materials and to foster a level of engagement that sparks an innate desire to learn (Chapter 6, page 117).

- What is/was your baseline?
- What is your goal?
- Where are you now?

STEP 4. ACADEMIC ASSESSMENT

I commit to selecting assessments and practicing assessment in a manner that aligns with culturally relevant instructional practices and is useful for driving equitable decision-making (Chapter 8, page 152).

- What is/was your baseline?
- What is your goal?
- Where are you now?

STEP 5. DATA-DRIVEN DECISION MAKING

I commit to data-driven decision making with an emphasis on reporting growth and mastery through an equitable grading system (Chapter 10, page 201).

- What is/was your baseline?
- What is your goal?
- Where are you now?

Do the Right Thing Well

Doing all the right things well means doing them with fidelity and integrity. It means examining your choices about what instruction you provide, how you provide it, how you assess, and how you grade through a lens of equity. It means being brutally honest with yourself, always pushing to become consciously competent in each action. It is heavily reliant on professional learning, self-assessment, peer assessment, and receiving feedback from our broader community to support a model of continuous improvement.

Let's reflect on what it looks like for you and your organization to do the right things *well* at each of the five steps of the CARTI Framework. Again, use the Four Equity Indicators and the Pathway to Cultural Competence as your framework for reflection. Respond to the questions below in your journal.

STEP 1. CULTURAL AWARENESS

I have an honest commitment to constantly working on improving my level of awareness and connectedness to the full range of cultures of my learners.

- How can I use the best available resources to support my development at this step?
- How can I engage all those who need to be involved to support systemic growth?
- What can I do better?

STEP 2. INSTRUCTIONAL METHODOLOGY

I provide instruction for equality of outcomes by using methods that are effective enough for every learner to end each year at or above grade level. I do this with fidelity and integrity in every classroom.

- How can I use the best available resources to check my fidelity and support development where gaps are found?
- How can I support all those who need growth and development to improve their classroom practices?
- What can I do better?

STEP 3. CURRICULUM CONTENT

I select and use culturally appropriate instructional materials where every learner can see themselves. Materials that have been vetted through the four equity indicators.

- How can I acquire instructional resources that meet culturally appropriate criteria in every subject area?
- What steps am I taking to ensure that I remain faithful to doing so?
- What can I do better?

STEP 4. ACADEMIC ASSESSMENT

I always, and in all ways, select and practice assessment in alignment with culturally relevant instructional practices to get data that can be used for equitable instructional decision making.

- How can I acquire assessments resources that meet culturally appropriate criteria in every subject area?
- What steps am I taking to ensure that I remain faithful to doing so?
- What can I do better?

STEP 5. DATA-DRIVEN DECISION MAKING

I commit to data-driven decision making with an emphasis on reporting growth and mastery through an equitable grading system.

- How can I monitor for fidelity and integrity the decisions I make about instructional placement, course assignment or eligibility, and grading based on the data I derive from assessment, particularly for marginalized learners?
- What steps am I taking to ensure that marginalized learners are not disproportionately negatively impacted by my decisions?
- What can I do better?

DO ENOUGH OF THE RIGHT THINGS TO EFFECT EQUITABLE CHANGE

There's a lot to do. There's a lot to check on to make sure you do the things you need to do well. But I'm asking you for more. Your learners, particularly those who've been historically marginalized, those you identified in Chapter 3 (page 50), deserve every opportunity for success. For them, I ask that you push yourself past the tipping point with this last self-assessment.

The Tipping Point

The tipping point in educational change, in shifting the culture to impact academic achievement for CLDLs and other marginalized learners, refers to that critical point where a relatively small input results in a significant change. It's like the boiling point of water—just a little more heat for a little bit longer. Once the tipping point of equity is reached, the shifts you seek will spread like a viral video. Everyone passes it along. And it can produce significant and sometimes unforeseen outcomes.

It may be that one more professional learning session that touches everyone and motivates a change. It may be the results of a high-stakes assessment that shows the increase in achievement based on work done so far that has everyone all-in for the next year. I remember that August day in 1998 as if it were yesterday—right down to the M&Ms I was sorting by color to help me keep my thoughts in my head and not spew from my mouth. The very first time I saw the results of equitable instruction pay off—at a time before "equity" was a thing.

Once your organization crosses that tipping point, the momentum for adoption of equitable practices becomes self-sustaining. It encourages even more commitment to equitable practices, resulting in even greater achievement. Identifying and leveraging your organization's tipping point is essential for effecting equitable change, especially given that the stakes are literally the futures—the lives—of your learners.

Doing enough of all the right things well means not only doing them with fidelity and integrity but doing so with a sense of urgency. It means sometimes becoming uncomfortable because you are being pushed to the very edge of your own zone of proximal development. It means keeping your foot on the gas until you see the change in learner outcomes happening. And then keeping it on the gas until those changes, those equal outcomes become the norm. Until every child is experiencing grade-level or above grade-level achievement.

Doing enough of the right thing means getting everyone to at least a level of conscious competence. What will that look like for you, for your organization? Write your response in your journal.

Conclusion

In this final chapter, I've given you a lot to think about, to reflect on. You've taken a look back and a look forward. Your reflections have been structured on three components we've worked with throughout this book: the CARTI Framework, the Four Equity Indicators, and the Pathway to Cultural Competence. Now, you have the self-assessment GPS to help guide you forward. Those three questions can be readily recalled when you find yourself in a quandary, or just checking your own—or someone else's—actions:

- Am I (are we/they) doing the right thing?
- Am I (are we/they) doing the right thing well?
- Am I (are we/they) doing enough of the right thing well?

You may find yourself asking these questions in faculty meetings, during your planning, or in conversation with your peers. That's a good thing.

Focus on these. Push to and through the tipping points. Effort creates ability and success breeds success. The curmudgeons who would dismiss or derail your efforts will either fade away or get on the equity bus.

Work hard. It gets easier. As your efforts become habits, they feel less like work and more like who you are and what you seek to become.

Before you know it, you'll find yourself in the growth zone, unconsciously competent, regularly engaging in transformative behaviors because it's become as much a part of your being as breathing. And know that I am here with you and for you, cheering for your success and ready to coach you when you feel like you're missing the next piece of the puzzle.

There's no Mindset Meter in this chapter either, just one final prompt based on your journey throughout this text:

> I used to think ______ but now I know ______.

And as always, don't worry about the things you cannot change. Change the things you can no longer accept.

APPENDIX A

Restorative Versus Retributive Disciplinary Practices

Restorative practices work to strengthen relationships: learners with learners and learners with educators. In a restorative practices model, social connections within the school community are emphasized. Practices revolve around the concept of building a sense of community, resolving conflicts, and repairing harm by promoting dialogue, mutual understanding, and cooperation.

The essential premise of restorative practice is that learners are happier, more productive, and more likely to make positive changes in their behavior when classroom educators and school disciplinarians do things with them, rather than to them. Methods and strategies for restorative practices include circles for speaking and listening, mediation, restorative conferencing, and other practices that work toward reparation of harm and rebuilding of trust. This approach helps foster a school environment that embraces dialogue and inclusivity, aiming to address wrongdoing while emphasizing the importance of learning and growth.

Retributive practice on the other hand is the historical theory of school discipline that holds that the best response to a misbehavior is a punishment, sometimes but not always, proportional to the offense, inflicted because the offending learner deserves the punishment. The fundamental principle behind this approach is "x-days suspension" for a specific offense, where school removal and withholding instruction as punishment is seen as a necessary and proportionate response to misbehavior. It is based on the premise that the offending learner must suffer.

Retribution is neither a deterrence (which aims to prevent future misbehaviors), nor a rehabilitation (which aims to reform the offender), nor a restoration (which aims to repair harm and build trust). In the retributive model, punishment is justified as a response to behavior.

APPENDIX B

Sociocultural Languages in U.S. Schools

African American English—a distinct, complex, and rule-governed linguistic system prevalent in Black American communities, characterized by distinct phonological, syntactic, semantic, and lexical conventions influenced by multiple African languages and historical, social, and cultural experiences of the Black American community and expressed in patterns divergent from School English (SE) (Green, 2002; Salikoko et al., 2022).

Appalachian English—a distinct, complex, and rule-governed linguistic system found in the predominantly White communities geographically situated in the Appalachian cultural area centered on southern West Virginia, southeast Kentucky, southwest Virginia, northeast Tennessee, and western North Carolina, with subregional differences. The language is influenced heavily by the heritage of Scotch, Irish, and Welsh immigrants who settled in the area (Hasty & Childs, 2021).

Chicano English—a distinct, complex, and rule-governed linguistic system prevalent in some Chicano-American communities, especially in the US Southwest, characterized by distinct phonological, syntactic, and lexical conventions influenced by Spanish and historical, social, and cultural experiences of the Chicano community and expressed in patterns divergent from School English (SE) (Fought, 1999; Penfield & Ornstein-Galicia, 1985).

French Creole—a stable natural language that developed from the ethnicity originating from the mix of French, Indigenous, and African cultures in the seventeenth century (Fontaine, 1981).

Gullah—a distinct, complex, and rule-governed language spoken by the Gullah and Geechee people of South Carolina, Georgia, and Florida. Originating as a pidgin language, Gullah is a mixture of West African and English languages.

Hawaiian Pidgin—also known as Hawaiian Creole English, is an underdeveloped creole language (Reinecke, 1938) originating, and primarily found, in Hawai'i. The language evolved as a form of communication between Hawaiian, Japanese, Chinese, Portuguese, and Filipino plantation workers and the English language of command in the nineteenth century (Marlow & Giles, 2008).

Jamaican Patois—a natural language spoken by the majority of Jamaicans as a native language; originally a creole language based in the vernacular and dialectical forms of English spoken by British and Scotch slaveholders nativized by West Africans in the seventeenth century (Davidson & Schwartz, 1995).

Lumbee Vernacular English—a distinctive English vernacular spoken by the Lumbee people, an Indigenous group primarily residing in Robeson County, North Carolina. Sometimes thought of as a variety of Southern English, the language is influenced by Iroquoian, Siouan, and Algonkian ancestral languages (Wolfram & Sellers, 1999).

Southern English—neither a singular dialect, vernacular, or language, Southern English is a broad term that encompasses a variety of regional accents, vernaculars, creoles, and dialects found across the Southern United States.

APPENDIX C

Setting SMART Goals for Cultural Awareness

If you've never written a SMART goal, or just need a refresher, follow the steps below. I'm using an imaginary, pie-in-the-sky goal I use as an exemplar in my workshops.

S IS FOR SPECIFIC

The goal must be clear, concise, and unambiguous. So, instead of:

- *I want to culturally connect to all my learners,*

I'll write:

- *I will develop a cultural connection with and sensitivity to my Southeast Asian learners who don't have faculty representation.*

Choose one of the bucket goals you brainstormed and work on making it more specific. This may mean clearly identifying a group, or a process. Keep it concise and avoid ambiguity.

M IS FOR MEASURABLE

Start with a baseline. You must be able to measure where you are, measure where you want to be when the goal is achieved, and track your progress using key performance indicators (KPIs). When I think about my goal, "I want to culturally connect to my Southeast Asian learners who don't have faculty representation," I need to know how I am doing now.

I need to think about the current racial composition of the learners. What percentage of my learners are Southeast Asian? How many was I able to truly connect with last year, or before I began this exercise? That's my baseline.

I need to know where I want to end up. That's my outcome. And I need to identify a KPI to use to measure my progress along the way. Let's say I did my homework on this and now have some numbers. My goal now reads:

- *I will develop a cultural connection with and sensitivity to the 32% of my learners who are Southeast Asian who don't have faculty representation and with whom I failed to connect last year, as measured by learner self-reporting on my end-of-year learner evaluations.*

Take your goal and work on making it measurable. What can you measure? What specifically do you want the outcome to be? How can you measure that? What KPIs do you have access to, or what can you create to use as a measurement?

A IS FOR ACHIEVABLE

Stretch your abilities but keep the goal in the realm of possibility. Looking at my last statement, and after a bit of reflection, I realized that connecting with all of them might be too much of a stretch. I need to consider the learner transiency rate and those who are habitually truant. That means my goal may not be plausible. But I think I can stretch to at least connect with 85% of my Southeast Asian learners. So, I revise my goal to read:

- *I will develop a cultural connection with and sensitivity to 85% of the 32% of my learners who are Southeast Asian who don't have faculty representation and with whom I failed to connect last year, as measured by learner evaluations.*

Go back to your goal and work on making it achievable. This requires some thought and refinement. It may even require some research.

R IS FOR RELEVANT AND REALISTIC

Align the goal to your other goals or perhaps to any strategic plan in place at your school or district. Make sure your goal fits into the values and vision of the educational agency you work for. This requires reflection. It may require reading the strategic plan or consulting with your coach or a system leader.

In my "Utopia Unified School District" that exists only in my writings, podcasts, and workshops, cultural awareness is a strategic priority. So, I know my goal is more than okay, it's supported at the top levels. What about yours?

Reflect on your goal. Is it realistic? Does it align with other goals and strategic plans or initiatives in place? Will it be accepted and supported by those in positions above you? Take a moment to think and journal any thoughts or questions you may need answered. Getting that information will be part of your completion work.

T IS FOR TIME-BOUND OR TIMELY

Establish a start and finish date and be politically sensitive to timelines connected to strategic initiatives, state or federal mandates, court orders, and so on. For my goal let's just imagine there is a bit of political time. Utopia Unified's strategic initiative has a target of achievement of all goals within five years. So, I'm going to add that to my goal:

- *I will develop a cultural connection with and sensitivity to 85% of the 32% of my learners who are Southeast Asian who don't have faculty representation and with whom I failed to connect last year, as measured by learner self-reporting on my end-of-year learner evaluations, and 98% by June 2030.*

And then I include my annual benchmark, to help keep me honest and focused.

- *I want to culturally connect with 85% of the 32% of my learners who are Southeast Asian who don't have faculty representation and with whom I failed to connect last year, as measured by learner self-reporting on my end-of-year learner evaluations, and 98% by June 2030, at a rate of 20% growth to goal each year.*

Make your goal time-bound and timely. Think about political time. Think about calendar time. When can you start? When do you need to, or will you, finish? What benchmarks can you include to help monitor your progress, so you'll know when to pivot, adjust, apply additional action or supports? Again, take a moment to think and journal any thoughts or questions you may need to have answered.

And that's it! You've written a SMART goal.

APPENDIX D

Memory-Enhancing Strategies

The use of memory-enhancing strategies looks different across the grade spans. Here are a few you can use across the grades.

> **Chunking.** Chunking refers to breaking information into smaller, manageable groups or "chunks." At the early grades, you might use chunking to learn the alphabet, days of the weeks, or the months of the year. Start with three to five items. When students know those, add on two more. Then two more, and so on until you can name any one and they can tell you the item that comes before and the one that comes after without hesitation.

At the higher grades, and in content areas, chunk lists of terms or concepts. Start by dividing them into meaningful groups. When I taught US History, I chunked the entire course. Rather than teaching it chronologically from Reconstruction to the present, I taught it in concepts: war and peace, poverty and prosperity, immigration and emigration, rights and responsibilities, innovation and traditionalism, and federalism and states' rights. This type of chunking made more sense to learners, supporting higher order thinking by connecting meaningful concepts and activities rather than lists of names, events, and dates.

Songs, Rhymes, and Raps. Using songs, rhymes, and raps to teach content makes the learning process enjoyable and memorable. Most of us learned and remember the alphabet song, which assists learners in remembering the sequence of letters.

For early American history, leveraging songs from the musical *Hamilton* is an engaging way to bring Alexander Hamilton and the history surrounding him to life. We had my grandson watch the film when he was twelve. Like many tweens and teens, he was so intrigued, he streamed it daily and memorized the entire production. It sparked questions and he could shortly thereafter talk about the history and the impact of the major characters of early American history.

A word of caution here: without meaningful engagement beyond the song, rhyme, or rap, learners may have to reproduce the entire content to get at a single item.

Mnemonic Devices. Use simple memory aids, such as acronyms, rhymes, or associations. For example, *Please Excuse My Dear Aunt Sally* is widely used to remember the order of operations in math. You might use *My Very Educated Mother Just Served Us Nachos* to remember the order of the planets. Longer mnemonic devices can be supported with chunking. For example, the 17 geological time periods should be chunked, as there are five that begin with the letter P. So, the mnemonic *Pregnant Camels Often Sit Down Carefully, Perhaps Their Joints Ache? Possibly Early Oiling Might Prevent Permanent Rheumatism,* while helpful, can still send a learner over the deep end.

Visual Aids. Use visual stimuli such as charts, diagrams, colorful drawings, and flashcards. Visual representations help simplify complex information and make it more digestible for younger and emergent bilingual learners. For example, a diagram that illustrates the life cycle of a butterfly. Learners can complete graphic organizers to show the relationships and traits of characters in a piece of literature. Though you'll need to cover them during tests, if learners have referenced them over time, they can look at the space, close their eyes, and visualize what was there.

Visualization. Encourage learners to create a mental image of concepts being taught. Making abstract ideas concrete in their minds fosters deeper understanding and retention. For instance, when discussing the water cycle, learners can visualize each stage, such as evaporation, condensation, and precipitation.

Massed and Distributed Practice. After initial instruction on a concept (massed practice), regularly review the information over time (distributed practice). For example, after providing instruction on addition and subtraction of fractions, and then moving on to multiplication of fractions, come back to a few addition and subtraction problems every few days. Over time, you can space that to two or three problems every few weeks. The higher the degree of perfection on the part of your learners, the more you can space out the distribution.

Routine and Consistency. Learners benefit from a structured environment. Establishing routines, like a daily review or recap of what was learned, can reinforce retention. Starting or ending a lesson with a recap acts as a mental bookmark.

Using strategies like these not only enhances the memory of your learners but also fosters an inclusive learning environment that accounts for diverse cognitive needs.

APPENDIX E

Total Physical Response (TPR)

Why teach sitting down? TPR involves using your body to teach, and learners using their bodies to demonstrate learning. TPR is a great tool for teaching action verbs, nouns, directions, prepositions, and other concepts that can be acted out.

Here are a few exemplars of what TPR can look like in the classroom. These examples aim to make the learning accessible and inclusive for all learners, including emerging multilingual learners.

INSTRUCTION ON PREPOSITIONS WITH EARLY LEARNERS

Teaching prepositions and spatial concepts, such as "above," to early learners can be highly effective and engaging when incorporating TPR along with hands-on, playful activities. This supports the developmental stages of young learners by making abstract concepts concrete and understandable. Here's a lesson to teach the concept of "above" that can be used to teach a variety of other prepositions.

Objective: Learners will understand and identify the spatial relationship denoted by the preposition *above*.

Materials: a variety of classroom objects (books, balls, stuffed animals, etc.); pictures illustrating the concept of "above"; a chair or a small table

TPR Activity Steps

1. Introduction with a Story or Visuals: Start by reading a story or showing pictures where the concept of "above" is evident and emphasized. For instance, a bird flying above the trees, or a cat perched above a bird cage. Discuss each example briefly to ensure learners grasp the concept.
2. Demonstration and Physical Engagement: Hold a chosen object (e.g., a stuffed animal) above a chair. Then say, "The [object] is above the chair." Invite a learner to hold the object above their desk and ask, "What is above the desk?" Guide them to understand that the object is above the desk.
3. TPR Movements: Have learners stand in an open space. Instruct them to place their hands above their heads. Say, "Your hands are above your head." This physical movement helps solidify their understanding of the concept. Encourage learners to find objects in the classroom and use their bodies to show "above" (e.g., standing and reaching above an object on the ground).
4. Interactive Game: Play a game of "Find and Show." Call out an object in the room and ask learners to point to an object that is above it. For example, "Find something that is above the chair." Repeat for additional objects. This encourages movement and active participation.

INSTRUCTION ON THE WATER CYCLE WITH INTERMEDIATE LEARNERS

Here is an example of how TPR can be used to teach the water cycle, a key science concept.

Objective: Learners will be able to identify and describe the four main stages of the water cycle: evaporation, condensation, precipitation, and collection.

Materials: diagrams or posters of the water cycle; water cycle vocabulary cards: evaporation, condensation, precipitation, collection.

TPR Activity Steps

1. Frontload Vocabulary: Introduce the water cycle stages using a diagram or poster. Explain each term (evaporation, condensation, precipitation, collection) and show its position in the water cycle.
2. Create Physical Movements:
   - Evaporation: Learners mimic the sun heating water by standing with feet apart and slowly rising on their toes while reaching arms up and wiggling fingers upwards, representing water vapor rising.
   - Condensation: Learners pull arms inwards and clench fists to represent water vapor cooling and condensing into clouds. They can also huddle together briefly to symbolize cloud formation.
   - Precipitation: From the condensation pose, learners extend arms and wiggle fingers downwards, simulating rain, snow, or other forms of precipitation falling to the ground.
   - Collection: Learners squat down and cup hands together, symbolizing water collecting on the ground, in rivers, lakes, and oceans.
3. Sequence Practice: Guide learners through the series of movements in order, correlating each movement with its stage in the water cycle. Repeat several times, increasing speed for fun and challenge, and then ask learners to perform the sequence in response to stage names or visual cues.
4. Role Play and Application: Divide the class into small groups and assign each group a stage of the water cycle. Each group creates a tableau or a short performance of their assigned stage, incorporating the physical movements. After each presentation, discuss how their stage fits into the overall cycle.

INSTRUCTION ON THE INDUSTRIAL REVOLUTION FOR MIDDLE GRADE LEARNERS

For a middle school classroom, TPR can effectively be applied to social studies, particularly in teaching historical events or concepts. Here's an example of using TPR to teach about the Industrial Revolution.

Objective: Learners will be able to identify and describe key aspects of the Industrial Revolution, including its causes, major inventions, and impacts on society.

Materials: timeline of the Industrial Revolution highlighting key inventions and events; images or replicas of major inventions (e.g., the steam engine, cotton gin); vocabulary cards with terms such as *Industrial Revolution, innovation, manufacture, labor,* and *society.*

TPR Activity Steps

1. Introduce the Industrial Revolution: Begin with a brief overview of the Industrial Revolution, emphasizing its timeline and global impact.
2. Frontload Vocabulary: Introduce the key vocabulary with the help of a timeline to visually represent key events and images of major inventions.
3. Create Physical Movements:
    - Innovation (Inventions): Learners mime the action of turning gears or levers, symbolizing the creation and operation of machinery.
    - Manufacture: Mimic assembly line work, such as passing objects (imaginary or realia) from one person to another, to represent mass production.
    - Labor: Show the transition from farming to factory work by first pretending to till the soil and then moving to mimic operating machinery.
    - Society: Demonstrate the shift from rural to urban living by walking in place slowly and then speeding up, indicating the move to faster-paced city life.
4. Sequence and Role Play: After practicing these movements, learners work in small groups to create a short role-play or sequence of movements that narrates the transition from pre-industrial to industrial society. Encourage them to incorporate the vocabulary and movements introduced.
5. Discussion and Connection: Facilitate a discussion on how the Industrial Revolution changed ways of living, working, and thinking. Encourage learners to connect these changes to present-day technological advancements and societal shifts.
6. Reflection and Creative Expression: Ask learners to reflect on what aspect of the Industrial Revolution they found most impactful and why. They can express their reflections through creative means such as a poem, rap, or drawing, incorporating TPR elements if possible.

HIGH SCHOOL WORLD LANGUAGE VOCABULARY ROUTINE

Incorporating TPR into high school world language instruction can significantly enhance learners' engagement and retention, especially when introducing new vocabulary or grammatical structures. Here's an example of a TPR activity designed for a high school Spanish class, focusing on teaching verbs related to daily routines.

Objective: Students will be able to understand, pronounce, and use verbs associated with daily routines in Spanish, such as "despertarse" (to wake up), "levantarse" (to get up), "comer" (to eat), "estudiar" (to study), and "dormir" (to sleep).

Materials: flashcards with the Spanish verbs; a list of sentences or phrases incorporating the target verbs.

TPR Activity Steps:

1. Introduction of Verbs: Use flashcards to introduce the verbs. Pronounce each verb clearly, and have students repeat after you to practice pronunciation.
2. Demonstration and Physical Engagement: Demonstrate each verb, through a simple action while using the verb in a simple sentence. For example, pretend to sleep when teaching "dormir" or mimic eating for "comer." Have students stand up and perform the actions with you as you say the verbs aloud, reinforcing the connection between the physical action and the verb.
3. Interactive Practice: Call out different verbs in random order and have learners perform the corresponding action without speaking. This helps solidify their understanding and recall of each verb. Next, introduce simple sentences incorporating the verbs, such as "Yo me despierto a las siete" (I wake up at seven). Perform the actions as you say the sentences, and have students mimic the actions and repeat the sentences.
4. Role-Playing Activity: In pairs, students create short skits, or dialogues that incorporate the verbs. Encourage them to use as many verbs as possible and to act out their routines. Each pair presents to the class, providing a fun and engaging way for students to practice speaking and listening in Spanish while also physically engaging with the content.

APPENDIX F

Interactive Notebooks

SCIENCE AND SOCIAL SCIENCES

Here's an example of how you might set up and use an interactive notebook for science or social science courses for intermediate and middle grades.

Materials Needed: composition or spiral notebooks with durable covers; colored pencils, markers, or crayons; scissors and glue; printed templates for foldables, charts, and maps (as needed)

SECTIONS OF THE NOTEBOOK

Table of Contents: Start with a table of contents at the beginning of the notebook. Each new entry should be added with its page number for easy reference.

Periodic Entries: Regular entries would include two primary components:

- *Vocabulary:* Each entry can feature vocabulary related to the lesson or reflective entry with foldables for key terms and definitions. Learners should leave the margins free for interactive feedback between you and them.

- *Lecture Notes and Class Discussions:* Learners should be encouraged to take notes taken during lectures or class discussions. Use the left side of the notebook (the back sides of the pages) for notes taken during class and the right side for summarizing the information in their own words, drawing diagrams, or creating charts. Learners should leave the margins free for interactive feedback between you and them.

Reflection and Analysis: After each unit, dedicate a page or two for reflection. Prompt with the questions you plan to use for reflective dialogue circles such as, "What was the most interesting aspect of _____?" or "How did geography influence _____?" Encourage personal connections, asking learners how they think their lives would be different if they had lived during that time.

Projects and Research Starters: Use the final section for project outlines; research notes; and brainstorming ideas for group presentations, models, reports, and so on.

Other elements that may be included:

- Timeline Foldables: Learners create timelines of major events for each era or unit. These can be accordion foldouts that extend beyond the notebook when opened.
- Character Flaps: For important historical figures, learners create flaps that lift to reveal facts, achievements, and their impact.
- Comparative Charts: Use Venn diagrams or charts to compare and contrast different civilizations or events, focusing on government, culture, achievements, and geography.

Literature

Here's an example of how you might set up and use an interactive notebook for middle or high school literature courses, focusing on analyzing themes, characters, and literary devices across various texts.

Materials Needed: durable composition or spiral notebooks; colored pens, pencils, and highlighters; scissors, glue, and tape; printed templates for graphic organizers, foldables, and analysis charts

SECTIONS OF THE NOTEBOOK

Table of Contents: Start with a table of contents at the beginning of the notebook. Each new entry should be added with its page number for easy reference.

Literary Terms Glossary: Each literary term or device (e.g., metaphor, symbolism, allegory) has its definition, an example from the text studied in class, and space for learners to add examples found in their personal reading.

Text Analysis Sections: Text analysis entries for each piece of literature or unit are written on the right-side pages (front). Encourage creative engagement including poetry, short story writing, and visual art that responds to or interprets themes and characters. For each text or unit, include:

- **Summary Pages:** brief summaries of the plot, setting, and characters.
- **Character Analysis Pages:** Use foldables or character maps to explore the development, motivations, and relationships of main characters.
- **Theme Exploration:** Create pages for each major theme, using text evidence and personal reflections to explore the theme's development and relevance.
- **Literary Device Tabs:** Insert tabs or flaps that highlight and analyze the use of literary devices within the text, linking them to themes and character development.

Comparative Analysis: Comparative analysis entries are written on the left-side pages (back) of pages opposite each component of the text analysis. This allows learners to compare and contrast themes, characters, or literary devices across different texts, in opposition to their analysis section. Encourage creative engagement including poetry, short story writing, or visual art here as well. Venn diagrams, charts, and tables can be effective here.

Critical Response and Reflection: At appropriate intervals, learners write a critical response, commentary, or reflection on the text. Prompt them with the questions you plan to use to start your reflective dialogue circles to encourage deep thinking and personal connection to the themes and characters. These can be included in designated sections of the notebook.

Projects and Research Starters: Use the final section for project outlines; research notes; and brainstorming ideas for group presentations, models, reports, and so on.

APPENDIX G

The Equity Checklist for Curriculum Content

In my work as a curriculum content (or textbook) reviewer, I needed a tool to use to consistently evaluate content through a lens of equity. Through research, application, practice, and revision, I came to develop what I call *The Equity Checklist for Curriculum Content*. Here is a simpler version of the tool you may use to check your instructional materials.

To determine whether your content meets the criteria of Equity Indicator 3—Impartiality, ask the following questions and use the criteria to examine and evaluate your materials.

Does this material:

1. build cultural awareness?
2. acknowledge, value, and preserve cultural and linguistic diversity?
3. promoting social progress?
4. represent diversity through imagery void of bias?
5. skew influence, privilege, and representation?

6. divide and isolate?
7. bias language and physical appearance?
8. demonstrate a commitment to delivering equitable instruction?

Build Cultural Awareness

The first question is, "Does this material build cultural awareness?" Your teaching materials should help your learners understand how knowledge is built. Using these materials, learners should create knowledge that shapes their understanding of how society sees itself. Look for the content to:

1. Clearly display and include a range of culturally diverse stories and events.
2. Provide instructor resources that offer guidance so that you may help your learners recognize and explore how hidden cultural beliefs, viewpoints, and biases in the subject affect how knowledge is formed within it.
3. Provide instructor resources that offer guidance to your learners in working collaboratively with people from racially, culturally, linguistically, and other diverse backgrounds to create new insights or knowledge that could not be created in isolation.

Acknowledge, Value, and Preserve Cultural and Linguistic Diversity

The second question is, "Does this material acknowledge, value, and preserve cultural and linguistic diversity?" Your teaching material should promote and support diverse languages, literacy, and cultures by maintaining both internal group and cross-cultural practices. Look for the content to:

1. Encourage learners to understand their cultural identity and recognize how various aspects of their identity shape their self-perception and experiences through both content and activities.

2. Prompt learners to continuously reflect on and explore how their personal identities and lived experiences influence their understanding of complex societal issues. This should be supported by the content and activities.
3. Be comprehensive, showcasing the traditions, practices, and contributions from a variety of communities, capturing both historical and evolving aspects.
4. Contain images and examples that are diverse and steer clear of clichéd portrayals, especially concerning race, gender, or abilities. (Refer to the Diversity Tally Scorecard on page 84 for guidance.)
5. Refrain from setting one cultural group's practices as a benchmark against which all other cultures are measured.

Promote Social Progress

The next question to ask is, "Does this material promote social progress?" Your teaching material should foster societal analysis and advocate for fair action. Look for the content to:

1. Urge learners to critically question societal norms.
2. Provide content for learners and instructional guidelines for teachers to showcase diverse perspectives, experiences, and problem-solving methods, emphasizing their equal significance.
3. Provide instructional resources that aid in fostering learners' connection to and utilization of tools and insights from various communities to critique prevailing norms.
4. Contain tasks that encourage learners to take actions that promote societal transformation for a fairer community.
5. Contain or suggest assignments that allow learners to freely convey their feelings, aspirations, and viewpoints, giving learners a platform to speak.
6. Contain tasks that inspire learners to take charge of their own paths and destinies.

Represent Diversity Through Imagery Void of Bias

The next question to ask is, "Does this material represent diversity through imagery void of bias?" Your teaching material should not overlook any group partially or completely. Look for the learner materials to:

1. Showcase visuals that represent individuals from a variety of backgrounds. (See the Diversity Tally Scorecard for guidance.)
2. Embody the cultural narratives, communal activities, and varied traditions of individuals from different origins.
3. Bring to light the stories, voices, and practices of various diverse communities.

In addition, teaching resources should provide guidance that does not endorse generic or reductionist views about specific groups, but rather support you with language and guidance that appreciates individual uniqueness. Whether in teaching materials or learner materials, look for the content to:

1. Re-evaluate traditional gender roles and cisgender identities, both in illustrations and text. For instance, show men as primary caregivers, while highlighting women for their professional achievements.
2. Portray individuals with dis/abilities considering their professional roles, societal contributions, and as engaged community members, not as merely disadvantaged or inspirational figures.
3. Steer clear of overarching assumptions about any community.
4. Contain tasks that inspire learners to recognize, question, and counteract biased or clichéd representations of specific groups or behaviors.
5. Depict individuals from the same racial or ethnic group with variance in appearance, highlighting a range of skin tones, eye and hair characteristics, and body shapes.
6. Depict different ethnicities and national origins accurately; for example, not all Asian-depicted families from China, and not every Latine representation is Mexican.

7. Depict a range of family setups, including single parents, adoptive or foster children, same-sex couples, multi-generational households, and so on, in images, photos, and illustrations.
8. Avoid disproportionately portraying characters of color in story conflicts as the root issue.
9. Avoid primarily portraying characters of color with financial struggles, limited education, or low income.
10. Avoid gender as the primary focus in stories. Present female characters in roles that can equally be occupied by male characters.
11. Portray diverse characters with clear cultural backgrounds rather than ambiguous ones.

Skew Influence, Privilege, and Representation

The next question is, "Does this material skew influence, privilege, and representation?" Your teaching resources should provide diverse interpretations of topics, situations, or communities, steering clear of simplifying or skewing intricate matters by excluding varying viewpoints. Look for the content to:

1. Refrain from suggesting that one group "bestows" privileges or rights upon another group.
2. Showcase historical viewpoints from various groups, integrating them into the overall structure of the text. Marginalized group stories aren't merely added but are integral to the overarching narrative.
3. Provide educational resources that highlight that significant scientific contributions come from diverse populations worldwide.
4. Provide teaching resources that embrace the historical perspectives and insights of different groups, recognizing both main narratives and alternate stories from diverse populations.
5. Affirm the authenticity and significance of knowledge rooted in communities of color, collective cultures, matriarchal societies, and non-Christian religious traditions.

In addition, teaching material should not gloss over or sidestep uncomfortable historical truths, such as prejudice, racial bias, discrimination, exploitation, oppression, gender bias, and conflicts between groups. Look for the content to:

1. Avoid painting an overly optimistic picture of the success of social programs and not imply these programs have entirely resolved community issues.
2. Delve into lingering societal challenges without suggesting simple solutions.
3. Portray historical incidents considering their sociopolitical backdrop, encompassing events shaped by racial bias, discrimination, exploitation, oppression, gender discrimination, and clashes among groups.

Divide and Isolate

The next question to ask is, "Does this material divide and isolate?" Your teaching material should not segregate or distinctly separate groups of people in visual depictions. Members of racial and ethnic groups should not be shown only mingling within their own communities but rather be portrayed interacting with diverse cultures. Look for the content to:

1. Provide educational resources that incorporate stories and historical recounts that highlight groups based on race, ethnicity, and gender as active participants in society and politics within the main text.
2. Weave the stories and histories of racial, ethnic, and gender-based groups in the core narrative, rather than isolate them in specialized sections, call out boxes, or supplemental curricula pieces.

Biased Language and Physical Appearance

The seventh question to ask is, "Does this material use biased language or physical appearances?" Your teaching material should avoid language and terms that reinforce stereotypes, biases, or the sidelining of specific groups through linguistic signals. Look for the content to:

1. Refrain from using terms like “roaming,” “wandering,” or “roving” when referring to the movements of Indigenous Peoples in the United States or elsewhere, irrespective of the era or location.
2. Steer clear of language implying that certain groups lacked structure or civilization compared to Western Europeans or White European-Americans.
3. Avoid phrasing that hints at certain communities requiring “rescue” or “assistance.”
4. Steer clear of male-centric terms such as “forefathers,” “mankind,” and “businessman,” which might undermine the roles and contributions of women.
5. Avoid any display of bias toward non-English speaking groups.
6. Challenge stereotypes, biases, and sidelining by emphasizing, spotlighting, and valuing stories from groups that aren’t always in the spotlight.

When examining your instructional materials, the aesthetic, what it looks like, should be consistent with its textual and inferential content. Materials should not rely on a “bias-free” flip test, which is a superficial marketing approach targeting curriculum selection committees and potential buyers who might only glance through a book without a deeper content evaluation. Look closely at the written content to make sure it:

1. Incorporates comprehensive stories (not just illustrations and highlight boxes) about female pioneers across fields like history, science, and mathematics.
2. Includes in-depth narratives (not just imagery) about influential figures from diverse racial backgrounds across various disciplines.
3. Delves deeper into the stories, backgrounds, and tales of people of color, those with dis/abilities, and members of the LGBTQ+ community beyond superficial imagery.
4. Is rich with genuine histories and stories from a spectrum of diverse backgrounds.

Demonstrate a Commitment to Delivering Equitable Instruction

And finally, we ask the question, "Does this material demonstrate a commitment to delivering equitable instruction?" This requires a look at pieces of teachers' guides we often ignore. Look at the resource guides, front matter, indexes, teaching notes in the margins, and resource ancillaries to see if:

1. The authors and contributors represent a spectrum of identities, including varied races, ethnicities, genders, and other potential identities.
2. Instructions emphasize recognizing one's personal biases and understanding the differences between one's own cultural background and that of learners.
3. Learners' diverse identities are appreciated as valuable assets that can enhance both individual and collective learning, rather than as challenges to be addressed.
4. Educators receive guidance on bridging academic content with the real-life context of the learners' local communities, their lived experiences, cultural influences, home environments, and community resources.
5. Recommendations allow learners to integrate their preexisting knowledge and lived experiences into topics, rather than solely reacting to classroom content.
6. Suggestions provide for learner involvement in culturally respectful hands-on learning experiences.
7. Advice is given on incorporating learners' families to enrich instructional content.
8. For some lessons, guidance includes understanding various possible reactions from learners. These reactions might be valid based on their unique backgrounds, viewpoints, and lived experiences.
9. Recommendations exist for adapting and enriching the curriculum to mirror the diverse cultures, histories, and interests of your diverse learners.

APPENDIX H

Media Literacy Activities

ACTIVITY 1. THE STORY OF TWO FRIENDS, GRADES 4–8

Learners must not only understand that every media source has its own perspective, agenda, and biases, but be able to justify how they know. Teach the difference between explicit bias (the conscious and intentional prejudices or stereotypes individuals hold towards others) and implicit bias (a natural phenomenon that exists in all humans, based on observed, taught, and reinforced behavior and ideas that cause prejudice). You may adjust the language and activities to accommodate older or younger learners. You may also choose a different text that conveys the same sentiments.

Objective: To help learners understand the difference between explicit (open and conscious) and implicit (hidden and unconscious) bias.

Materials Needed: *The Sneetches and Other Stories* by Dr. Seuss or another text that portrays two characters with differing explicit and implicit biases.

1. Start by explaining that explicit bias is when we openly express our opinions or preferences about something, while implicit bias is when we have hidden feelings or ideas that we might not even realize we have.

2. Read *The Sneetches*, focusing on the part where some Sneetches have stars on their bellies and others do not. This leads to explicit bias, as the Star-Belly Sneetches openly treat the Plain-Belly Sneetches differently.
3. Ask the learners to identify examples of explicit bias in the story, such as how the Star-Belly Sneetches openly exclude the Plain-Belly Sneetches from their activities.
4. Create a scenario related to the story that involves implicit bias. For example, a Sneetch who doesn't realize they are favoring others with the same belly stars as them, but says they treat all Sneetches equally.
5. Ask the learners to discuss what the implicit bias was in the scenario. This can lead to a conversation about how sometimes people don't realize they have hidden biases.
6. Place the learners in small groups and have them create short skits that show explicit and implicit biases, using the explicit and implicit biases from the book and scenario.
7. Have each group present their skit to the class.
8. Lead a class discussion to reflect on what students have learned about the differences between explicit and implicit bias. How can they recognize these biases in themselves and others? How can understanding these biases help us treat others fairly? Emphasize that, just like the Sneetches learned to accept and include one another, recognizing and understanding our biases can help us treat everyone fairly.
9. Have learners create Bias Awareness posters or drawings that depict what they learned. Display these in the classroom.

ACTIVITY 2. NEWS DETECTIVE, GRADES 4–12

Learners must master analyzing difference sources. Create activities where learners engage with multiple news sources, both traditional and alternative, especially on contentious issues. Encourage them to notice differences in reporting, tone, emphasis, and what's left out.

Teach your learners to evaluate the source before delving into the content. Who produced the information? Why? Who funded it? Is it a reputable source? What might their biases be?

Stress the importance of fact-checking. Develop a list of reliable fact-checking websites for your content area. Provide it to your learners as well as their parents and caregivers and teach them how to use these tools effectively.

Objective: To guide learners in comparing and analyzing how different news sources report on the same issue, emphasizing distinctions in tone, focus, and content.

Preparation:

1. Select a current and contentious issue that's appropriate for your grade level.
2. Identify various traditional and alternative news sources (newspapers, magazines, online articles, etc.), both print and online, covering the chosen issue.

Activity:

1. Explain to learners that they will become "News Detectives" to investigate how different sources report on the same issue.
2. Place learners into small groups and provide each group with access to the news sources covering the issue.
3. Provide an activity sheet, guide, or graphic organizer, or write questions and prompts on the board to help the groups analyze the news sources. Include questions such as:
   - What are the headlines?
   - How is the issue framed?
   - What words or images are used?
   - What information is included or excluded?
   - What seems to be the tone or perspective of the article?
   - Is there any evident bias?
4. Allow time for the groups to read, compare, and discuss their findings. Provide supports and scaffolds for younger learners or struggling readers.
5. Have each group create a visual comparison (such as a chart or Venn diagram) that highlights the differences and similarities they've discovered between the sources.
6. Invite groups to present their visual comparisons to the class, followed by a guided discussion. Encourage learners to share what surprised them, what they learned, and how they might approach news consumption differently in the future.

7. Optional: Ask learners to write a short reflection on what they've learned and how it might impact their understanding of media and news consumption. This may be a few sentences and a picture in elementary school, or a paragraph or more at middle and high school.
8. Optional Extension: Have learners follow the issue over time, noting changes in reporting and reflecting on why those changes may have occurred.

ACTIVITY 3. WHAT YOUR EYES TELL YOU, GRADES 9–12

In an age of memes and infographics, understanding visual media, including recognizing when images are manipulated, is crucial. Equity Indicator 3—impartiality—is all about representation. Discuss this with students and provide instruction on how the media represents diverse groups, especially racial, gender-identity, religious, cultural, and socioeconomic. Ask students to consider impartiality or fairness in these representations. Are they stereotypical? Who is left out?

Teaching high school learners to analyze and interpret visual media is an essential skill, particularly in a digital age rich with visual content. This activity cultivates awareness of the power and responsibility that comes with both consuming and creating visual media, particularly in representing diversity fairly and impartially.

Objective: To guide learners in analyzing visual media, including memes, infographics, and advertisements, with a focus on manipulation, representation, and impartiality related to racial, gender-identity, religious, cultural, and socioeconomic groups.

Materials Needed: selection of diverse visual media (memes, infographics, advertisements, etc.); image editing software (optional); activity sheets or graphic organizers (print or digital) for analysis

1. Start with an introduction to visual literacy, emphasizing the importance of critical thinking in interpreting visual media, including recognizing manipulation and considering fairness in representation.

2. Place learners into small groups and provide each group with a selection of visual media. Ask them to analyze the images for:
   - manipulation (e.g., use of image-editing software)
   - representation of diverse groups
   - tone, message, and intended audience
   - fairness and impartiality
3. Provide an activity sheet or guide with questions and prompts to help groups delve deeper into their analysis. Include questions such as:
   - How are diverse groups represented?
   - Are there stereotypes or biases evident?
   - Is there evidence of image manipulation?
   - How might different audiences interpret this image?
4. Facilitate a class discussion where groups share their analyses and creations. Focus on how different visual elements convey messages and how biases may be present.
5. Ask learners to write a reflection on what they learned about visual literacy, including how they might apply this understanding to their own consumption and creation of visual media.
6. Optional: If possible, have learners create or modify an image using simple image editing software. Encourage them to create a meme or infographic that represents a diverse group fairly and without stereotypes.
7. Extension: Have learners engage in a project where they analyze visual media from a specific outlet or source over time, identifying trends, biases, or consistencies in how diverse groups are represented.

ACTIVITY 4. DIGITAL FOOTPRINT TRAIL, GRADES 4–12

Teaching learners about their digital footprint and the lasting nature of online posts is essential in developing media literacy. This visual and hands-on activity provides a concrete representation of the abstract concept of a digital footprint. By creating and discussing their footprint trails, learners across different grade levels can engage with the concept in a way that's tangible and memorable, fostering responsible online behavior.

Objective: To help learners understand what a digital footprint is and the long-lasting nature of online posts, comments, likes, and shares.

Materials Needed: paper cut-outs of footprints (one set per learner); markers, pens, or pencils; tape or glue

1. Start by explaining what a digital footprint is. You might say, "Everything we do online leaves a trail, like footprints in the sand, but these footprints don't wash away."
2. Give each learner a set of footprint cut-outs and markers. Ask them to write or draw something they might do online on each footprint, such as posting a photo, liking a post, or writing a comment.
3. Have the learners tape or glue their footprints on the floor or a long sheet of paper, creating a trail. Emphasize that once something is online, it stays there, just like their footprint trail.
4. Facilitate a discussion about the implications by asking questions such as:
   - What happens if you share something online you wish you hadn't?
   - How can you be careful about what you post or share?
   - Why is it important to think before you post?
5. Optional Extension for Grades 7–12: Dive deeper by discussing privacy settings, the potential impact on future opportunities (like college or jobs), and the importance of digital citizenship.
6. Have learners write or draw a quick reflection on how they'll be be mindful regarding their digital footprint or what they'll do differently.
7. Optional: Have learners create a small footprint reminder to take home or place in their notebooks, summarizing what they've learned.

ACTIVITY 5. MEDIUM MATTERS

It's important for learners to understand how different mediums can influence the way a message is conveyed. Here's an activity designed for eighth graders that compares a TikTok video, a newspaper editorial, and a podcast, focusing on how each medium conveys the same information differently. When learners analyze different mediums on the same subject, they develop a critical understanding of media literacy, recognizing that the medium isn't just a platform for a message but an integral part of how that message is received and understood.

Objective: To guide learners in analyzing how the medium (TikTok video, newspaper editorial, podcast) affects the presentation and reception of information on the same topic.

Materials Needed: access to a TikTok video, newspaper editorial, and podcast on the same or similar subject; activity sheets (print or digital) for analysis

1. Start with an explanation of how different mediums can present the same information in various ways, influencing how the audience perceives the message.
2. Crowdsource the selection of a relevant and engaging topic that's been covered in a TikTok video, newspaper editorial, and podcast. Engage learners who regularly consume TikTok content. It could be a current event, a historical figure, or a cultural phenomenon.
3. Place learners into three groups, assigning each group one of the mediums to analyze.
4. Provide an activity sheet or guide with questions to help the learners analyze their medium. Include questions such as:
   - How is the information presented?
   - What elements (visual, auditory, textual) are used?
   - How does the medium influence the tone or perspective?
   - What might be the advantages and limitations of this medium?
5. Allow ample time for groups to explore their assigned medium and discuss their findings.

6. Ask each group to create a chart or visual comparison that highlights the specific characteristics of their medium and how it influenced the presentation of the information.
7. Invite groups to present their analyses and comparisons, encouraging a discussion about how each medium can shape our understanding of the information.
8. As a class, create a large comparative chart that captures the insights from all three groups. Discuss what was learned about how medium influences message.
9. Have learners write a brief reflection on what they've learned and how they might apply this understanding to their own consumption of media.
10. Optional Extension: Have learners individually or in small groups create their own short content (a TikTok-style video, an editorial, or a podcast) on a chosen subject, reflecting on how the medium influenced their approach.

APPENDIX I

Exemplar Conversations With Parents and Caregivers

In Chapter 9, you critiqued three hypothetical conversations teachers had with parents. You should have noted some glaring concerns. Below are exemplars of ways these conversations could have gone if the teachers had higher levels of cultural competence.

Since the task was to mark up the teacher's side of the conversation, I've included only those revisions.

SCENARIO 1

Teacher: "Hello, Mrs. Rodriguez. Thank you for taking the time to come in and meet with me. I know it's not always easy to get here during the school day and I truly appreciate your helping me do the best I can for Juan.

"I'm genuinely concerned with how Juan has done on his recent reading tests. I'm a little worried about his progress, but only with reading independently. Can you tell me if Juan has a favorite book or two? Perhaps I can find some books that he finds more interesting. That way, when we work on his reading smoothly, quickly, and with understanding, it will be something he wants to read instead of has to read.

"On the plus side, I've noticed he loves his culture and brings that into his answers when we're talking about familiar situations where there are some cultural differences. This tells me that Juan is thinking at a very high level. His ability to make connections across cultures is a desirable skill. We want to continue to support and nurture that."

SCENARIO 2

Teacher: "Hello, Mr. and Mrs. Jackson. Thank you both for taking the time to come in and meet with me. It's wonderful that you both were able to make it. I truly appreciate your helping me do the best I can for Malik in my English class.

"I see something in his writing and I'm hoping we can work as a team to foster what I think may be a budding literary career. Does Malik speak multiple languages? I've noticed his careful use of African American English in his essays. It brings a certain authenticity to his characters that would be lost if he only wrote in School English.

"Let me share his journal entries where he has responses to some quick write prompts.

"I don't want to stifle that creativity and fluid use of multiple languages. Unfortunately, we are limited in the choices of literature we can use in class. And we'll need to make sure that when it's time for the state test that Malik only uses School English.

"In the meantime, I'm open to any other suggestions you might have about supporting him."

SCENARIO 3

Teacher: "Hello, Mr. Nguyen. Thank you for taking the time to come in and meet with me. I'm honored you were able to make it. I appreciate your helping me do the best I can for Tuân in my math class. I've noticed he's struggling a bit. I get the sense that math might not be his favorite subject. What can you tell me about his history with math and, well . . . math teachers?

"Well, if he loves music and art, that might be our key to connecting what he loves to what he doesn't. You see, music and math are intertwined; rhythms involve counting, and scales showcase patterns. These are key math concepts that can make learning it more engaging for music lovers like Tuân.

"And art and math are connected as well. Geometric shapes, symmetry, and proportions in art rely on mathematical principles. This will make math real and creative for our art enthusiast Tuân.

"Thank you so much for that insight! I tell you what. I'll create some lessons that make these connections. I'll use them with the whole class so that Tuân doesn't feel singled out. I'll also find some resources that are designed for parents to use and share those with you to work with him at home."

APPENDIX J

The Work of the Professional Learning Community

Whether through book study, podcast study, a consultant, or other professional learning, setting the foundation of equitable grading in your school or district is work best done as a community. While individual instructors may refine their own practices, students are impacted by multiple educators each year.

It may be that you begin with professional learning just in determining the purpose of grading for your school. Perhaps you need to discuss as a community what role grades play in evaluating students' knowledge and skills, and motivating them to learn, and even your perspective as a collective on grades to support college admissions and future opportunities.

Perhaps you go all out and do the work outlined in Chapter 5 as a committee group for your entire school, district, or larger education agency or organization. You could even bring in an expert facilitator to help guide that work.

Achieving impartiality and grading may involve learning about and developing strategies like blind grading (where the grader does not know whose work they are grading), using clear and detailed rubrics, and providing anonymous peer feedback on grading policy. Expert training should provide educators deep work on recognizing and counteracting their biases. This type of work is not a "one and done," two-hour after-school session. Recognizing and mitigating bias takes time.

Learning how to use strategies such as culturally responsive instruction and objective grading rubrics, and creating an inclusive curriculum that reflects the experiences and contributions of diverse cultures and races, is not light work. It's important to regularly assess and reflect on grading policies and practices to ensure that they're as fair and as unbiased as possible.

This means working not only on us but our students as well. Given the insidiousness of stereotype threat in culturally and linguistically diverse learners, explicit professional development on how to reduce its effects and help our culturally and linguistically diverse learners succeed without fear of discrimination is essential. Consider that some interventions have shown that simply making learners and their instructors aware of stereotype threat reduces its effect. Just educating our learners on a growth mindset, the idea that intelligence is a learned and not a fixed trait, can majorly reduce stereotype threat. In one study, Black students who were encouraged to view intelligence as a malleable trait reported greater enjoyment and engagement in education and obtained higher grade point averages than control groups (Aronson et al., 2002).

As educators, we can learn how to instruct on intelligence as a trait that can be changed through the learner's own effort and attention. We can provide instruction such that our learners fully comprehend that a growth mindset makes their performances less vulnerable to stereotype threat. We can help them maintain engagement without doubting their abilities. We too benefit from this training. We benefit by increasing our own cultural awareness and cultural competence, understanding and respecting cultural differences in attitudes toward education and grading.

APPENDIX K

Model Rubrics for Grading Culturally Relevant Thinking and Practices

CULTURALLY RELEVANT RUBRIC FOR INTERMEDIATE GRADES—520 LEXILE

	Not Clearly Shown There isn't much proof presented. Improve your skills.	**Somewhat Shown** There is proof, but it could be better. Get even better.	**Fully Shown** Proof is always there and you show how you know. Keep doing well.
Understanding and connecting to people who are different from you.	**To get better**, use your own experiences in your work. This helps you understand more.	**Keep doing well.** Try to understand different people a little better. Think about how they think and live. Connect your life to theirs. This will help you understand.	**Keep up this good work.** Keep using your own experiences. You're showing how making connections helps you understand more.

(Continued)

(Continued)

Understanding and applying what you learn	**To get better,** always think about different ways of thinking and where things happen. Use what you learn in real life or when it fits.	**Keep doing well!** Build on what you know. Always show what you learn with details. Also, keep thinking about different ways of thinking and where things happen. Use what you learn in real life or when it fits.	**Keep up this good work** by always showing what you learn with details. Also, keep thinking about different ways of thinking and where things happen. Use what you learn in real life or when it fits.
Thinking and understanding different views. Show that you can look at and understand information from other cultures.	**To make your work better,** practice understanding different views from many cultures. This helps you understand things better.	**To get even better,** try doing this more and going deeper. This helps you see the whole picture.	**Keep doing well** by always being good at understanding different views from many cultures. This is a strong point in your work and really helps you understand things well.
Communication Show how good you are at saying what you think. Be nice to people from different places. Make sure your information is easy to understand. Listen to what others say and be open to different ideas.	**To make your work better**, focus on talking better. Try to say your ideas well and be nice to people from different places. Also, make your information easy to understand and be open to hearing new and different ideas.	**To get even better**, try saying your ideas well while always being nice to people from different places. Make your information easy to understand and be even more open to hearing new and different ideas.	**Keep doing well** by always being good at saying your ideas well, being nice to people from different places, and making information easy to understand. Also, keep being open to hearing new and different ideas. This helps your talking a lot.
Working in Groups Show that you can be nice to others and like their ideas in groups. Show that you can work well with different people in teams and use their strengths.	**To work better with others**, try being nice to others in groups and working well with them. Try to get better at using everyone's strengths.	**To get even better,** try to be nice more and share the work more evenly. That means always being nice to others in groups and using everyone's strengths.	**Keep doing well** by always being good at being nice to others in groups and using everyone's strengths. This is a strong point in your work.
Language and Expression Show that you know it's important to respect how different people talk. When you write or speak,	**To make your skills better**, understand how people use different ways of speaking. Also, make sure your writing and speaking are clear	**To get even better**, try to do this more. Always understand how people use different ways of speaking. Keep working on being	**Keep doing well** by continuing to be good at understanding how people use different ways of speaking. Also, keep being

make sure it's clear and makes sense. Also, understand that people use language in different ways.	and make sense. Be nice to different ways of using language.	clear and making sense when you write or speak. Respect different ways of using language.	clear and making sense when you write or speak. Respect different ways of using language. This is a strong point in your work.
Creativity and Innovation Show that you use things from different cultures in your creative projects or ideas. Be creative on your own, but also be respectful and get ideas from different cultures.	**To make your skills better,** use things from different cultures like drawings, poetry, or quotes. Also, be creative and respectful when you get ideas from different cultures. This makes you even more creative.	**To get even better,** always use different cultural things like drawings, poetry, or quotes in your creative projects or ideas. Keep being creative and respectful when you get ideas from different cultures.	**Keep doing well** by always using different cultural things in your creative projects or ideas. Also, keep being creative and respectful when you get ideas from different cultures. This makes your creative work richer and deeper, and it's a strong point in your work.
Self-and Peer Reflection Show that you think about your own learning and experiences in connection to bigger cultural situations. Also, when you give feedback to peers, make sure it helps and be careful about cultural differences.	**To make your skills better**, think about your own learning and experiences in connection to other cultural situations. Also, work on giving feedback to peers in a helpful way and be careful about cultural differences. This is important for self- and peer reflection.	**To get even better**, always think about your own learning and experiences in relation to broader cultural contexts. Keep giving helpful feedback to peers while being careful about cultural differences.	**Keep doing well** by always reflecting on your own learning and experiences in connection to broader cultural situations. Also, keep excelling in giving helpful feedback to friends while being sensitive to cultural differences. This makes your self- and peer reflections richer and more meaningful, and it's a strong point in your work.
Community and Real-World Connection Show that you understand the things you learn by connecting them to real-life situations or things happening in your community. Also, use community resources or experiences well in your assignments or projects.	**Work on understanding** better by connecting to real-world situations or community issues. Also, focus on connecting community resources or experiences more effectively into your assignments or projects.	**To get even better,** always connect to real-world situations or community issues. Keep striving to connect community resources or experiences into your assignments or projects.	**Keep doing well** by showing you understand the content through real-world connections. Keep excelling in the integration of community resources or experiences into your assignments or projects. This makes your work more meaningful.

(Continued)

(Continued)

Growth and Effort Show how you've improved in understanding and appreciating different viewpoints over time. Put in the effort to understand, respect, and include different cultural elements.	**To improve**, work on getting better at understanding and appreciating different viewpoints. Also, put in more effort to understand, respect, and include different cultural elements.	**To get even better**, always focus on understanding and appreciating different viewpoints. Keep putting in effort to understand, respect, and include different cultural elements.	**To maintain excellence,** consistently show improvement in understanding and appreciating different viewpoints. Keep putting in the effort to understand, respect, and include different cultural elements. This is a strong point in your work.

CULTURALLY RELEVANT RUBRIC FOR MIDDLE SCHOOL—665 LEXILE

	Insufficiently Demonstrated: There is little to no evidence provided.	**Limited Demonstration:** Evidence is occasionally presented, but it lacks consistency and depth.	**Strong Demonstration:** Evidence is often provided with depth and understanding.	**Exceptional Demonstration:** Evidence is consistently and thoroughly provided with depth and understanding.
Cultural Relevance and Responsiveness Demonstrate an understanding of diverse cultural perspectives within the content. Skillfully integrate your own cultural experiences into your responses.	**To make your work better,** focus on integrating your own cultural experiences into your responses. This can deepen your understanding.	**To get even better,** try to get a better grasp of diverse cultural viewpoints in the material. Continue integrating your own cultural experiences into your responses.	**Keep doing well** by consistently providing evidence with depth and understanding. Deepen your grasp of diverse cultural perspectives while maintaining the integration of your own cultural experiences for a more comprehensive approach.	**Keep up this good work.** Keep consistently providing evidence with depth and understanding, showcasing a commendable comprehension of diverse cultural perspectives, and skillfully integrating your own cultural experiences into your responses.

Understand the core content deeply. Consistently consider diverse viewpoints or cultural contexts. Apply knowledge effectively in real-world or culturally relevant scenarios.	**To make your work better,** focus on deepening your understanding of what's been taught. Always consider diverse viewpoints or cultural situations. Apply your knowledge effectively in real-world or culturally relevant scenarios.	**To get even better,** aim for greater consistency and depth in showing what you've learned. Make a stronger effort to always consider diverse viewpoints or cultural situations. Practice applying your knowledge in real-world or culturally relevant scenarios.	**Keep doing well!** Build on your strong foundation. Keep evidence with depth and understanding of core content. Additionally, continue to adeptly incorporate diverse viewpoints or cultural contexts and maintain your skillful application of knowledge in real-world or culturally relevant scenarios.	**Keep up this good work** by consistently providing evidence with depth and understanding of core content. Keep excelling in considering diverse viewpoints or cultural contexts while skillfully applying your knowledge in real-world or culturally relevant scenarios.
Critical Thinking and Perspective Taking Show the ability to look at and understand information from many different cultural viewpoints.	**To make your work better**, work on your ability to analyze, evaluate, and synthesize information from many different cultural viewpoints. This is important for understanding different perspectives deeply.	**To get even better**, try to do this more consistently and go deeper in your ability to analyze, evaluate, and synthesize information from various cultural viewpoints. This will help you give a fuller perspective.	**Keep doing well** by consistently analyzing, evaluating, and synthesizing information from various cultural viewpoints. This is generally clear in your work and helps you understand different perspectives.	**Keep up this good work** by always showing a strong ability to analyze, evaluate, and synthesize information from many different cultural viewpoints. This is a strong point in your work and really helps you understand different perspectives well.
Communication: Show how well you can express your thoughts and ideas. Make sure to show respect for different cultural viewpoints.	**To make your work better,** focus on improving your communication skills. Try to express your ideas well and show respect for different cultural	**To get even better**, try to do this more consistently and go deeper in your communication skills. That means expressing	**Keep doing well** by consistently expressing ideas effectively, respecting diverse cultural perspectives, and making information clear. Also, keep	**Keep up this good work** by always showing a strong ability to express ideas effectively, respecting diverse cultural perspectives, and making

(Continued)

(Continued)

Be clear when you share information. Be open to feedback and different points of view.	viewpoints. Also, work on making your information clear and be more open to feedback and different opinions.	ideas effectively while always respecting diverse cultural perspectives, making your information clear, and being even more open to feedback and different viewpoints.	being open to feedback and different opinions. This helps your communication a lot.	information clear. Also, keep being open to feedback and different viewpoints. This is a strong point in your work and helps your communication a lot.
Collaboration and Group Work Show how well you respect different ideas and contributions in group settings. Show your ability to work well with others in diverse teams, using everyone's strengths.	**To improve your skills,** focus on showing respect for different ideas and contributions in group settings. Also, work on getting better at collaborating effectively in diverse teams and using everyone's strengths.	**To get even better,** try to do this more consistently and go deeper in your skills. That means respecting different ideas and contributions in group settings all the time. Also, keep improving your ability to collaborate effectively in diverse teams and use everyone's strengths.	**Keep doing well** by consistently showing respect for different ideas and contributions in group settings. Also, keep getting better at collaborating effectively in diverse teams, using everyone's strengths. This is a strong point in your work.	**Keep up this good work** by always showing a strong ability to respect different ideas and contributions in group settings. Also, keep excelling at collaborating effectively in diverse teams, using everyone's strengths. This is a strong point in your work.
Language and Expression Show that you understand the importance of how different people speak. Be clear and make sense when you write or speak, even when you use different languages.	**To improve your skills,** work on understanding how different languages and when they're used are important. Also, focus on being clear and making sense when you write or speak, even when you use different languages.	**To get even better,** try to do this more regularly and go deeper in your skills. That means always understanding the why using different languages can be important. Keep working on being clear and making sense when you write or speak, even when you use different languages.	**Keep doing well** by consistently showing different languages and when they're used are important. Also, keep being clear and making sense when you write or speak, even when you use different languages. This is a strong point in your work.	**Keep up this good work** by always showing a strong ability to understand the value of different language forms and their usage. Also, keep excelling in being clear and making sense when you write or speak, even when you use different languages. This is a strong point in your work.

Creativity and Innovation Show how you use different cultural elements in your creative projects or solutions. Be original while also respecting and finding inspiration from different cultures.	**To improve,** work on using cultural elements, like drawings, poetry, or quotes. Also, focus on being original while respecting and finding inspiration from various cultures, as this is important for being more creative.	**To get even better**, always use different cultural elements, like drawings, poetry, or quotes' in your creative projects or solutions. Keep working on being original while also respecting and finding inspiration from various cultures.	**Keep doing well** by consistently using different cultural elements in your creative projects or solutions. Also, keep being original as you respect and find inspiration from various cultures. This helps make your creative work richer and deeper.	**Keep up this good work** by always showing a strong ability to use different cultural elements in your creative projects or solutions. Also, keep excelling in being original while respecting and finding inspiration from various cultures. This is a strong point in your work.
Self-and Peer Reflection Show how you think about your own learning and experiences in relation to broader cultural situations. Give feedback to peers in a helpful way, while being sensitive to cultural differences.	**To improve,** actively think about your own learning and experiences in relation to other cultural situations. Also, work on providing constructive feedback to peers with sensitivity to cultural differences, as these are important aspects of self- and peer reflection.	**To get even better**, try to do this more consistently and go deeper in your skills. That means always reflecting on your own learning and experiences in relation to broader cultural contexts. Keep working on giving constructive feedback to peers while being sensitive to cultural differences.	**Keep doing well** by consistently reflecting on your own learning and experiences in relation to broader cultural contexts. Also, keep excelling in providing constructive feedback to peers with cultural sensitivity. This makes your self- and peer reflections richer and more meaningful.	**Keep up this good work** by always showing a strong ability to reflect on your own learning and experiences in relation to broader cultural contexts. Also, keep excelling in providing constructive feedback to peers with cultural sensitivity. This is a strong point in your work.
Community and Real-World Connection Show how well you understand the content by relating it to real-world situations or community issues.	**To improve,** work on understanding better by connecting to real-world situations or community issues. Also, focus on connecting	**To get even better**, try to do this more consistently and go deeper in your skills. Always connect to real-world situations or community issues. Keep	**Keep doing well** by consistently understanding the content through real-world connections. Also, keep excelling in the integration of community	**Keep up this good work** by always showing a strong ability to understand the content through real-world connections. Also, keep excelling in

(Continued)

(Continued)

Incorporate community resources or experiences effectively into your assignments or projects.	community resources or experiences more effectively into your assignments or projects.	improving on connecting community resources or experiences into your assignments or projects.	resources or experiences into your assignments or projects. This makes your work more meaningful.	the integration of community resources or experiences into your assignments or projects. This is a strong point in your work.
Growth and Effort Show how you've improved in understanding and appreciating different viewpoints over time. Put in the effort to understand, respect, and include different cultural elements.	**To improve,** actively work on better understanding diverse viewpoints over time. Also, put in more effort to understand, respect, and include different cultural elements, as this is crucial for personal growth in this area.	**To get even better,** try to do this more consistently and go deeper in your efforts. Always show understanding and value diverse perspectives. Keep making a consistent effort to understand, respect, and integrate diverse cultural elements into your work.	**Keep doing well** by consistently understanding and valuing diverse perspectives. Also, keep excelling in your effort to understand, respect, and integrate diverse cultural elements into your work. This contributes to your ongoing growth in this area.	**Keep up this good work** by always showing a strong ability to demonstrate understanding and valuing diverse perspectives. Also, keep excelling in your effort to understand, respect, and integrate diverse cultural elements into your work. This is a strong point in your approach.

CULTURALLY RELEVANT RUBRIC FOR HIGH SCHOOL—1200 LEXILE

	Not Clearly Evident Little to no evidence is shown.	**Minimally Evident** Evidence is shown on occasion, but it is inconsistent or lacks depth.	**Somewhat Evident** Evidence is demonstrated, but there's room for further consistency and depth.	**Consistently Evident** Evidence is frequently provided with depth and understanding.	**Fully Evident** Evidence is consistently and thoroughly provided with depth and understanding.
Cultural Relevance and Responsiveness Evidence of understanding diverse cultural perspectives presented in the content.	**To improve your work,** focus on integrating your own cultural experiences into your responses, as this can significantly	**To further improve your work,** enhance your understanding of diverse cultural perspectives presented in the content	**To enhance your work,** continue integrating your own cultural experiences into your responses. This will contribute to a more	**Continue to excel,** strive for even greater consistency in providing evidence and continue to deepen your understanding of diverse	**Maintain this standard,** continue to consistently provide evidence with depth and understanding and

Integration of one's own cultural experiences in responses.	enhance the depth of your understanding.	and strive to integrate your own cultural experiences into your responses.	consistent and profound understanding.	cultural perspectives while maintaining the integration of your own cultural experiences for a more comprehensive approach.	demonstrate a commendable comprehension of diverse cultural perspectives along with skillful integration of your own cultural experiences in your responses.
Content Mastery Depth of understanding of the core content; consideration of diverse viewpoints or cultural contexts; application of knowledge in real-world or culturally relevant scenarios.	**To improve your work,** focus on enhancing the depth of your understanding of core content, actively considering diverse viewpoints or cultural contexts, and applying your knowledge in real-world or culturally relevant scenarios.	**To further improve your work**, strive for greater consistency and depth in demonstrating your understanding of core content, make a concerted effort to consistently consider diverse viewpoints or cultural contexts, and practice applying your knowledge in real-world or culturally relevant scenarios.	**To enhance your work,** aim for greater consistency and depth in presenting your understanding of core content, continue to explore and integrate diverse viewpoints or cultural contexts consistently, and seek opportunities to apply your knowledge in more nuanced real-world or culturally relevant scenarios.	**Continue to excel,** build upon your strong foundation by consistently demonstrating evidence with depth and understanding of core content, continue to incorporate diverse viewpoints or cultural contexts adeptly, and maintain your skillful application of knowledge in real-world or culturally relevant scenarios.	**Maintain this standard,** continue to consistently provide evidence with depth and understanding of core content, and continue to excel in considering diverse viewpoints or cultural contexts while skillfully applying your knowledge in real-world or culturally relevant scenarios.
Critical Thinking and Perspective Taking Ability to analyze, evaluate, and synthesize information from multiple cultural viewpoints.	**To improve your work,** focus on developing your ability to analyze, evaluate, and synthesize information from multiple cultural viewpoints, which is essential for a deeper understanding	**To further improve your work,** strive for greater consistency and depth in your ability to analyze, evaluate, and synthesize information from multiple cultural viewpoints, as this will enable you to	**To enhance your work,** aim for greater consistency and depth in your ability to analyze, evaluate, and synthesize information from multiple cultural viewpoints, which will lead to a more nuanced understanding.	**Continue to excel,** strive for greater consistency in your analysis, evaluation, and synthesis of information from multiple cultural viewpoints as this skill is generally evident in your work and contributes to a well-rounded understanding	**Maintain this standard,** continue to consistently demonstrate the ability to analyze, evaluate, and synthesize information from multiple cultural viewpoints, as this is a strength in your work and contributes

(Continued)

(Continued)

	of diverse perspectives.	provide a more comprehensive perspective.		of diverse perspectives.	significantly to a comprehensive understanding of diverse perspectives.
Communication Effectiveness in expressing ideas, ensuring that diverse cultural perspectives are acknowledged and respected. Clarity in presenting information, while being open to feedback and alternate viewpoints.	**To improve your work,** focus on enhancing your communication skills, with an emphasis on effectively expressing ideas and ensuring that diverse cultural perspectives are acknowledged and respected. Additionally, work on presenting information with clarity and being more open to feedback and alternate viewpoints.	**To further improve your work,** strive for greater consistency and depth in your communication skills. This includes effectively expressing ideas while consistently acknowledging and respecting diverse cultural perspectives, as well as presenting information clearly and being more open to feedback and alternate viewpoints.	**To enhance your work,** aim for greater consistency and depth in your communication skills. This involves consistently and effectively expressing ideas while ensuring that diverse cultural perspectives are acknowledged and respected. Additionally, work on presenting information with clarity and being receptive to feedback and alternate viewpoints.	**Continue to excel** by consistently and effectively expressing ideas while actively acknowledging and respecting diverse cultural perspectives. Maintain clarity in presenting information and remain open to feedback and alternate viewpoints, as this contributes to your strong communication effectiveness.	**Maintain your high standard** of communication excellence by consistently and effectively expressing ideas while consistently acknowledging and respecting diverse cultural perspectives. Continue to present information with clarity and remain open to feedback and alternate viewpoints, as this is a notable strength in your work.
Collaboration and Group Work Demonstrated respect for diverse ideas and contributions in group settings. Ability to work collaboratively in diverse teams, leveraging the strengths of all members.	**To improve your skills,** focus on demonstrating respect for diverse ideas and contributions in group settings. Additionally, work on developing the ability to collaborate effectively in diverse teams by leveraging the strengths of all members.	**To further improve your skills,** strive for greater consistency in demonstrating respect for diverse ideas and contributions in group settings. Improve your ability to collaborate effectively in diverse teams, ensuring that you leverage the strengths of all members.	**To enhance your skills,** aim for greater consistency in demonstrating respect for diverse ideas and contributions in group settings. Continue developing your ability to collaborate effectively in diverse teams, ensuring that you consistently leverage the strengths of all members.	**Continue to excel** in your collaborative and group work skills by consistently and effectively demonstrating respect for diverse ideas and contributions in group settings. Maintain a high standard of collaboration by continually developing your ability to work collaboratively in diverse teams, ensuring that you leverage the strengths of all members.	**Maintain your high standard** of excellence in collaborative and group work by consistently demonstrating respect for diverse ideas and contributions in group settings. Continue to excel in working collaboratively in diverse teams, consistently leveraging the strengths of all members. This is a notable strength in your work.

Language and Expression Recognizing the value of multiple language forms, including African American Vernacular English (AAVE) or other culturally specific dialects, while also understanding the context in which they're used. Clarity and coherence in written and spoken language, while valuing linguistic diversity.	**To improve your skills,** focus on recognizing the value of multiple language forms and understanding the context in which they're used. Additionally, work on achieving clarity and coherence in both written and spoken language while valuing linguistic diversity.	**To further improve your skills**, strive for greater consistency and depth. This includes consistently recognizing the value of multiple language forms and understanding their contextual usage. Additionally, aim for clarity and coherence in both written and spoken language, while continuing to value linguistic diversity.	**To enhance your skills,** aim for greater consistency and depth. This involves consistently recognizing the value of multiple language forms and continually understanding their contextual usage. Additionally, work on achieving greater clarity and coherence in both written and spoken language, all while maintaining a strong commitment to valuing linguistic diversity.	**Continue to excel** by consistently recognizing the value of multiple language forms and understanding their contextual usage. Maintain a high standard of clarity and coherence in both written and spoken language, while valuing linguistic diversity, as this contributes to your strong language and expression abilities.	**Maintain your high standard of excellence** by consistently recognizing the value of multiple language forms and consistently understanding their contextual usage. Continue to excel in achieving clarity and coherence in both written and spoken language while upholding a strong commitment to valuing linguistic diversity. This is a notable strength in your work.
Creativity and Innovation Incorporation of diverse cultural elements in creative projects or solutions. Demonstrating originality while respecting and drawing inspiration from various cultures.	**To improve,** focus on incorporating diverse cultural elements into your creative projects or solutions. Additionally, work on developing originality while respecting and drawing inspiration from various cultures, as this is essential for fostering creativity.	**To further improve**, strive for greater consistency and depth. This includes consistently incorporating diverse cultural elements into your creative projects or solutions and further developing your originality while respecting and drawing inspiration from various cultures to infuse depth into your creative work.	**To enhance your work,** aim for greater consistency and depth. This involves consistently incorporating diverse cultural elements into your creative projects or solutions and continually honing your originality while respecting and drawing inspiration from various cultures, which will elevate the quality of your creative endeavors.	**Continue to excel** by consistently incorporating diverse cultural elements into your creative projects or solutions. Maintain a high standard of originality while respecting and drawing inspiration from various cultures, as this contributes to the richness and depth of your creative work.	**Maintain your high standard** of excellence by consistently incorporating diverse cultural elements into your creative projects or solutions. Continue to excel in demonstrating originality while respecting and drawing inspiration from various cultures. This is a notable strength in your work.

(Continued)

(Continued)

Self-and Peer Reflection Reflecting on one's own learning and experiences in relation to broader cultural contexts. Providing constructive feedback to peers with cultural sensitivity and understanding.	**To improve** your skills, focus on actively reflecting on your own learning and experiences in relation to broader cultural contexts. Additionally, work on developing the ability to provide constructive feedback to peers with cultural sensitivity and understanding, as these are essential components of effective self- and peer reflection.	**To further improve** your skills, strive for greater consistency and depth. This includes consistently reflecting on your own learning and experiences in relation to broader cultural contexts and providing more consistently constructive feedback to peers with cultural sensitivity and understanding.	**To enhance** your skills, aim for greater consistency and depth. This involves consistently reflecting on your own learning and experiences in relation to broader cultural contexts and continually enhancing your ability to provide constructive feedback to peers with cultural sensitivity and understanding.	**Continue to excel** in your skills by consistently reflecting on your own learning and experiences in relation to broader cultural contexts. Maintain a high standard of providing constructive feedback to peers with cultural sensitivity and understanding, as this contributes to the depth of your self- and peer reflections.	**Maintain your high standard** of excellence by consistently reflecting on your own learning and experiences in relation to broader cultural contexts. Continue to excel in providing constructive feedback to peers with cultural sensitivity and understanding. This is a notable strength in your work.
Community and Real-World Connection Demonstrating understanding of content by making connections to real-world situations or community issues. Integration of community resources or experiences in assignments or projects.	**To improve** your skills, focus on demonstrating a better understanding of content by making connections to real-world situations or community issues. Additionally, work on integrating community resources or experiences more effectively into your assignments or projects.	**To further improve** your skills, strive for greater consistency and depth. This includes consistently demonstrating understanding of content by making connections to real-world situations or community issues and making a more consistent effort to integrate community resources or experiences into your assignments or projects.	**To enhance** your skills, aim for greater consistency and depth. This involves consistently demonstrating understanding of content by making connections to real-world situations or community issues and continually improving the integration of community resources or experiences into your assignments or projects.	**Continue to excel** in your skills by consistently demonstrating understanding of content through meaningful connections to real-world situations or community issues. Maintain a high standard of integrating community resources or experiences effectively into your assignments or projects, as this contributes to the depth of your work.	**Maintain your high standard** of excellence by consistently demonstrating understanding of content through meaningful connections to real-world situations or community issues. Continue to excel in the integration of community resources or experiences into your assignments or projects. This is a notable strength in your work.

Growth and Effort Demonstrated growth in understanding and valuing diverse perspectives over time. Effort put into understanding, respecting, and integrating diverse cultural elements.	**To improve,** focus on actively working toward a better understanding of diverse viewpoints over time. Additionally, put more effort into understanding, respecting, and integrating diverse cultural elements, as this is crucial for personal growth in this area.	**To further improve**, strive for greater consistency and depth. This includes consistently demonstrating growth in understanding and valuing diverse perspectives over time and making a more consistent effort to understand, respect, and integrate diverse cultural elements into your work.	**To enhance** your growth and effort, aim for greater consistency and depth. This involves consistently demonstrating growth in understanding and valuing diverse perspectives over time and continually putting effort into understanding, respecting, and integrating diverse cultural elements, which will lead to more profound growth.	**Continue to excel** in valuing diverse perspectives by consistently demonstrating growth in understanding over time. Maintain a high standard of effort in understanding, respecting, and integrating diverse cultural elements into your work, as this contributes to your continued growth in this area.	**Maintain your high standard of excellence** by consistently demonstrating growth in understanding and valuing diverse perspectives over time. Continue to excel in your effort to understand, respect, and integrate diverse cultural elements into your work. This is a notable strength in your approach.

GLOSSARY

access—the opportunity for all learners to participate in and benefit from educational services, regardless of their socio-economic status, race, gender, disability, or other factors. It suggests a lack of barriers and equal opportunities in learning environments.

African American English (AAE)—a distinct, complex, and rule-governed linguistic system prevalent in Black American communities, characterized by distinct phonological, syntactic, semantic, and lexical conventions influenced by multiple African languages and historical, social, and cultural experiences of the Black American community and expressed in patterns divergent from School English (SE).

asset allocation—the strategy of providing resources, instruction, and services among various groups of learners based on need to optimize the behavioral and academic outcomes of all learners based on a goal of all learners achieving at- or above-grade-level performance each year and eliminating disproportionalities in areas such as referrals to special education or suspensions and expulsions.

automaticity—the ability to read connected text without spending cognitive energy processing low-level details.

bias—a predisposition or prejudice in favor of or against something, often based on personal beliefs, experiences, or stereotypes, influencing objective judgment.

BIPOC—Black, Indigenous, and people of color; an inclusive acronym used to refer to members of nonwhite communities that acknowledges the unique histories and struggles faced by all people of color but placing specific emphasis on the two most marginalized racial and ethnic groups in the United States: Black and Indigenous peoples.

Chicano English—a distinct, complex, and rule-governed linguistic system prevalent in some Chicano-American communities, especially in the US Southwest, characterized by distinct phonological, syntactic, and lexical conventions influenced by Spanish and historical, social, and cultural experiences of the Chicano community and expressed in patterns divergent from School English (SE).

code-switching—the use of elements from both the learner's home language and School English. A strategy promoting linguistic flexibility that helps students navigate between different linguistic contexts.

collectivist—related to the practice or principle of giving a group priority over each individual in it.

comorbidity—in school demographics, the presence of two unalterable demographic markers in a learner that have historically impacted academic success through no fault of the learner.

contemporary commentary—analyses, opinions, or reflections on current events, cultural shifts, societal issues, or trends that are produced during the same time period as the events or issues themselves.

creole—a stable natural language that develops from different languages simplifying and mixing into a new form (often a pidgin) that expands and establishes itself as a native or heritage language over one or more generations; in America, most commonly recognized as French Creole, a language developed through the ethnicity originating from the mix of French, Indigenous American, and African cultures in the 17th century.

cultural awareness—awareness of the information, norms, values, behaviors, and morals of groups of people who share an identity; awareness of the socially transmitted norms, values, behaviors, and morals of a group of people.

culturally and linguistically diverse learners (CLDLs)—learners whose home culture is not mainstream, middle-class, and White and/or whose language background reflects anything other than School English.

culture—the information, norms, values, behaviors, and morals of a group; socially transmitted norms, values, behaviors, and morals of a group of people.

emergent bilingual—an inclusive term used to refer to English language learners, English speakers of other languages, limited English proficient learners, not (or non-) English proficient learners, and, in this book, School English learners.

equality—a state of being equal or having the same status, rights, or opportunities; in education, especially in provision of instruction, disciplinary actions, and opportunities for achievement.

equity—without bias against or favoritism for.

equity warrior—one who actively advocates for equity; one who works to ensure no person, especially no child, is disadvantaged by prejudice or bias.

ethnicity—the shared cultural, linguistic, or ancestral characteristics of a group of people serving to differentiate populations based on commonalities such as heritage, language, religion, or historical experiences, providing a sense of belonging and identity, distinct from race or nationality, within larger societal contexts.

explicit—stated clearly and in detail, leaving no room for confusion, misinterpretation, or doubt.

explicit bias—the conscious and intentional prejudices or stereotypes individuals hold towards others, based on race, gender, age, religion, culture, and other known or assumed social or genetic factors that we can name, see, and call out, usually in a way that is unfair and/or harmful.

formative assessment—an ongoing process used to collect data on learner understanding and skills; assessment used to inform instructional adjustments and provide feedback to learners for improvement, rather than for grading purposes.

identity—the conception, qualities, beliefs, and expressions that make a person or group distinct, encompassing aspects such as culture, ethnicity, gender, and personal experiences; who or what a person is; similarity or affinity to a group.

impartiality—equal treatment of all members of a community, group, rivals, or disputants; fairness; without bias, favoritism, or prejudice; ensuring equal consideration in treatment.

implicit—implied, or suggested, although not specifically or plainly expressed.

implicit bias—a natural phenomenon that exists in all humans, based on observed, taught, and reinforced behavior and ideas that cause prejudice in favor of or against a thing, a person, a group, or a culture, usually in a way that is unfair and/or harmful.

mastery—a deep and comprehensive understanding of a subject or skill, allowing an individual to apply, teach, or adapt the knowledge effectively in various contexts; comprehensive knowledge or skill in a subject.

media literacy—the ability to access, analyze, evaluate, and create media; an understanding of how media messages shape our culture and society; the ability to make informed decisions related to media consumption.

meritocracy—holding of power by people in a system or organization on the basis of their ability.

metacognition—awareness and understanding of one's own thought processes.

metacognitive knowledge—the capacity to understand what we know and what we don't know; the knowledge about when and how to use particular strategies for learning or problem-solving.

metacognitive regulation—the ability to plan how to approach a given task, monitor one's own ability, and evaluate the progress toward the completion of that task.

microaggression—a subtle, often unintentional, form of prejudice expressed through brief verbal, behavioral, or environmental slights; remarks or actions that convey negative stereotypes or insensitivity, often directed at marginalized groups, reflecting underlying biases or misunderstandings.

microassault—explicit, intentional actions or slurs, often racially driven, meant to hurt the intended victim; usually conscious and deliberate actions or words displaying overt bigotry or bias toward a marginalized group, generally unambiguous in their discriminatory intent.

microinsult—subtle, often unintentional, verbal or behavioral communications that convey rudeness, insensitivity, or demean a person's racial heritage or identity; remarks or actions perpetuating negative stereotypes and reflecting underlying biases; subtle belittlements of a targeted individual or group.

microinvalidation—comments or actions that negate, dismiss, or nullify the feelings, experiences, or identities of individuals from marginalized groups; suggestions that the person's experiences aren't genuine, relevant, or based on real societal issues, undermining their reality or feelings.

newcomer—a non-English-proficient learner, newly arrived in the United States from a non-English-speaking country.

objective standardized testing—a consistent form of assessment using uniform procedures and scoring to measure knowledge or skills across individuals.

Patois—a natural language spoken by the majority of Jamaicans as a native language; originally a creole based in the vernacular and dialectical forms of English spoken by British and Scotch slaveholders nativized by West Africans in the 17th century.

pidgin—a simplified form of language developed as a means of communication between two or more groups that do not share a common language; not a primary or heritage language, but rather English that has been influenced by other local and heritage languages and thus creating a unique linguistic system.

primary sources—original documents or records that provide firsthand testimony or direct evidence of a topic, event, person, or period. They are unaltered records created at the time of the event or by someone who experienced the event firsthand.

proficiency—a high degree of competence or skill; expertise.

provision gap—the difference between demonstrated academic ability as measured by high-stakes assessments, often annual state testing, and the required benchmarks of a grade level; the gap that is created by the use of ineffective instructional methods and culturally inappropriate curriculum.

psychological safety—the ability of people in a group (classroom, school, organization) to feel safe to participate, to learn, to speak up without fear of punishment, ridicule, or embarrassment.

race—from a sociological perspective, a category of people who are perceived to share distinct physical characteristics that are deemed socially significant. In the United States, the major races are White-European, Indigenous (Native American or Alaska Native), Black (African American), Hispanic (referred to in this text as Latine), Asian, and Pacific Islander; the concept used to legitimize social hierarchies and justify discrimination and exploitation.

realia—objects and material from everyday life that may be used as visual aids; realistic toys that are exemplars of real objects, such as dinosaurs, cars, trucks, tools, etc.

restorative practice—a conflict resolution approach focusing on repairing harm and rebuilding relationships emphasizing dialogue, accountability, and understanding the impact of one's actions, fostering community and trust among participants.

retributive practice—an approach to discipline centered on punishment for wrongdoers, emphasizing the infliction of penalties proportionate to the offense; prioritizes deterrence and retribution.

rote—the technique of learning information through repetition without necessarily understanding its deeper meaning, emphasizes recall over comprehension, often leading to the ability to recite details without grasping their contextual significance.

schema—cognitive frameworks or concepts that help learners organize and interpret information; mental maps or structures used to organize knowledge, beliefs, and understandings; a requisite to incorporating new information into existing knowledge to support ease of comprehension.

School English (SE)—the linguistic system called on by the state standards that is taught, spoken, and assessed in schools, featuring the grammar, usage, and mechanics of the English language and accepted as the standard for instruction in the United States; may also be referred to as Standard English or academic English.

social identity threat—the fear individuals feel when they believe they'll be judged or stereotyped based on their group membership, potentially leading to underperformance or stress.

sociocultural language—a language that encompasses the intricate relationship between language and the social and cultural contexts in which it is used; a language that both mirrors and molds societal norms, values, and identities; language that is not merely a tool for communication, but a deep tie to lived experiences, cultural practices, ideologies, and power dynamics.

standards—levels of quality or attainment; ideas or things that may be used as measures, norms, or models in comparative evaluation or performance.

stereotype—widely held but fixed and oversimplified image or idea of a particular type of person or thing; a fixed or overgeneralized belief about a particular group or class of people; a set idea people have about what someone or something is like, especially negative.

stereotype threat—the anxiety or distress a person feels when at risk of confirming negative stereotypes about their social group, affecting performance and behavior.

stereotyping—the act of ascribing or assigning generalized traits or behaviors to an entire group, often based on oversimplified perceptions or preconceived notions frequently rooted in cultural, racial, or gender biases.

summative assessment—an evaluation of a learner's achievement at the end of an instructional period, often for grading or accountability purposes; a measurement of mastery of content and skills, typically through exams, projects, or papers.

systemic—relating to a system, especially as opposed to an individual or a single part.

systemic bias—pervasive, ingrained prejudice within a system or institution that results in unequal treatment or outcomes for a particular group, often based on race, gender, or other characteristics.

unfinished learning—skills or concepts learners have not mastered that they need for their current or future grade level.

White ethnocentrism—the belief in the inherent superiority of White culture and norms, leading to the evaluation of other cultures from a White-centric perspective.

REFERENCES

Abrams, Z. (2023). Teaching social-emotional learning is under attack. *Monitor on Psychology, 54*(6), 28.

Adams, J. (1777, May 22). *Letter to Abigail Adams.* Massachusetts Historical Society. www.masshist.org/digitaladams/archive/doc?id=L1 7770522ja

Ahmed Abdel-Al Ibrahim, K., Cuba Carbajal, N., Zuta, M. E. C., & Bayat, S. (2023). Collaborative learning, scaffolding-based instruction, and self-assessment: Impacts on intermediate EFL learners' reading comprehension, motivation, and anxiety. *Language Testing in Asia, 13*(1), 16.

Applebee, A. N. (1989). *A study of booklength works taught in high school english courses. Report series 1.2.* Center for the Learning and Teaching of Literature.

Applebee, A. N. (1992). Stability and change in the high-school canon. *English Journal, 81*(5), 27–32.

Aronson, J., Fried, C. B., & Good, C. (2002). Reducing the effects of stereotype threat on African American college students by shaping theories of intelligence. *Journal of Experimental Social Psychology, 38*(2), 113–125.

Azizi, Z., & Farid Khafaga, A. (2023). Scaffolding via group-dynamic assessment to positively affect motivation, learning anxiety, and willingness to communicate: A case study of high school students. *Journal of Psycholinguistic Research, 52*(3), 831–851.

Baker, D. J., Skinner, B. T., & Redding, C. H. (2020). Affirmative intervention to reduce stereotype threat bias: Experimental evidence from a community college. *Journal of Higher Education, 91*(5), 722–754.

Barron, K. (2021). *The literary canon: What's in it, and who makes the list?* TCK Publishing blog. tckpublishing.com/the-literary-canon/

Berger, D., & Wild, C. (2017). 'Forgotten lore': Can the socratic method of teaching be used to reduce the attainment gap of black, Asian and minority ethnic students? *Higher Education Review, 49*(2), 29–55.

Berry, A. L. (2023). *Effecting change for culturally and linguistically diverse learners*, Second Edition. Shell Education.

Bishop, R. S. (2012). Reflections on the development of African American children's literature. *Journal of Children's Literature, 38*(2), 5–13.

Bleckmann, E., Lüdtke, O., Mueller, S., & Wagner, J. (2023). The role of interpersonal perceptions of social inclusion and personality in momentary self-esteem and self-esteem reactivity. *European Journal of Personality, 37*(2), 187–206.

Bradley, B. (2021, June 3). Sales of K–12 instructional materials soaring, new industry estimates show. *EdWeek Market Brief.* marketbrief.edweek.org/marketplace-k-12/sales-k-12-instructional-materials-soaring-new-industry-estimates-show/

Bryant, D. A., & Carless, D. R. (2010). Peer assessment in a test-dominated setting: Empowering, boring or facilitating examination preparation? *Educational Research for Policy and Practice, 9*, 3–15.

Butler-Barnes, S. T., & Inniss-Thompson, M. N. (2020). "My teacher doesn't like me": Perceptions of teacher discrimination and school discipline among African-American and Caribbean Black adolescent girls. *Education Sciences, 10*(2), 44. https://doi.org/10.3390/educsci10020044

Cawley, M. J. (2015). *Required reading and the literary canon: An introduction.* Pennsylvania State University Education Reform Weblog. sites.psu.edu/educationreform/2015/03/16/required-reading-and-the-literary-canon-an-introduction/

Cegolon, A. (2023). Soft skills and general education. *Form@ re-Open Journal per la formazione in rete, 23*(1), 112–122.

Cisneros, S. (2004). *The house on Mango Street.* Bloomsbury.

Clark, T. R. (2020). *The 4 stages of psychological safety: Defining the path to inclusion and innovation.* Berrett-Koehler.

Davidson, C., & Schwartz, R. G. (1995). Semantic boundaries in the lexicon: Example from Jamaican patois. *Linguistics and Education, 7*(1), 47–64.

Davis, J., & Martin, D. B. (2018). Racism, assessment, and instructional practices: Implications for mathematics teachers of African American students. *Journal of Urban Mathematics Education, 11*(1/2), 45–68.

Drugaș, M. (2022). Screenagers or "Screamagers"? current perspectives on generation alpha. *Psychological Thought, 15*(1), 1–11.

Ehri, L. C. (1998). Grapheme-phoneme knowledge is essential for learning to read words in english. In J. L. Metsala & L. C. Ehri (Eds.), *Word recognition in beginning literacy* (pp. 3–40). Erlbaum.

Fontaine, P. M. (1981). Language, society, and development: Dialectic of French and Creole use in Haiti. *Latin American Perspectives, 8*(1), 28–46.

Fought, C. (1999). A majority sound change in a minority community: /U/-fronting in Chicano English. *Journal of Sociolinguistics, 3*(1), 5–23.

Gates, & Senna. (1993). Keep your eyes on the prize. *Newsweek, 122*(16), 89.

Green, L. J. (2002). *African American English: A linguistic introduction.* Cambridge University Press.

Greenberg, J., & Rosenfield, D. (1979). Whites' ethnocentrism and their attributions for the behavior of blacks: A motivational bias. *Journal of Personality, 47*(4), 643–657.

Hansen, A. L. (2005). *Multiculturalism, public policy, and the high school United States and American literature canon: A content analysis of textbooks adopted in the state of Florida in 1991 and 2003.* University of South Florida.

Hasty, J. D., & Childs, B. (2021). Investigating Appalachian Englishes: Subregional Variation in the New Appalachia. *Journal of Appalachian Studies, 27*(1), 69–88.

Heflebower, T., & Hoegh, J. K. (2014). *A school leader's guide to standards-based grading.* Solution Tree Press.

Hendratmoko, A. F., Madlazım, M., Wıdodo, W., & Sanjaya, I. G. M. (2023). The impact of inquiry-based online learning with virtual laboratories on students' scientific argumentation skills. *Turkish Online Journal of Distance Education (TOJDE)*, *24*(4), 1–20.

Homayouni, M. (2022). Peer assessment in group-oriented classroom contexts: On the effectiveness of peer assessment coupled with scaffolding and group work on speaking skills and vocabulary learning. *Language Testing in Asia*, *12*(1), 61.

Institute of Education Sciences. (n.d.). Deciphering state education standards. *Regional Educational Laboratory Southeast*. Retrieved April 5, 2023, from https://ies.ed.gov/ncee/edlabs/infographics/pdf/REL_SE_Deciphering_State_Education_Standards.pdf

Ireland, D. T., Freeman, K. E., Winston-Proctor, C. E., DeLaine, K. D., McDonald Lowe, S., & Woodson, K. M. (2018). (Un)hidden figures: A synthesis of research examining the intersectional experiences of Black women and girls in STEM education. *Review of Research in Education*, *42*, 226–254.

Jones, J., Jenkin, M., & Lord, S. (2006). Maintaining teacher performance through self-reflection. In J. Jones, M. Jenkin, & S. Lord (Eds.), *Developing effective teacher performance* (pp. 45–74). Sage.

Kumar, T. (2022). Where are their voices? authors of color in the secondary ELA curriculum. *Multicultural Education*, *29*(1/2), 15–24.

Kurian, G. T. (2013a). Monochronic culture. In G. T. Kurian (Ed.), *The AMA dictionary of business and management* (1st ed.). AMACOM, Publishing Division of the American Management Association.

Kurian, G. T. (2013b). Polychronic culture. In G. T. Kurian (Ed.), *The AMA dictionary of business and management* (1st ed.). AMACOM, Publishing Division of the American Management Association.

Marlow, M. L., & Giles, H. (2008). Who you tink you, talkin propah? Hawaiian Pidgin demarginalised. *Journal of Multicultural Discourses*, *3*(1), 53–68.

Marzano, R. J. (2006). *Classroom assessment and grading that work*. ASCD.

Meissner, C. A., & Brigham, J. C. (2001). Thirty years of investigating the own-race bias in memory for faces: A meta-analytic review. *Psychology, Public Policy, and Law*, *7*(1), 3–35. https://doi.org/10.1037/1076-8971.7.1.3

Mizrav, E. (2023). Segregate, discriminate, signal: A model for understanding policy drivers of educational inequality. *Educational Policy*, *37*(2), 554–581. https://doi.org/10.1177/08959048211029026

National Academy of Sciences. (2013). *Next generation science standards*. nextgenscience.org/

National Association of School Psychologists. (2012). School-family partnering to enhance learning: Essential elements and responsibilities [Position Statement]. Bethesda, MD: Author.

National Center for Education Statistics. (2020). *Percentage of students suspended and expelled from public elementary and secondary schools, by sex, race/ethnicity, and state.*

National Center for Education Statistics. (2021). *Percentage of students suspended and expelled from public elementary and secondary schools, by sex, race/ethnicity, and state*. nces.ed.gov/programs/digest/d21/tables/dt21_233.40.asp

National Center for Education Statistics. (2022). *Percentage of students suspended and expelled from public elementary and secondary schools, by sex, race/ethnicity, and state.*

National Council for the Social Studies. (2010). *National curriculum standards for social studies: A framework for teaching, learning, and assessment.*

National Equity Project. (n.d.). *Definition for equity*. Retrieved July 19, 2024, from nationalequityproject.org/education-equity-definition

Nkrumah, T. (2023). The inequities embedded in measures of engagement in science education for African American learners from a culturally relevant science pedagogy lens. *Education Sciences, 13*(7), 739.

Oliveri, M. E., & Lawless, R. (2018). The validity of inferences from locally developed assessments administered globally. *ETS Research Reports Series, 2018*(1), 1–12.

Penfield, J., & Ornstein-Galicia, J. L. (1985). *Chicano English: An ethnic contact dialect.* Benjamins.

Peterson, R., & Eeds, M. (2007). *Grand conversations: Literature groups in action.* Scholastic Teaching Resources.

Phogat, P., Ajji, S. K., Verma, S., & Yadav, M. (2023). Assessing the impact of online education on mood and feelings physical activity, sleep, and consequent internet addiction during COVID-19 on adolescents in Delhi-NCR. *Indian Journal of Health and Wellbeing, 14*(4), 443–448.

Poore, M. (2014). Why use social media in your studies and research? In *Studying and researching with social media* (pp. 2–18). Sage.

Prison Policy Initiative. (2021). *States of incarceration: The global context 2021.* prisonpolicy.org/global/2021.html

Raden, D. (2003). Ingroup bias, classic ethnocentrism, and non-ethnocentrism among American whites. *Political Psychology, 24*(4), 803–828.

Ravitch, D. (2003). *The language police: How pressure groups restrict what students learn.* Knopf.

Reinecke, J. E. (1938). "Pidgin English" in Hawaii: A local study in the sociology of language. *American Journal of Sociology, 43*(5), 778–789.

Ryan, C. S., Hunt, J. S., Weible, J. A., Peterson, C. R., & Casas, J. F. (2007). Multicultural and colorblind ideology, stereotypes, and ethnocentrism among Black and White Americans. *Group Processes and Intergroup Relations, 10*(4), 617–637.

Salikoko, S.M., Rickford, J.R., Bailey, G. & Baugh, J. (Eds.). (2022). African American English: Structure, history, and use. Routledge

Santos, P., Cook, J., & Hernández-Leo, D. (2015). M-AssIST: Interaction and scaffolding matters in authentic assessment. *Journal of Educational Technology and Society, 18*(2), 33–45.

Setemen, K., Sudirtha, I. G., & Widiana, I. W. (2023). The effectiveness of study, explore, implement, evaluate E-learning model based on project-based learning on the students conceptual understanding and learning agility. *Journal of Technology and Science Education, 13*(3), 583–596.

Shaywitz, S. E., & Shaywitz, J. (2020). *Overcoming dyslexia: Second Edition.* Knopf Doubleday Publishing Group.

Snelgrove, D. (2020). Power: Its role in society and education. *Journal of Philosophy and History of Education, 70*, 49–65.

Ssemugenyi, F. (2023). Teaching and learning methods compared: A pedagogical evaluation of problem-based learning (PBL) and lecture methods in developing learners' cognitive abilities. *Cogent Education, 10*(1), 1–20.

Steele, C. M., Spencer, S. J., & Aronson, J. (2002). Contending with group image: The psychology of stereotype and social identity threat. In M. P. Zanna (Ed.), *Advances in experimental social psychology* (Vol. 34, pp. 379–440). Academic Press.

Sue, D. W., Nadal, K. L., Capodilupo, C. M., Lin, A. I., Torino, G. C., & Rivera, D. P. (2008). Racial microaggressions against Black Americans: Implications for counseling. *Journal of Counseling and Development, 86*(3), 330–338.

Tawil, M., Said, M. A., & Suryansari, K. (2023). Authentic assessment development science to assess student competency. *International Journal of Education and Practice, 11*(2), 194–206.

TNTP. (2018). *The opportunity myth: What students can show us about how school is letting them down—and how to fix it.* tntp.org/publication/the-opportunity-myth/

Totonchi, D. A., Perez, T., Lee, Y. K., Robinson, K. A., & Linnenbrink-Garcia, L. (2021). The role of stereotype threat in ethnically minoritized students' science motivation: A four-year longitudinal study of achievement and persistence in STEM. *Contemporary Educational Psychology, 67*, 102015.

Townsend, B. L. (2000). The disproportionate discipline of African American learners: Reducing school suspensions and expulsions. *Exceptional Children, 66*(3), 381–391.

United Nations Department of Economic and Social Affairs. (2022). *World population prospects.* population.un.org/wpp/

United States Census Bureau. (2024). *U.S. and world population clock.* census.gov/popclock/world

Ursu, O., & Ciortescu, E. (2021). Exploring cultural patterns in business communication. Insights from Europe and Asia. *Centre for European Studies (CES) Working Papers, 13*(2), 149–158.

Watson, L. M. (2023). The anti-"Critical Race Theory" campaign: Classroom censorship and racial backlash by another name. *Harvard Civil Rights-Civil Liberties Law Review, 58*(2), 487–549.

Widiana, I. W., Kertih, I. W., Kristiantari, M. G. R., Parmiti, D. P., & Adijaya, M. A. (2022). The effect of project based assessment with value clarification technique in improving students' civics learning outcomes by controlling the family environment. *European Journal of Educational Research, 11*(4), 1969–1979.

Wilkerson, I. (2020). *Caste: The origins of our discontents.* Random House.

Wolfram, W., & Sellers, J. (1999). Ethnolinguistic marking of past be in Lumbee Vernacular English. *Journal of English Linguistics, 27*(2), 94.

Woodson, J. (2014). *Brown girl dreaming.* Nancy Paulsen Books.

Ye, F. T. F., Gao, X., Sin, K. F., & Yang, L. (2023). Remote learning and mental health during the societal lockdown: A study of primary school students and parents in times of COVID-19. *BMC Public Health, 23*(1), 1106.

Zinshteyn, M. (2021, November 19). UC officially ditches any tests for undergraduate admissions. *CalMatters Higher Education.* calmatters.org/education/higher-education/2021/11/uc-admissions-no-tests

INDEX

CORWIN
A Sage Company

Zeitfracht Medien GmbH
Ferdinand-Jühlke-Straße 7
99095 Erfurt, Deutschland
produktsicherheit@kolibri360.de